CHANGING CULTURES

Tázlár: a village in Hungary

CHANGING CULTURES
General Editor: Jack Goody

The aim of this series is to show how specific societies and
cultures, including sub-groups within more complex societies,
have developed and changed in response to conditions in the
modern world. Each volume will draw on recent fieldwork
to present a comprehensive analysis of a particular group,
cast in a dynamic perspective that relates the present both to
the past of the group and to the external forces that have im-
pinged upon it. The range of volumes in the series reflects the
developing interests and concerns of the social sciences,
especially social anthropology and sociology.

Also in this series

The Nayars Today by Christopher J. Fuller
The Skolt Lapps Today by Tim Ingold
The Yoruba Today by J.S. Eades
The Western Isles Today by Judith Ennew

Tázlár: a village in Hungary

C. M. HANN

Department of Social Anthropology
University of Cambridge

CAMBRIDGE UNIVERSITY PRESS

CAMBRIDGE

LONDON   NEW YORK   NEW ROCHELLE

MELBOURNE   SYDNEY

CAMBRIDGE UNIVERSITY PRESS
Cambridge, New York, Melbourne, Madrid, Cape Town, Singapore, São Paulo, Delhi

Cambridge University Press
The Edinburgh Building, Cambridge CB2 8RU, UK

Published in the United States of America by Cambridge University Press, New York

www.cambridge.org
Information on this title: www.cambridge.org/9780521295710

First published 1980
Re-issued in this digitally printed version 2009

A catalogue record for this publication is available from the British Library

Library of Congress Cataloguing in Publication data
Hann, C. M. 1953–
Tázlár, a village in Hungary.

(Changing cultures)
Bibliography: p.
Includes index.
1. Tázlár, Hungary – Rural conditions. 2. Villages–
Hungary–Case studies. I. Title.
HN420.5.T39H35   301.35′2′094391   79–14810

ISBN 978-0-521-22591-5 hardback
ISBN 978-0-521-29571-0 paperback

Contents

v

Contents

Illustrations and Tables

Illustrations and tables

Tables

Preface

Before I went to live in Tázlár in Autumn 1976 I spent a year in Budapest, learning Hungarian and about Hungary. Because of its unusual Turkish origin, the very name of Tázlár rang strange to my Budapest friends. The community belongs to a world far removed from that of Hungary's sophisticated capital, a world unfamiliar to any urban Hungarians. Despite the work of sociologists and ethnographers, and the burgeoning of a literary sociography in the last decade, the reality of the Hungarian countryside in communities such as that of Tázlár remains insufficiently understood inside Hungary. Although this book is naturally intended to help fill a very large gap in Western perceptions of socialist rural society, it is also hoped that some of its points would not be too harshly received if read by those capable of acting and improving upon present conditions in Hungary.

I first visited Tázlár in May 1976. Further short visits then preceded ten months of continuous residence, from October 1976 to August 1977, after which I returned for a fortnight in the summer of 1978, and for further brief stays thereafter. The ethnographic present of the book refers to the first half of 1977, except where specific indications to the contrary are given.

The choice of Tázlár as a community to study was far from fortuitous. In spring 1976 I walked around a number of villages in the concentrated szakszövetkezet zone administered from the town of Kiskőrös. I decided to study this particular village when, while seeking some basic statistical data on Tázlár at the main administrative offices in Kiskőrös, a number of officials expressed to me their unanimous distaste for that community, and suggested that any other village in the district would be more suitable for study and analysis. They would have far preferred me to undertake the study of a more 'model' community. Tázlár is not a model community; on the contrary, it is characterised by the persistence of elements of pre-socialist socio-economic organisation into the socialist period. It was for this very reason, and for the opportunity it presented of studying the ways in which a traditional peasant society had adapted to socialism, that I chose to study it. It is therefore obviously questionable how representative Tázlár is of Hungary as a whole. However, I did not set out to describe a 'typical' community, but rather, during both the fieldwork and the ensuing writing, to describe and to analyse a contemporary Hungarian rural community not only unfamiliar to the West but also largely unknown and ignored in Hungary itself.

The book is based primarily upon traditional, though perhaps unusually 'passive' participant observation. Non-academic Hungarian friends, unfamiliar with Western fieldwork practice, tended to think of my work as a *'felmérés'*, which usually implies a quantitative survey, and, certainly, I did attempt to use the statistics available, as well as collecting some of my own. By and large, I was assisted in this by the local administration, both at the szakszövetkezet and at the council offices. However, not all of the arguments and conclusions of this book can be defended with statistics. Some judgements are explicitly subjective, and these are obviously open to question.

The data quoted to illustrate patterns in the nation as a whole, for comparison with Tázlár, are generally taken from the Hungarian Pocket Statistical Handbook for 1977. Otherwise, with the exception of the figures which I obtained myself in the community (see note to Chapter 4), statistics are taken from diverse, accessible publications of the Hungarian Central Statistical Office. In general, I have avoided cluttering the text with references which are neither indispensable to the specialist nor of much value to the average English reader.

A minimal number of Hungarian words are used and explanations of those used more than once are provided in the glossary. Some of the proper names are fictitious and those of the individuals have been written in the English manner, with the Christian name first. The conversion of Hungarian currency presents a greater problem. The official rate of around 35 forints (abbreviated to fts) to a pound is now only some two-thirds of the rate which prevailed in the early 1970s; the effects of inflation in Hungary have been partly alleviated by the continued large subsidies on basic goods such as foodstuffs and public transport. To give some indication of costs, average monthly wage packets at the time of the fieldwork were approaching 3,000 forints; the price of a new Soviet-made Zsiguli, although it had remained fixed since the car was introduced in the early 1970s, was 80,000 forints. Other prices, including housing, and increasingly foodstuffs as well, have been continually rising in recent years.

I am grateful to the Social Science Research Council and the administrators of the Anglo-Hungarian Cultural Exchange Programme for financial support; to Corpus Christi College, Cambridge, for a travel grant in 1978; and to my supervisors Tibor Bodrogi and Mihály Sárkány in Budapest, and Jack Goody in Cambridge. I wish to thank Nigel Swain and Sándor Dúl, now the Secretary of the Hungarian Socialist Workers Party cell in Tázlár, and my many friends in that community. Thanks also go to Claude Rosenfeld and to 'Öcsi', for developing most of the photographs.

October 1978   C.M.H.

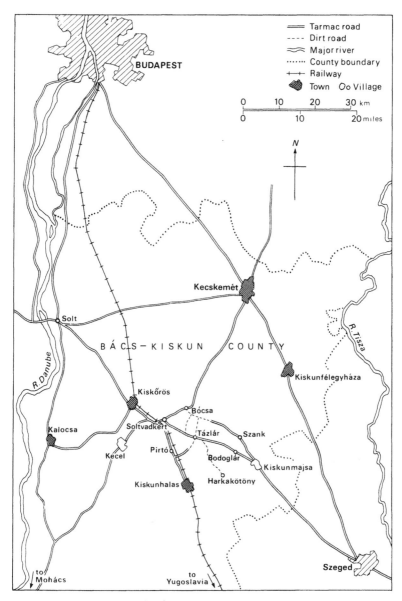

Map 1 Regional communications

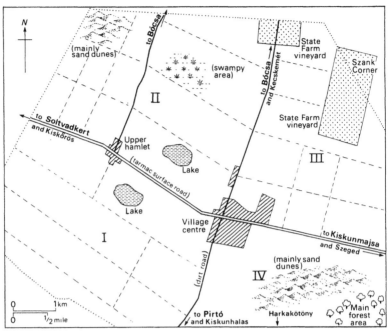

Map 2 The village zones

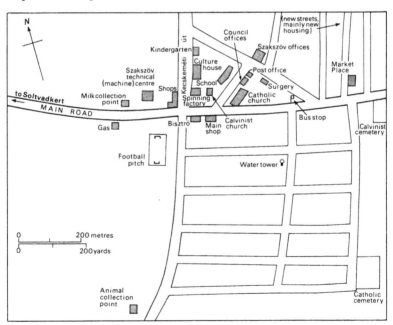

Map 3 The centre of the village

1 Introduction

Two Hungarian words are essential to the problematic of this book and must be introduced at the outset. Together they contain the key to the 'atypicality' of Tázlár, and unless the reader has some grasp of them at the beginning he will not appreciate the arguments in later chapters, which attempt to relate this atypicality back to the contemporary national context.

The first of these terms is 'the tanya problem'. The literal meaning of this phrase could be given as 'the problem of the isolated farm', but in Hungarian, even today, the phrase carries a heavy emotional and analytical load. For example, according to Erdei (1970, p. 3), 'If a family has no house in the village in addition to their tanya accommodation the connotation is clearly that of a rural slum.' Western travellers to Hungary in the eighteenth and nineteenth centuries created an image of the entire Great Plain as a wild and romantic *puszta* (steppe), and this image was officially maintained, largely for the benefit of the tourist trade, at least until the inter-war period. It was left to Hungarian novelists and sociographers in the first half of this century to describe the real 'tanya problem', particularly as it existed in the conditions created by the penetration of capitalism. Population growth and pressure upon the land led to the establishment of fully autonomous tanyas (units of production and consumption without any connection with larger nuclear settlements), sometimes in previously uninhabited regions. Tázlár provides a good illustration of this particular settlement phenomenon and of the full range of social problems posed by all types of scattered settlement.[1]

The second term with which the reader must familiarise himself is 'szakszövetkezet' (pronounced 'socksövetkezet'), which can be rendered as 'specialist cooperative'. The szakszövetkezet is a self-administering association of farmers, the sovereign authority of which is the general assembly of all the members. This assembly elects an executive committee and a full-time salaried chairman from amongst its members. Other full-time officers such as agronomists and accountants are responsible for managing the activities of the cooperative, both in the socialist sector (i.e. the land which is cultivated collectively) and in the dealings with individual members. In addition, there is a substantial number of manual workers employed at the machinery centre, and some members may work for the szakszövetkezet part-time or on a seasonal basis, although the majority of individual members devote their main energies to their personal farms.

1

Introduction

The reasons for the establishment of this unusual type of cooperative in Tázlár will become clear in Chapters 2 and 3. They have much to do with the importance of the tanya in the history of the community and the technical difficulties of collectivising in areas of scattered settlement: 'From a purely organisational point of view, scattered buildings suitable only for a few animals and their fodder . . . could not be considered for the purposes of collective farming' (Fekete, 1973, p. 23). However, the persistence of the szakszövetkezet in this area is also bound up with structural problems of post-collectivisation agriculture in Hungary. Its main feature is the scope which it affords to individual small-farming. The members of this association are not obliged to change their traditional pattern of farming and a majority has carried on farming traditional family farms. The evolution of the szakszövetkezet over the last two decades is a reflection of government policies towards the rest of the small-farm sector (primarily the members of full 'production cooperatives' who have rights to a household plot), and to some extent of the evolution of the economic system itself, especially since the introduction of the New Economic Mechanism in 1968. It has frequently been difficult to reconcile the practical need for the production of the small-farm sector with basic ideological commitments and, in the case of the szakszövetkezets, with a commitment to the eventual completion of collectivisation. The latter have flourished for some years now, despite the threat of imminent extinction. The reader should bear in mind that in Tázlár, while many private farmers were flourishing, poor performances in the small 'socialised sector' of the szakszövetkezet, and serious disturbances in the leadership, made uncertainty unusually acute in 1977. Many farmers were convinced that outside forces would put an end to individual farming on substantial family holdings by 1980 at the latest.

The concern of this book is to examine the changes which have occurred in this one particular community during the socialist period, and to show how various forms of pre-socialist socio-economic organisation have persisted, adapted to, and been accommodated in the socialist period. It analyses the way in which a traditional peasant economy has responded to the imposition of collectivisation, and also the effects which this collectivisation has had on social and cultural life. It is hoped that, while the community itself is not typical, some of the issues raised here can shed some general light on State socialist society. Occasionally these issues may be 'sensitive', in the minds of either Hungarian or Western readers. It may dismay many to realise the current reliance of Hungarian agriculture upon its small-farming sector and to accept that the government regulates its relationship with this sector primarily through the price mechanism and material incentives. However, I should make it clear that I do not argue that the small-farms constitute some kind of autonomous 'private sector'. In fact, I agree with the repeated claims of the authorities that most small-farms, including those of the szakszövetkezet community, should be considered as a more or less integrated component of modern socialist agriculture.

2

Introduction

Unlike some sociologists critical of State socialist societies, I also believe that changes in ownership relations are far from superficial, and, even in the szakszövetkezet community, the ownership of land has been displaced as the basic criterion of social status. At the same time, I find it useful to consider the persistence of elements of a 'peasant mode of production' within the small-farm sector and, despite ideology and despite some empirical evidence for the equalisation of rural and urban incomes in Hungary in recent years, to reconsider at the end of the book the question of continuing disparities between town and countryside and the emotive issue of 'exploitation'.

The community which is the subject of this book is known as Tázlár. For a period after 1907 it was called Prónayfalva (Prónay's village), having taken the name of a well-known politician and noble, who had no connection with the settlement, but from whom the local administration of the time hoped for patronage and financial assistance. The lord was apparently willing for the community to bear his name, but less forthcoming with material aid. The original name was restored in 1947. Confusion reigns today only in the heads of certain outside employees at the council offices, who puzzle about the location of Prónayfalva, the recorded birthplace of the majority of the population of Tázlár today.

The community name is not the only name which has changed over the years. The streets in the centre have acquired official names in the socialist period, but many of the older people have not learned them and regularly use the old forms. Certain buildings too have changed their function, but have retained their popular designation. When a new *bisztró* (bar), including an expresso coffee section and providing meal services, replaced the former *kocsma* (inn) in the early 1970s, the new name took a long time to stick, and many of those for whom there has been no change of function still tend to prefer the term '*kocsma*'.

Moreover, the people themselves have changed their names. One occasionally hears the boast in Tázlár that this is a pure Hungarian community in an ethnically very mixed district. Kiskőrös was populated by Slovaks in the early eighteenth century and Tázlár's immediate neighbour, Soltvadkert, was settled by *Sváb* Germans shortly afterwards. In fact, many of the early settlers in Tázlár came from these two older communities. Both these and others later changed foreign-sounding family names to similar-sounding Hungarian forms, for patriotic reasons. Thus Plametz became Pusztafi. Fogl became Földi or Földvári, and Haskó became Hadfi, to give but a few examples of family names common in Tázlár today. Immigration into Tázlár continued until after the First World War, when a number of families from Transylvania arrived in the community. They had possibly the best claim of all the settlers to a pure Hungarian ethnicity.

At any rate, the name Tázlár is indubitably more ancient. The first reference to a settlement of this name dates from 1429 (Károly, 1904

3

p. 603), and it is likely that there was a well-developed network of small villages in this area in the later period of Kun settlement. The Kuns or Cumanians were a nomadic eastern-Turkish people who arrived in several waves in the Carpathian Basin and were settled by medieval Hungarian kings principally in the region between the Rivers Danube and Tisza. The names of Tázlár and those of its immediate neighbours Bócsa, Bodoglár and Kötöny are all of Kun-Turkish origin (Rásonyi, 1958). Nothing is known of the medieval settlement. According to a legend widely repeated today, but with scant archaeological support, the original settlement was on a slightly raised area, about 1 kilometre from the village centre, known as Church Hill. Stones found here are said to have been used in the construction of modern tanyas in the 1870s. Almost the entire Danube-Tisza interfluve was abandoned following the Turkish invasion and their decisive victory over the Christian armies at Mohács in 1526. Thus the lands of Tázlár were uninhabited for some three centuries in all, although this did not imply that they were not used, nor that their ownership was not important and subject to occasional legal wrangling. The social structure of Turkish-controlled Hungary was highly complex. While in some areas villagers paid taxes to both the Turk and to the nominal Hungarian landlord, elsewhere the emergence of large and substantially autonomous agrarian towns undermined feudalism. The latter tendency was stronger in the Danube-Tisza interfluve. In the middle of the seventeenth century Tázlár was rented for pasture by the citizens of Szeged, to the south-east (Borovsky, 1910). Later, at the very end of the Turkish occupation, a peasant from Kiskunhalas lost his life after venturing beyond the town boundaries into Tázlár. (Nagy Szeder, 1926, Document 52.)

The expulsion of the Turks began a new epoch in the eighteenth century, characterised by the general reimposition of feudal controls, a Second Feudalism which sent the country into a developmental process in many ways the reverse of that under way in western Europe. The reconstituted enclaves of Kun settlement, including the most southerly on the interfluve, the Kiskunság, are partial exceptions to this process. They retained their anomalous status in the Hungarian state until the middle of the nineteenth century. But the new Kiskunság had no connection with the original Kun settlers, and Kiskunhalas for example was repopulated in the main by Hungarians from south Transdanubia. Furthermore, the geographical correspondence with the old Kun territory was imperfect. Tázlár was excluded, and linked instead, together with five other uninhabited properties, all described as *pusztas*, to the new settlement of Kiskőrös, which was granted by the monarchy to the Wattay family in gratitude for political and military services rendered (Sarlay, 1934). This family then populated the settlement with poor peasants from Slovakia in 1718 (Tepliczky, 1880).

In the course of the eighteenth century the Wattay serfs travelled out regularly to Tázlár for summer grazing. The noble family lived in Pomáz, north of Buda, and its archives record in detail the rents paid from its many widely-distributed possessions. They also show that an inn was established, probably at the crossroads of the Soltvadkert-Szeged and the Kecskemét-Kiskunhalas roads, the same intersection which still marks the centre of the community today. The consumption of spirit (*pálinka*) was high here during the summer months, when it was proportionately low in Kiskőrös; in winter, when the animals were kept in the town, the pattern was reversed. During this period Tázlár developed the same outlaw traditions as did neighbouring regions of the Kiskunság. These flourished until well into the nineteenth century, when, according to some, the famous outlaw Sándor Rózsa sought refuge here for a time after his escape from gaol in Szeged. A case of violent assault and robbery on the 'Tázlár *puszta*' which rendered a local man incapable of work for some months is recorded in Kiskőrös in 1807, in terms which suggest that the event was far from unusual.[2]

A few years after this, the Wattay property began to fragment. This process intensified as the century proceeded, and is very typical of the fate of large sections of the Hungarian nobility of the period (Mályusz, 1924). Tázlár was separated from Kiskőrös and the more northerly of the six *pusztas*. It was linked instead, both administratively and ecclesiastically, to Soltvadkert, and, according to the ecclesiastical records, permanent settlements began in 1822, probably from Soltvadkert. The annual population counts throughout the first three-quarters of the nineteenth century show very considerable fluctuations in Tázlár, and a maximum population density of less than one person per square mile (2.6 square kilometres). Permanent settlement here in 1881 was still very limited in extent, in contrast to the developed nuclear community of Soltvadkert.

The modern age began with heavy waves of settlement in the 1870s and coincided with the tragic decades of the 'tanya movement' in Hungary. By this time the *puszta* had been divided between several large landowners, but the name Tázlár still designated an area far larger than that of the present community. It included the whole of Bócsa and Harkakötöny, plus fragments of other neighbouring communities, making a total territory of over 100 square miles (260 square kilometres) (Galgóczy, 1876). In 1872, an independent local administration over this territory was formed, on principles which were not fundamentally altered for a further three-quarters of a century (see Chapter 5 below). A former manor house was used temporarily as a school in Upper Tázlár. It was converted into a church in the first decade of the twentieth century, after the construction of a new schoolhouse, the single classroom of which is still in use today. Tázlár was separated from Bócsa and new council offices were built in what is now the village centre, still sometimes referred to as 'Lower Tázlár'.

Despite these changes and the growth of organised religion and education, the tanya world was growing very rapidly during these years, with minimal administrative interference. The individualist spirit of frontier pioneers replaced the bonds and social control of a cohesive community.[3]

Introduction

Population growth is shown in Table 1. The process of parcellisation attracted the poorer strata, and especially the landless, from surrounding black-soil regions, including large numbers from beyond the Tisza. However, by the 1930s in Tázlár also there was a significant proportion without land. The diaries and records of the Catholic Church for the inter-war period reveal considerable poverty, and susceptibility to disease and to alcoholism in certain sections of the population. Yet the census data of 1935 (Table 2) are open to a rather different interpretation. Compared to other Hungarian communities at this time, Tázlár has a high proportion of peasants with plots over 5 *hold* (2.8 hectares) and, even allowing for the poor quality of much of this land, one might presume the existence of a large, mainly self-sufficient 'middle peasantry'. In some respects the farm production of this peasantry, notably in animal-breeding, compares favourably with production levels in the community today.

Table 1 Total population 1880–1978

1880	1890	1900	1910	1920	1930	1941	1949	1960	1970	1978
392	515	876	2,268	2,447	3,103	3,147	3,408	2,994	2,466	2,121

Note: Figures prior to 1910 are official estimates from the totals which then included Bócsa and other territories. The figure for 1978 was obtained at the Tázlár council offices and is the official figure on 31 May.

Table 2 Land ownership 1935

			(area in *hold*)					
	Less than 1		1–5	5–50	50–100	100–500	500+	Total
	without ploughland	with ploughland						
No. of farms	27	61	279	507	55	26	4	959

1 *hold* = 0.58 hectares (5,755 square metres)

The aim of this book is to examine the changes in the community that have taken place in the socialist period. However, to understand these one must begin from the ambiguous achievement of the pre-socialist society and the compatibility of extremes of inequality and poverty with an apparently 'open', private peasant economy, tanya-based and subject to no effective community control, in which certain families were highly mobile and indeed very prosperous.

Introduction

Tázlár is situated on low-lying sandy soils in the centre of the Danube-Tisza interfluve, about 80 miles (130 kilometres) south-east of Budapest. The sand is characteristic of large areas of the interfluve, although in recent decades the notorious shifting sands (*futó homok*) have been brought under effective control by planned forestation. In Tázlár the problem has always been most acute in the fourth zone, which borders Kötöny and Bodoglár. This has always been the most sparsely populated area, and was forested on a large scale in an early phase of resettlement by the absentee landlord, Earl Vigyázó, after whom the entire forest is still popularly named. The settlers of the 1870s were all exhorted to plant trees in order to restrict the movement of the sand (Galgóczy, 1876).

Despite the very low average value of agricultural land, there is a considerable variety of soil types. The territory is now divided administratively into four zones which are roughly equal in size and which meet in the village centre (see map 2). The first resettlers occupied what is generally regarded as the best black earth, to the west and north-west of the village centre in the first and second zones. The third zone, to the east and northeast, like the fourth, is of lower average quality than the first two, especially as one moves away from the village centre in the direction of Szank, the so-called 'Szank corner'. Most of the land in this zone has been taken over by the Kiskőrös State Farm. Apart from a small area of forest, two successful large-scale vineyards were established in this zone by the State Farm in the 1960s. This success highlights a factor which applies equally to private peasant farming. The pioneers learned over time that it was possible to carry on certain types of agriculture on apparently unattractive soils, and that careful manuring would improve results significantly in all but the most hopeless areas of shifting sand. Only in recent years have scientific soil analyses preceded the execution of costly investments. The large-scale vineyards now planned by the szakszövetkezet for the early 1980s should not fail in the same way as earlier szakszövetkezet projects of the 1960s.

Detailed climatic information has to be taken from data for Harka-kötöny, Soltvadkert and Kecskemét. There is an annual average of 2,051 hours of sunshine, and 25 inches (635 millimetres) of rain (14 (355 millimetres) of which fall between April and September). Cloudbursts are very common during the summer, and May and June are the wettest months of the year. The average temperature in July is 21.9°C., in January -1.8°C. (with a January record minimum of -32.2°C. and record maximum of 17°C.). The people of Tázlár feel that their winters have become milder in recent years, and certainly the quantity and duration of snow cover appears to have diminished. The essential climatic uncertainties of great relevance for agricultural production have, however, persisted. The first frost on average occurs on 20 October, but frost has been known as early as September. Similarly, the 50-year average for the last spring frost is 10 April, but frosts have been known to occur late in May. Hailstorms in spring or early summer have frequently destroyed an entire year's grape

7

production, while the wind, which moves the sands, is also a recurring hazard which often makes work in the fields impossible. The main branches of agriculture have not changed fundamentally since resettlement. The production profile of most farms was initially decisively influenced by the conditions of tanya settlement and the isolation of Tázlár from outside markets, even after the opening of the railway at Soltvadkert in 1882. Grain was not produced for sale on these soils, but animal-breeding continued on larger properties with the old extensive methods. Later, following intensive parcellisation, the local council administered a public pasture which afforded even smaller farmers at least summer-grazing rights. The census of 1895 records a total of 3,265 head of Hungarian cattle on the territory then administered from Tázlár. By 1935, on a territory reduced by more than half, this number had fallen to 1,463, and a much larger area was devoted to intensive crop production, especially to maize. However, fruit and wine production was probably of greater marketability from the outset, and was given by many families as the main reason for their migration to Tázlár. The Danube-Tisza interfluve is not one of the great traditional wine-producing regions of Hungary, but because of the incidence of phylloxera in those regions, grape cultivation spread rapidly in the decades of heavy resettlement in Tázlár. Thus fruit and wine production also established itself in both the ideal and the actual composition of peasant farm output. Richer farmers, able to produce their own wine, found this a highly marketable commodity in the inter-war period; but even poorer settlers, those unable to keep large animals, still had an area of vines for their own consumption and, perhaps through some exchange with richer farmers, found many opportunities to satisfy their consumer demands in wine also.

Map 1 shows the position of Tázlár and its regional communications. The only tarmac road runs from north-west to south-east and is traversed twice daily in each direction by the long-distance bus. Almost all other bus services link the community to the west, to the rich community of Soltvadkert (population presently around 8,500), and to the towns of Kiskőrös (population 15,000) and Kiskunhalas (population 28,000) on working-days only. However, there are no buses in this direction after six o'clock and on Sunday there is only the long-distance bus, which leaves soon after four. Hence public transport, and in particular access to the railway station at Soltvadkert 6 miles (10 kilometres) away, still leaves much to be desired, and contributes to the importance of private means of conveyance.

It is obvious from Map 1 that to go from Tázlár to Kiskunhalas via Soltvadkert is a somewhat circuitous route. However, the earth road which provides a more direct link is frequently quite unsuitable for motor transport, and the same is true of the earth road which joins Tázlár to Bócsa, in the direction of Kecskemét. Many Tázlár people allege that the condition of these roads is connected with the presence in the vicinity of Soviet and Hungarian military bases, and the shooting ranges at Bócsa and Kötöny. Certain sections of the entire earth road grid established over the community during tanya parcellisation are regularly rendered impassable by long convoys of military vehicles. These generally travel at night, and soldiers are not often seen in the village centre.

Bócsa, Pirtó, Bodoglár and Harkakötöny are neighbouring 'tanya centres', the first two roughly comparable in size and settlement pattern to Tázlár, the latter less developed and administratively subordinate to Kiskunmajsa and Kiskunhalas respectively. Tázlár people commute to both of these towns (commonly abbreviated as Majsa and Halas), but there are no formal administrative links. Instead, Tázlár remains, as it was in the eighteenth century, the south-eastern extremity of a district administered from Kiskőrös. There is no longer an elected district council, but Kiskőrös contains nevertheless a large Party-State apparatus which, as will be examined in this book, plays a very important role in events in Tázlár. The town, famous as the birthplace of the great revolutionary poet Sándor Petőfi, also contains a court-house and a large surgery; it has grown rapidly since its promotion to the rank of town in 1972, but still lacks a substantial industrial base and as a market centre it attracts from Tázlár only those dependent upon public transport. For the marketing of their own produce and for exceptional consumer needs, in addition to the local Thursday market in Tázlár itself, the twice-weekly market in Soltvadkert is sufficient.

1. The local market

For other needs, the fashion is increasingly to take longer trips, either to Szeged or to the county-town of Bács-Kiskun county, Kecskemét. The latter also exercises considerable direct administrative control over Tázlár, and local officials must travel here almost as often as they are called to Kiskőrös. Tázlár men work in all these towns and in the capital itself. Those young people who study beyond the compulsory eight-grade 'general school' in the village are even more widely spread.

Ecclesiastically, Tázlár falls into the Catholic diocese of Kalocsa, in a district formerly based on the larger village of Kecel. Episcopal visits are rare nowadays and no longer demand a mounted guard of welcome at the community boundary (which point is still marked, however, by a large wooden crucifix at the side of the road). Kalocsa is also the centre of the dairy enterprise to which Tázlár's daily milk output is sold.

The internal communications and landscape of Tázlár are quickly described. Upper Tázlár (*a felső telep*), about 2 kilometres nearer Solt-vadkert, and the site of the earliest manor houses and of the first church and school, was the original tanya-centre. Even today there is some new house-building here, because some tanya-dwellers of the vicinity prefer to move here than to build in the village centre. All the buses stop in Upper Tázlár, and there is a shop and a private grinder. The population of the hamlet is around 130, their houses border the main road and two small side-streets, and the average age of the inhabitants is somewhat higher than the average in the village.

The regular plan of the main village (Map 3) was laid down in the first decade of the century, yet in the 1970s a few of the house-plots in these old streets were still awaiting their first dwelling, and were temporarily functioning as gardens. The final street on the eastern side, north of the main road, is old and distinctive. Its small, identical houses were constructed in the 1930s specifically for poorer families with many children, one of a range of direct relief measures taken by the State in the years after the depression. The street is still known by the nickname bestowed at the time of construction and also retains a little of its past in the character of its inhabitants today. The last street on the other side of the main road has an utterly different character, having been more recently built up by richer farmers moving in from tanyas. Most new housing is scheduled for the area north of the main road. The allocation of all building plots is now carefully controlled by the council. Its latest long-term development plan for the community has designated a large marshy area within the inner village (*belterület*) for landscaping as a park. The road which leads in the direction of Kecskemét and is officially named the *Kecskeméti út* has been built up so as to link it to the most proximate tanya row, which it now incorporates as part of the inner village.

Tanyas are not randomly scattered over the land, but are in general found at regular intervals along an earth road, sometimes still bearing exact witness to the original scheme of parcellisation. Some have profited from specific natural features and built beside one of the two large shallow lakes, or in the shelter of a permanent sand-hill, or in the cover of a pre-existent copse or glade. Others were built wherever their families were able to make a plot available, and this explains the existence today of several rows of dwellings built as close to each other as village houses are, and commonly named after a single family. The tanya was usually surrounded by trees, so that it was visible to the stranger only in winter. The complete fencing in of the farmyard is, however, a more recent development. It is associated in the state farm area of the third zone with a measured 'household plot', the norm for which in the nation as a whole since mass collectivisation has been 1 *hold* (0.58 hectares). All the principal earth road arteries have popular names, usually signifying the dominant family along a particular track, or some conspicuous feature such as a windmill.

Today almost all public buildings and facilities are concentrated in the village, most of them in a very small area at the centre. At the perimeter one finds the two cemeteries, the sports field, the dairy and animal collection points and the machinery centre of the szakszövetkezet, its granaries and grinder. Otherwise, everything has developed within a stone's throw of the ancient crossroads. This is the site of the modern *bisztró*, where the Communist Party offices stood in the 1950s. Next door, on the site of the former *kocsma*, is the main self-service shop. There are also separate butchers', clothing and household-goods shops, which operate in the

2. A tanya of the second zone. It is inhabited, but has no garden plot and only a small yard. It is surrounded by collectively-owned pasture

11

framework of a Consumers' Cooperative based in Soltvadkert. This total falls considerably short of the number of private shops which functioned in the 1930s. Across the road from the *bisztró* and shop a small park has been established. Behind it, the former village hall (*népház*) has been recently converted into a spinning factory, controlled from Kiskunhalas and employing some 50 persons, most of them female. Next door is the calvinist church, built in the mid-1960s, while a little further down the *Kecskeméti út* are the large culture house, opened in 1961 and fulfilling many of the old functions of the *népház*, and the new kindergarten. The main school was built on the same block in the 1960s and replaced a previously fragmented network of classrooms founded, and until the late 1940s maintained, along sectarian lines by the two major Churches. In the same street as the school are the administrative offices of the szövetkezet, in a converted former private house, the new post office (opened in 1963), the new council offices (1965) and the new surgery (1973). The largest building in the community remains the Roman Catholic church, built beside the main road after decades of planning and wrangling with the authorities, largely through self-help and subscription in the difficult years of the 1950s, and finally consecrated in 1958.

The physical environment of both village centre and tanya world has been transformed in the socialist period. In the village the 1970s brought a steep increase in house prices, but dwellings continued to increase in size and to follow ever more novel designs. The first two-storeyed house was built in 1971 by a private motor mechanic, and not emulated until five years later by a private builder and by the then treasurer of the szakszövetkezet. Pavements have been laid down in all the village streets by the council, which in an energetic phase in the 1960s also established a piped-water system and contributed towards the costs of electrification. Not all households drew immediate benefit from these services, as the costs to individuals remained considerable. There are still a few families today who use petroleum lights in winter evenings, and draw their water from pumps in the street or from wells. The village skyline is now also adorned with television aerials. In 1978 there were officially 228 sets in the entire community, including some battery-powered models in tanyas; there were also 337 radios, plus one or two unofficial (i.e. unlicensed) colour television sets. Bicycles remain the ubiquitous form of transport. The traditional horse-drawn carriage was replaced by a rubber-tyred version in the 1960s. Slowly, of course, horses are themselves being replaced by motor vehicles, but recent tax changes designed to encourage small-farming, through eliminating the tax on horses, may weaken this trend still further in Tázlár.

Change in the tanya environment has been no less-far-reaching. Tanyas themselves crumble very quickly once abandoned, even if the roof and other sections are not immediately dismantled for use elsewhere. In certain areas, especially in the first and second zones, the land has already been transformed by the formation of large fields or *táblas*, which are farmed by the szakszövetkezet on a large scale, principally for cereal production. On the other hand, there are numerous areas in every zone where land has fallen into disuse in recent decades. In 1977 the treasurer of the szakszövetkezet estimated privately that between one-quarter and one-third of the total surface area of Tázlár might fall into this category. In the following year a major campaign was launched in the nation as a whole to restore all abandoned lands to efficient cultivation. In Tázlár strenuous efforts were made but, for reasons which will become clear in later chapters, the task was proving impossible and the szakszövetkezet, according to the new laws, was having to face heavy fines. New forests and large-scale vineyards were mentioned above. The other major change in the landscape has resulted from costly investment in irrigation channels, which now link the major lakes of the community and also join up with similar schemes in neighbouring communities. The total project is of questionable final advantage to the szakszövetkezet, but nevertheless absorbed most of its investment resources in the 1970s.

This introductory outline is developed in Chapter 2, which concentrates upon the problems associated with tanya settlement and the task of 'community building' in the socialist period. Tanya settlement in itself is shown, however, to be an insufficient explanation for the contradictions which have arisen from half-hearted collectivisation in Tázlár, although

3. A new village street on the northern side, after rain

tanya residence has continued to play a significant role in farm production for a certain section of the population. Chapter 3 follows Tázlár's recent history in its national context. It begins with the origins of the cooperative movement in the 1940s and continues through the reversals of 1956 to the accomplishment of mass collectivisation between 1959 and 1961 and the formation in Tázlár of simple cooperative groups and later of szakszövetkezets. The theory and practice of the szakszövetkezets is related to basic premises of Hungarian development strategy, and also to the reform of the national economic mechanism introduced in 1968, i.e. the launching of the so-called 'guided-market economy'.

Chapters 4, 5 and 6 examine various aspects of the szakszövetkezet community. Each contains detailed analysis of the situation which prevailed at the time of fieldwork and some form of prognosis for the 1980s. Although the list of topics covered is far from exhaustive, it becomes clear that the influence of the szakszövetkezet upon the development of the community has been profound and certainly cannot be restricted to any narrow 'economic' sphere. Chapter 7 reverts to certain theoretical implications of the earlier analysis, which mainly concern the transformation of the peasantry and the basic character and relevance of the 'Hungarian Road', in both collectivisation and general development policy.

2 The tanya question

The late Ferenc Erdei, one of Hungary's greatest social scientists, in his early sociography of the Danube-Tisza interfluve, classified Tázlár with a small group of tanya communities which 'lacked any germ of a village' (Erdei, 1957, p. 174). At the same time he made it clear, both here and a few years later in his definitive treatise on the tanya question (Erdei, 1976), that this form of tanya settlement was exceptional and that therefore the problems which it posed would lie outside the general scope of 'tanya policy', which in any case Erdei regarded as a poorly formulated panacea unable to remedy the fundamentally misguided policies of the Horthy government. In contrast to the typical settlement pattern of the Great Plain with its ancient nomadic origins, the tanyas of Tázlár were permanent and self-contained productive and residential units. Because they had not developed through any specific relation with a neighbouring town or older nuclear settlement they did not, strictly, deserve to be called tanyas. Moreover, the sum of these self-contained units had developed only minimal community institutions and even these were, for the most part, externally imposed by the requirements of the State administrative system. Because of the diversity of the immigrants and the absence of nuclear settlement the application of any concept of 'community' to Tázlár has, until quite recently, been quite unreal. Today, despite deliberate emphasis upon community-building in the socialist period, there is still a tanya problem which needs to be faced. This is not necessarily the same problem as that now typical of the rest of the country, where the tanya system had different origins and closer links with traditional communities, and has often played a different role in the transition to a collectivised agriculture in the socialist period.

There is an immediate and obvious contradiction between the goals of large-scale, collectivised agriculture and fragmented tanya settlement of the kind which took place in Tázlár. This problem is often discussed in the literature and was the main justification for effectively excluding Tázlár and a number of similar communities from mass-collectivisation in the early 1960s (Orosz, 1969). The task of this chapter is threefold: first of all to define the relationship between Tázlár's atypical tanya settlement pattern and the character of peasant economy in the capitalist period; secondly, to assess the impact of socialist policies, of specific measures to stimulate migration into the village centre and the criteria likely to influence the choice of residence in the near future; and thirdly, to consider

15

what role, if any, the tanya has played in the farming economy of the socialist period.

I Tanya settlement and the peasant economy of the capitalist period

The break-up of the unified *puszta* which had belonged to the Wattay family began in the early part of the nineteenth century. It intensified after the 1870s and reached a climax in the first decade of the twentieth century. This was the period in which agriculture was begun, on land previously utilised only for summer grazing. These decades also saw heavy immigration, mass migrations in the national context, and the full impact of capitalist penetration from western Europe. In the mid-1870s there were already numerous manors and tanyas of various sizes (Galgóczy, 1876). The founder of the Lazár family is said by his descendants to have arrived at this time from Szeged and to have purchased 600 *hold* (340 hectares) of the best soil, and to have lived for a few years in huts dug into the ground before gathering the materials for tanya construction. Later, the parcels which larger landowners offered for sale through regional banks became much smaller. Several old men still recall the parcellisation of the Schwáb property in 1905 by the Kalocsa Bank. This was sold off in 30-*hold* (17-hectare) parcels, some of which were taken up by immigrants from Soltvadkert, who constructed what became known as the Hirsch row of tanyas at just over 2 kilometres from the lower village centre. This cluster is still fully populated today and, having been electrified, is likely to remain so. However, four of the Schwáb parcels, totalling 134 *hold* (75 hectares), were taken up by a single family of earlier settlers who were already prospering on the rich soils of this zone.

Despite the tendency for larger properties to fragment, which continued until the end of the capitalist period and reached a climax in the Land Reform of 1945, inequalities remained very pronounced throughout this period. For example, there are records of essential welfare relief in the community being undertaken by the local council from the 1870s onwards. There is considerable difference of opinion in the recollections of informants concerning the period prior to the Liberation. Many middle peasants assert that they never had any difficulty in buying land when they wished to expand, but were frequently unable to find a ready market when they wished to sell; some blamed this fact specifically upon the security enjoyed by the landless and farm-servant strata in Tázlár, which gave them no incentive to set up independent farms. During the Second World War there were one or two properties which were owned by absentee landlords and exploited in a more 'capitalist' manner. But even these were a far cry from the system of large noble estates which remained dominant in the country as a whole, and in Tázlár the largest farms were owned by rich peasants who were frequently well liked and respected by the people who worked for them, in permanent or temporary capacities.

On the other hand, there are many objective reasons for supposing that the greater mobility of the first generation of settlement in the heyday of the tanya movement, when even poor immigrants fortunate in the location of their parcel had a real opportunity for self-enrichment, had been stifled by the sheer volume of settlement and by the economic conditions of the inter-war period. For example, later immigrants who obtained between 5 and 15 *hold* (3 and 9 hectares) of poor soil on peripheral zones such as the Szank corner were faced with a daunting subsistence task. Most men in this neighbourhood were always in need of work as farm servants or as day-labourers. They generally kept one cow, but only a few kept a horse as well; almost all had about 1 *hold* (0.58 hectare) of vines. Today this zone has been considerably depopulated by the expansion of the State Farm, and only two young families remain.

The formation of a community from such disparate tanya elements was in a number of ways impeded by the peasant economy of the period. There was no public market activity in the form of exchange of goods within the territory, and only larger farmers were able to develop external trading links, usually with Jewish merchants in Soltvadkert and Kiskunhalas. But despite the constraint on mobility by worsening economic conditions and the limited extent of external marketing, the organisation of farm work did not encourage the integration of tanya households. In fact, tanya farming is remembered by most middle peasants as isolated and individualised. It contrasts fundamentally with the mutual-aid patterns found in most peasant economies, as for example with the cooperation described by Fél and Hofer in their study of a traditional community of the Great Plain (Fél and Hofer, 1969, pp. 179—80). It is through both the individualisation of production and consumption on the tanya, and the new pattern of stratification which followed, emphasised by unilateral transfers of labour to richer farmers, that the tanya system in Tázlár revealed the scope it afforded capitalist forces. This was in spite of the unfavourable environment and the fact that the system was built by those in flight from the consequences of capitalist penetration elsewhere in the countryside.

It is very important to understand the character and extent of capitalist relations in Tázlár in this period and to realise that the character of capitalist penetration in other, more traditional, village communities was quite different. It is true that in its regional context Tázlár has always been regarded as a poor and backward settlement, and with some justification. It has also been perceived as socially very heterogeneous, and it is still considered as such today. It is easy to forget about this social diversity when the main aim is to stress the relative deprivation of the entire community, and this is very much the case with Erdei (1957). At this time Erdei was considering the process of embourgeoisement (*polgárosódás*) of the peasantry from a material and technical point of view, basing his judgements upon the development of the forces of production, and neglecting the class relations which were then developing within the peasantry. Erdei welcomed this process. Moreover, in many of the older nuclear communities of the region, including Kiskőrös, he understated the class differences and emphasised the unity and the social homogeneity of the village (Erdei, 1957, p. 168). Later, in his foreword to the third edition of *Futóhomok*, Erdei retracted this analysis. Instead he declared that there were two aspects to the process of embourgeoisement and that he was concerned with the development of both forces and relations, though a certain ambiguity would have to remain through the use of the single term *polgárosódás*. The distinction is nevertheless important for the analysis here. In Kiskőrös Erdei saw that the forces of production were rapidly developing in response to capitalist stimuli, but that the attendant process of class formation was rendered much less acute by the unity of the community. In Tázlár the absence of any such unity was a condition for the formation of classes which developed along capitalist lines in spite of the high proportion of self-sufficient family farms, and the number of other factors which inhibited the development of productive forces (market isolation, etc.).

One further aspect of the economy of this region in the capitalist period should be stressed as a condition for the social relations which prevailed in Tázlár, and which created a very different situation from that which prevailed in the country as a whole. Because of fruit and wine production, the latter exceptionally labour-intensive, there was no fundamental problem for anyone here in making a living from the land. Despite the heavy settlement of the tanya period, the land was always able to absorb more immigrants. Significantly, it was the poor who led the way in the planting of vineyards, but when the richer farmers followed and Hungarian wines became increasingly popular on the German market, casual labour opportunities were guaranteed, and at times of the year which did not prevent subsistence production from continuing in other branches. Erdei makes the point in relation to Soltvadkert (Erdei, 1957, p. 171) but it applies just as well to Tázlár: the 'rural labour surplus' in Tázlár was not condemned to the fate suffered by landless labourers in so many other parts of the country (such as seasonal migration or non-agricultural work). This was so in the earlier phase of the tanya period because of the general availability of land, and, as land became increasingly scarce, because of changes in the composition of production and the market conjuncture in wine. Consequently, despite the restricted mobility of the later tanya period, everyone was able to make some sort of living from the land inside his native community. Thus, in comparison with other regions of Hungary, much social conflict was not thrown so sharply into relief here. However, this must not blind us to an awareness of conflict and of its underlying causes.

Can we relate this discussion to anthropological theory of peasant economy, and postulate a link between tanya settlement and the peasant economy of Tázlár in the capitalist period? A late settlement community of scattered peasant farms is qualitatively different from the nuclear community on which much of the traditional theory of peasant economy has been founded. It is not necessary for the settlement to be nuclear for the village to be considered as a production entity and not simply a 'granular mass of households' (Georgescu-Roegen, 1970). It is common to assume

that the village is cohesive in every way, that cooperation between households will complement production on the family farm, and even that the
unity of the village as a community ('Gemeinschaft') is a simulation at
a higher level of the organisation of the peasant family itself. Now, given
that the village community does have some determining influence over
the sphere of operation of individual farms, it is only a short step to posing
the community as a barrier or shield which can protect those productive
units from the market principles which increasingly impinge from outside in the period of capitalist penetration. This has led to the construction of an autonomous domain of peasant economy within a capitalist
national framework, and also to Erdei's failure to notice the changes in
social relations brought about by capitalism in the 1930s. There is no
place for class differentiation in the theory of the traditional village.
Moreover, even in Lenin's classical analysis of the Russian countryside there
is some recognition of the resistance offered by the traditional community
to the successful implantation of capitalist relations; in the short term
and under certain conditions the community is able to preserve the unity
of a 'stratum of peasants' and to prevent the emergence of a peasantry
which is differentiated along urban-capitalist lines.[1]

These versions of the traditional theory are clearly of little use for the
analysis of the pre-war situation in Tázlár. The majority of the tanya
peasantry were isolated, atomised producers. They *were* a 'granular mass'.
From this point of view they can, however, be taken to illustrate another
recurring theme in the analysis of peasant economy, associated in particular with vulgar interpretations of the theories of Chayanov, according
to which the isolation and the 'natural state' of peasant economy can be
explained exclusively at the level of the household. Undoubtedly, poor
communications and farm isolation had severe cultural implications and
contributed to the absence of a community sentiment. They also contributed
to economic backwardness, emphasised subsistence production and the
autonomy of individual farms, and minimised both cooperation in the
agricultural labour process and dependence on an outside capitalist market.
In these aspects the tanyas of Tázlár fulfil certain criteria of the traditional
model of peasant economy, which stress the 'domestic economy/consumption'
functions at the expense of its character as a productive enterprise. This
model too assumes the unity of a peasant stratum which is not susceptible
in these conditions to the class differentiation which only capitalism can
induce.

There is some questionable support for this model in the very large
number of farms of between 5 and 50 *hold* (3 and 29 hectares) shown in
the 1935 census data (see Table 2). But it would be necessary to have a
more detailed breakdown of this category and of the quality of the land
they were farming to estimate what proportion of them were able to live
from their own land alone. And even if this was a considerably higher
proportion than in most areas of the country at this time, alongside the
proud autonomous middle peasantry there were those whose production

19

was primarily intended for the market and many others who could only dream of self-sufficiency. We must remember that tanya settlement in Tázlár grew out of the penetration of capitalism into other areas of the Hungarian countryside, and perhaps detailed knowledge of the characteristics of those who bought land and settled in Tázlár would help explain the peculiar vulnerability of the tanya community itself to capitalist forces. Those forces resulted in a very wide span of differentiation and in a very active labour market which was much more highly developed than the analysis of Chayanov will allow. We may conclude that despite the low level of productive forces, and even though many producers were not involved directly in significant production for the market, and for a long period land remained relatively abundant, nevertheless the settlement of this 'frontier' was from the beginning governed by the capitalist mode of production. Furthermore, the stratification which resulted in Tázlár may have corresponded rather better than the typical pattern in villages elsewhere in the country to the Leninist ideological assumptions upon which anti-peasant policies and eventually collectivisation came to be founded.

II The drift away from the tanya

Nuclear settlement has developed in the lower centre of Tázlár in the socialist period, i.e. in a period of intensified industrialisation in the national economy and of conditions generally associated with the disintegration of peasant communities. The lower centre is commonly referred to as 'the village' and it has been the consistent policy of the government to persuade tanya-dwellers to build and resettle there. In historical perspective, the socialist ban on farmstead construction, which in practice for a long time extended also to farm amelioration, and to the repairing and replacing of essential buildings, is in effect a return to pre-settlement restrictions (perhaps less effectively enforced, and designed to buttress feudal controls over the population).[2] Whatever the underlying objectives of socialist policy towards the tanya, in terms either of social control or of raising the economic level of the peasantry, it appears to have had far-reaching effects, both in Tázlár and throughout the country. In 1949 Tázlár had a population of 2,650 living outside the two tanya centres, out of a total population of 3,408 (78 per cent). By 1978 out of a total of 2,121, just over 50 per cent were living on tanyas. Almost all the growth in the nuclear population had taken place in the lower centre, and of the remaining tanyas a high proportion was close to the centres or to the main road. These results were not achieved by the use of force. Only those residents of the third zone whose farms fell within the area redeveloped by the State Farm in the 1960s were obliged to leave their tanyas, although situations similar to this were still arising in the late 1970s as the szakszövetkezet embarked upon similar large schemes. When a middle-aged widow lost her home to the State Farm, she had a small tanya built by the family in another area of the third zone, and defended this action on the grounds that the compensation provided was insufficient for the purchase of any dwelling within the village centre. She nevertheless paid a small fine. A considerably larger fine was levied upon a rich farmer whose permanent abode lay in Soltvadkert but who, in the traditional manner in which tanyas originated, built a conspicuously elegant tanya beside his fruit plots near the Soltvadkert boundary (see plate 4). Almost a full two storeys in height, it incorporated cellars and a garage. Recently, many families have renovated buildings and even erected new ones without incurring punishment. The main practical difficulty, which several tanya-dwellers criticise strongly and claim is forcing them to migrate, is that the Savings Bank will not provide loans for tanya-building work. Against this, it is clear that for many families the well-known lines of official policy are a pretext or at most a secondary factor behind a decision to emigrate, the real causes of which must be sought elsewhere; in other words, State policy merely facilitates a process which it is unable to control or actively to precipitate.

Ideally, the drift away from the tanya should be linked with a general analysis of rural emigration and of the motives and behaviour of different categories within the peasantry, all within the context of State policy and the distinctive features of 'extensive' industrialisation in Hungary. Because there are no reliable statistical data for the social patterns of emigration from Tázlár and because the typical patterns of other communities cannot be assumed to apply here, there can only be some conjecture, supported by the evidence of today and the opinions of informants. All levels of the

4. A fully modernised, electrified tanya, with surrounding orchards

peasantry were affected. The tiny elite of absentee owners and rich peasants had been speedily eliminated by the end of the 1940s. The exodus of the former agricultural proletariat has been a more gradual process. Some obtained larger properties following Land Reform and prospered as small-holders, surviving within the framework of the szakszövetkezet up to the present day. Others could not respond to the challenge of independent farming and preferred to join the cooperative farms which functioned from 1949. Most of this group have left the community and very few remain on tanyas today. As for the middle peasants, although in general their children have profited from new educational opportunities, and have obtained skills and qualifications and then emigrated, many of this wide band have flourished in the szakszövetkezet community. A high proportion of the most impressive new housing in the village centre is the fruit of their labour in private small-commodity production.

In the campaigns which have been regularly mounted by the media as a result of countless analyses of the 'tanya problem', much stress is always laid upon the cultural and material advantages of residence in the socialist village community. Given the obvious attractiveness of the village, despite high building-costs and despite better transport and other improvements which have reduced the discomforts of the tanya, it is useful to ask in what sense this expansion has strengthened bonds of community, and whether this community now has a specifically socialist character.

Undoubtedly, the presence of certain socialist institutions in the village centre was no incentive to tanya-dwellers and in the past certain bureaucratic organs may have been a considerable disincentive. Later, in an improved political and economic climate, a non-interfering bureaucracy was no longer perceived as a threat to private peasant economy; and it is argued in Chapter 4 how well the limited cooperative type, the szakszövetkezet, served a certain manner of community integration. However, it is doubtful whether the major public investments of a novel, socialist character, such as the culture house, contributed much to the popularity of village residence. Even the closure of tanya schools and the construction of a large new school in the village was no great inducement, for most tanya families now have close kin in the centre and there is always a place where a child can stay during those brief periods in winter when the daily journey may prove impracticable. Moreover, certain indirect consequences of the new order have had a negative effect. For example, the traditional private shops and taverns have been replaced by new establishments under cooperative control from Soltvadkert, but the services provided are not reckoned to be of a high standard. The quality of the bread and the inadequacy of meat supplies were especially delicate problems in 1977. As for the *bisztró*, the only official public tavern, in families where a wife preferred to have her husband drink at home this too worked against resettlement in the village.

Nevertheless, if socialist policy is taken more broadly to include public works and the various aspects of successive community development plans, then the achievement has been considerable. The improvements of the 1960s greatly increased the attractiveness of village residence. Furthermore, the installation of basic amenities to households called for careful negotiation between council and individuals, who were required to make high advance contributions to the investment costs. These public utility provisions may not seem extravagant, but in this context, where, for example, social security at this time extended only to a small minority of the population, it is difficult to exaggerate the importance of the initiatives taken by the council and of the financial collaboration organised between households at community level, involving for the first time all sections of the population. Significantly, the 'free rider' problem has been an obstacle recently to the spread of electrification in the tanya areas where the higher material contributions could have been met by a cluster of tanyas, but where the households individually were unable to agree and to make their demand effective.

Improvements in public facilities are still going ahead on a smaller scale, mainly through additions to existing buildings or to the network of pavements around the village. Much more important, however, are the changed opportunities for employment, including, in the early 1970s, the opening of the spinning factory, for which the council was in part responsible. This was the first important source of non-agricultural wage-labour in the community, and it absorbed principally unskilled female labour, thus complementing the simultaneously expanding opportunities in agriculture for male wage-labour. However, since the spinning factory demanded regular night-shift work, tanya-dwellers were at a clear disadvantage. Although a few workers at the factory, as well as some other daily commuters, do travel in from tanyas and affirm that they have no intention of changing their abode, the majority of the industrial workforce lives in the village. Modifications in traditional peasant economy and the increasing popularity of external commuting on a daily basis have inevitably encouraged the movement in from the tanyas. There is a general demand for wage-labour, not only among the young. But young women in particular have been attracted by recent State family allowance policies. The child-care allowance introduced in 1967, which permits a female in employment to take three years' maternity leave with a substantial monthly allowance, is one of a few socialist measures universally praised by the people of Tázlár. Moreover, women are assisted in their return to work by the excellent nursery facilities, another major bonus of village residence. In Tázlár in 1977 approximately 43 women were on paid maternity leave, and of this number 35 were resident in the village.

Thus the growth of the village centre in Tázlár has been influenced by socialist policies, but this has been due more to higher national standards in public facilities and the integration of the community into the national economy than to either tanya policy *per se* or to the establishment of specifically socialist institutions in the village. There are many other factors at work, some of which can be quantified — the economic factors analysed below — and some of which cannot. It is reasonable to suppose that the process of emigration from tanya areas is self-reinforcing, i.e. that conditions which are known to be shared by a number of households in an area become less tolerable when the neighbours emigrate, either to the village or to some urban destination. Thus depopulation has not proceeded evenly over the entire territory, but has left empty pockets which cannot be completely explained by the quality of the land, by the impact of land confiscations, by distance from the centre or by any other quantifiable variable. Despite the radio and many other innovations on the tanya, with family size now much reduced and agriculture less demanding than in the past, and with younger members of the family expressing unambiguous preferences for the village, it may be that behind the decision of many a tanya family to move to the village there lies a positive desire to discover 'community'. Such a move will frequently mark a transition in the life-cycle of the household, or in that of the head of the household only, perhaps the latter's definitive abandonment of peasant farming.

Other aspects of the village housing market and in particular its role in prestige competition are considered in Chapter 6. The process of building always makes very heavy demands upon family labour and may be very protracted (although there is often a panic at the end to meet the official deadline when a mortgage has been raised). But when a tanya farmer completes his house today there is no guarantee that he will move in at once. Some houses have been sold, let, or simply left to stand empty for years, providing insurance for an owner who, perhaps for specific economic reasons, chooses to stay a little longer farming on the tanya. These economic motives and the economic conjuncture of the later 1970s, in which some farmers scrambled to sell tanyas while others simultaneously renounced all intention of migration to the village, will be considered in the next section.

III The tanya and the integration of peasant economy

The origins and development of tanya settlement in Tázlár can be explained in terms of a particular mode of peasant economy tied up with the penetration of capitalist relations in Hungary. Let us now examine the relation between the settlement pattern and the persistence of a modified peasant economy in the socialist period. The main question is whether the consequences of tanya policy and the drift to the village centre are in accord with the more recent vital objective of the socialist state, not specific to dispersed-settlement communities. This objective is the maximum utilisation of 'marginal' peasant labour in small-commodity production, in the case of Tázlár to take place within the organisational framework of the szakszövetkezet.

Apparent confirmation of the contradiction between tanya settlement and socialist collectivised agriculture is abundant in Tázlár. On the perimeter of the third zone the State Farm expanded on private territory, took over rather more land than it was able to farm, and by the 1970s was leasing back large areas to the few surviving tanya-dwellers. The same pattern is characteristic in neighbouring communities where full cooperatives were formed in place of szakszövetkezets, and this suggests that an active land policy would have had highly deleterious consequences for production in Tázlár also. In any case, many tanya farms have been more or less voluntarily abandoned and their land ceded to the szakszövetkezet, which has been unable to utilise the land. It is probable that there was a continuing decline in the area of arable land before the late 1970s, and by 1978 there was still no fundamental improvement. Amongst tanya-dwellers rumours of the impending completion of collectivisation were strengthening the desire to emigrate. Amongst even the leaders of the szakszövetkezet, few had much confidence in its ability to make good the inevitable losses in production. The contradiction between the maximisation of economic resources and collectivisation in tanya areas will persist at least until the large investment of capital enables a cooperative fully to replace private tanya production. In Tázlár and many similar communities only a 'second-best optimum' has been pursued so far. There has been a gradual drift away from the tanya, for reasons not primarily bound up with local land policy and collectivisation, and an even slower expansion of the socialist nucleus within the szakszövetkezet. Since this transitional period has now lasted almost two decades it may be asked at what political and social cost it has been achieved and what evidence there is today to link a high level of private small-commodity production with dispersed settlement.

If one begins from bourgeois locational theory one might expect a negative relation between the distance of a farm from the main road or the centre of the village (or possibly of the upper hamlet if that is nearer) and the volume of its production, on the grounds that for farms nearer the village shorter distances and better communications should have a positive effect on production potential. Now, it is true that the szakszövetkezet has indeed brought the entire tanya world into contact with the external 'market' and it has integrated tanya farmers in the same 'vertical' manner in which it has integrated the farmers of the village. There is a general dependence on the szakszövetkezet for marketing produce, for machinery services and for material inputs, fodder supplies, etc. Moreover, the greater propensity to abandon tanyas in peripheral zones has been noted, whilst the proportion of cultivable land which has fallen out of use in the proximity of the centre is exceedingly small. One could adduce individual examples of farmers whose output increased significantly when they moved from a very remote tanya to one better situated nearer the centre.

Nevertheless, the overall picture of the 172 tanya enterprises which marketed some produce through the szakszövetkezet in 1976 shows that the distance from the centre has no significant influence upon the level or type of farm production. If, in addition, the tanya production figures are compared with those of farmers based in the village, similarly we find few significant differences. The total number of farm units in the main village centre is still smaller than the tanya total (for more detail on these statistics and the definitions behind them see Chapter 4). Rather more tanya enterprises produced wine than did village farms, but the average value of the quantity sold by the latter was slightly higher. Pigs were sold by more units in the village than on tanyas, and again the average value produced was greater in the village. This barely holds in the case of milk production, where the number of tanya producers is 176 compared to the village's 69. Only 100 enterprises in the village had pasture land of their own, compared with 214 tanya units, and the average size of the plot was also higher for the tanyas. Tanya holdings of arable land also exceeded village holdings and 312 tanya enterprises had one or more plots, compared with only 209 in the village. Despite these differences, if we consider only those economic units which did market some produce through the szakszövetkezet in 1976 (261 out of 410 tanya units, 210 out of 372 village units), the average total value of production comes to 24,955 forints for tanya-based units and 26,999 forints for those based in the village.

Such evidence is important because it contradicts the often implicit assumption that tanya residence in itself and independently of the organisational framework of production confers significant economic advantages, which individuals would be deprived of if they were resettled in nuclear settlements. It would seem that in Tázlár in 1976 either few such advantages existed or that if there were such objective advantages they were no longer perceived or taken up by tanya-dwellers. The data are especially interesting in view of the official reasons for avoiding full collectivisation in Tázlár. If both villagers and tanya-dwellers respond in the same way to the institution of the szakszövetkezet, then both the need for a distinct cooperative type in tanya zones and the justifications for the adoption of an alternative type everywhere else are called into question.

The fact is that the tanya world has been integrated, but not in a bourgeois way. The land requirements for the maintenance of a peasant farm today are very small, indeed for some units they are zero. The abstractions of locational theory do not apply because nearness to the plot is not essential to the farmer. He now farms on only a few holdings and produces more intensively, wasting little time in travel between plots and making full use of fertilisers and machinery that were not available prior to the formation of the szakszövetkezet. At the same time, minor differences between the tanya and the village farming pattern persist. Village farmers do make rather more use of the services of the cooperative than do tanya farmers. The more remote do experience difficulty in transporting supplies and in bringing in their animals to collection points. If such factors do have some influence upon the composition of farm output, they appear to be offset by certain survivals of the 'natural state' advantages of the tanya, contingent upon its location but still not necessarily upon the ownership of land. For example, on the periphery it is easier to rent pasture land either privately or from the szakszövetkezet or State Farm. This may account for the higher milk production of tanya households, especially during certain months, and compensates for the villagers' ease of access to directly purchased supplies at the szakszövetkezet shop. However, even tanya dairy production cannot be regarded as unintegrated, since it is the szakszövetkezet which guarantees the daily collection of output of even the most remote producers.

The community-wide vertical integration of farmers into the szakszövetkezet must not blind us to the importance of other patterns of integration which have developed in the peasant economy in the socialist period. One such pattern relates specifically to the tanya problem. Types of dual residence, which have long been thought central to the origins and development of the Hungarian tanya, have become important in Tázlár only in the socialist period and their appearance can be taken as symbolic of the reintegration of the community into the national society. There were partial exceptions to atomised isolation in the past but these were mainly immigrants from nearby communities who retained their kinship ties, and perhaps property interests as well, and in a few cases moved back to the older village upon retirement from agriculture. Nowadays, although not officially encouraged, dual residence provides many more families with the means of combining the comforts of village residence with the tanya's economic advantages over the annual production cycle.

There are only a few families resident in the village (or in neighbouring villages and towns, or even in Budapest) who move out to occupy a tanya during the agricultural season, i.e. for some period between March and October. In theory, Hungarian law prevents a person from owning more than one permanent dwelling, but this is not the problem. In fact the spirit of this law is not observed by anyone nowadays, although a rich widow who had not bothered to transfer one of her houses to another family member was having to face confiscation of one property in 1978. There is a larger group of villagers who make limited use of an abandoned tanya, primarily during the summer months; but a routine of daily commuting makes it difficult to keep animals on such a tanya, and, besides, buildings that are not lived in tend to decay very quickly.

By far the most interesting links are those which have developed between large numbers of village-dwellers and their immediate family who inhabit tanyas. In many cases production links are intimate and all marketing takes place under the same family identification, although budgets are very seldom jointly managed. Sometimes the older generation has invested in village housing for their child or children, but has preferred to remain on the tanya with informal rights upon the labour of the younger generation at peak periods until a late age. The younger generation does not establish a separate farm and undertakes production only of a very marginal type at the village house. As the incentives to private agriculture have increased in the 1970s an inverse type has again become common. Here, the older generation moves into the village, and possibly into semi-retirement, whilst the young spend their most productive years on a tanya. Such a pattern is not new. The first tanya-dwellers who built houses in the centre before the Liberation were careful to preserve the family tanya. They only moved in to the new house when a newly-married couple was ready to take over the tanya, but they seldom handed over all of their land at this point. It was common for two prosperous families to buy a tanya from a third party in order to set up a young couple. Nowadays, few young couples are keen to remain in full-time peasant farming in the long term, either on a tanya or in the village. Nevertheless, many will accept free, or almost free, tanya accommodation and the currently highly remunerative opportunities of agriculture in the short term. The financial motivation is strong, and the tanya is said to 'die' only when the children follow their parents into the village, or migrate further afield.

Dual settlement may often be only a transient stage, which is unlikely to keep life on the tanya for very long, but in the present context it cannot be ignored. It is noteworthy how it upholds the traditional family base of peasant farming, at least at peak periods on the production side, even after the family has ceased to reside under one roof. Of course, this effect is also achieved by the return at peak periods of family members who have emigrated outside the community; some of those who return no longer have any kin in the community at all, but still return to cultivate a few vines. But it seems reasonable to maintain that what has loosely been termed 'duality of settlement' denotes a phenomenon which is concealed in the statistics and which may disguise the continued importance of a tanya base for peasant farm output.

A further trend of the 1970s may yet suggest a more permanent future for the tanya. There is some evidence in Tázlár to show that electrification can check the exodus, and perhaps change the social characteristics of emigration as well. By 1977 only a few conveniently-located clusters of tanyas had been provided with electricity, though the proportion was possibly above the national tanya average. The problems of persuading individuals to cooperate in order to obtain the most rational electricity distribution system have been noted (p. 23), and naturally there has been no demand amongst the very poor and the old. But it is several years now since the first tanyas were electrified and there has been no tendency to emigrate from these. One which came on to the market in 1977, when a widow moved to another tanya to live with her daughter, fetched almost as high a price as a comparable village dwelling. This should further caution against exaggerating the success of socialist policies in explaining the exodus which has taken place until now. There is at least one case of a prosperous farmer who built a large new house in the village centre at a time when it was reckoned unlikely that his tanya would be scheduled for electrification. Then, having installed electricity in the tanya, he successively postponed the decision, and finally, even after taking up a salaried post at the szakszövetkezet in the centre, decided to remain on his tanya, though he did not hurry to sell the new house.

A caveat should be entered here. Those tanyas which can be electrified — so far those lying up to about 2 kilometres from the main road or from the village centre — have been those which would in any case command a price on the market. They tend to belong to richer members of the peasantry who have traditionally farmed the higher-quality soils near the centre, and whose very proximity to the centre, together with their longstanding identification with their patrimony, reduces their incentive to migrate.

Let us return to the farmer in the example above and consider his reasons for remaining on the tanya after going to all the trouble of building a house in the village. This man, although his stepmother lives in the village and although he cooperates in production with a village household, has remained fundamentally the head of a family-labour farm (most of the labour being that of his wife). He insists that he would not be able to run the same farm in the village. If the szakszövetkezet were to collectivise the land immediately surrounding his tanya, he says he would still not fence in his yard and his checkens would continue to wander on the rich grass. The statistics may suggest that the man is bluffing, but this is very difficult to prove.

The problem is that a static statistical description of the situation which prevailed in 1976 is no basis for assuming that the present tanya producers could be easily chivvied into the village without changing the pattern of their production. There has been a steady decline in the number of productive units based on tanyas, and the recent rise in production levels is limited to quite a small group. It has been pointed out that some farmers take advantage of the move away from the tanya to reduce the scale of their private farming. If tanya farmers are now obliged to move into the village as the result of new land appropriations by the szakszövetkezet, or if they simply lose their land, there is likely to be a serious decline in production. For many of those still producing on tanyas today the size and proximity of the landholding is probably intimately related to their production in a way that is no longer the case for villagers. In other words, the old bases of peasant production have been less effectively undermined for the tanya population as a whole than for the village population. We have seen this already with respect to dairy production, which would inevitably suffer from hasty collectivisation today. But the same applies in other branches. There is no relation between the extent of the arable landholdings of village units and the value of the pigs they sell through the szakszövetkezet, whereas for tanya units there is a good statistical relation. It cannot be assumed that the present tanya population would adapt to a new process of production, even if we take it for granted that the szakszövetkezet has all the feed and other materials they may need.

There are also important differences between tanya and village populations, which must be taken into account. The average age of the head of a tanya household is over 55, compared with 52 in the village, in spite of the number who have moved into the village in retirement. There is a similar difference in the ages of the heads of actively producing enterprises (49 in the village, 52 on the tanyas). A large number of solitaries live on tanyas (65 compared with 39 in the centre), and there are still many more full-time farmers in the tanya population than there are in the village, for all age-groups. In view of these factors it cannot be assumed that the comparable global averages in the production of tanya and village units indicate any identity of social structure.

An active policy of land appropriation is now threatening the tanya farmers and the village farmers in a different way, although production statistics do not show this. Firstly, there is the phenomenon of dual residence, in particular the number of village farmers who still make use of a tanya base, which is not apparent in the statistics. Secondly, there is the problem of consciousness. Tanya farmers for the most part firmly *believe* that only through living on the tanya and farming the land they currently farm can they maintain their accustomed level of production. Thirdly, there is the range of social differences in the structure of the two populations. For all these reasons an active campaign now to dispense with the tanya would entail serious consequences for agricultural production. The tanya today is more than just a dispersed residence: it remains an economic unity that has not yet been fully integrated by the socialist farm.

One feature in the present social structure of the tanya population deserves special emphasis. It has become more polarised than the population of the village. At one extreme there is a large number of households with a very small population, of high average age, including many solitaries, and only minimally productive. At the other extreme there is a group which regularly markets a large surplus, shows considerable willingness to modernise, and owes its current prosperity to the szakszövetkezet and to the success of national policies to encourage private production. Some of these policies have not been designed specifically for the szakszövetkezet community, but they have brought special benefits to the szakszövetkezet members. This group is made up mainly, but not exclusively, of former middle peasants. It is present in the village also, and indeed, as in the example quoted above, many of these farmers have already taken the precaution of investing in village housing. It seems unlikely that their children will remain in farming full-time, and one must therefore hesitate to speak of a future for the modern 'farm-tanya'.[3] But even if electrification can make the tanya sufficiently attractive as a residence, the persistence of its role in production, even in the short term, is crucially dependent upon the continuation of present policies and the survival of the szakszövetkezet in its present form, or something very similar.

If what might be seen as the logic of the transition to full collectivisation is now too forcefully pursued – and the nature of the threat will become clear in later chapters – then global small-farm production is bound to suffer. Much will depend upon how the policies are put into practice. The confiscation of land in itself may not be the worst blow. It might have the effect of encouraging more farmers to move into the village, but would not necessarily push them out of full-time farming, although many insist *a priori* that it would. They might, in other words, make the same adjustment as that made by many village farmers already and become fully integrated szakszövetkezet members. The biggest problem would arise if they were obliged to work on the collective sector of the szakszövetkezet, as is usual on production cooperatives, and were denied the services and supplies they need from the szakszövetkezet to maintain and increase their former levels of production. The danger in the elimination of full-time farming as an occupation is not experienced to the same degree by the farmers of the village, a larger proportion of whom already combine farming with some wage-labour activity.

If we now step back and consider the entire evolution of the tanya problem in Tázlár, certain conclusions can be drawn. It seems likely that the crude political goal proclaimed in the late 1940s, the total abolition of tanyas wherever they appeared, will not now be realised. Electrification will ensure the survival of a number of outlying farm-residences, which will probably be inhabited by older people and by individuals with a dislike of larger settlements. However, an absolute onslaught on the tanya was not the policy espoused by all, even in the early socialist period. Erdei in particular argued for the careful reintegration of tanyas into larger units, bearing in mind the continued role of the tanya in small commodity production even after the socialisation of agriculture. Although his arguments were not designed for communities such as Tázlár, which had to a large extent developed independently of any traditional community, they nevertheless became particularly pertinent after the establishment in Tázlár of a limited cooperative type, the szakszövetkezet. It has been the framework of the szakszövetkezet which has slowed the exodus from the tanyas and at the same time preserved their role in peasant farming. Szakszövetkezet tanyas are classified by Romány as virtually the only remaining tanyas of a type which was much more important in the past, on which the peasant family lives and produces in the traditional atomised manner (Romány 1973 cf. Kulcsár in Erdei, 1976). But the szakszövetkezets are explicitly a transitional institution. Despite the substantial economic benefits they have brought, it would seem that after two decades a further decision must be taken. The State may still fear the losses in production which would result if it were now to end the long experiment with the szakszövetkezet and pushes through full collectivisation. On the other hand, this would secure ideological consistency and, in the light of what has been noted above, the state may hope by such a step to avoid the re-emergence of a rich peasant or even capitalist 'farmer' stratum out of the ranks of the former middle peasantry. An obvious compromise for the authorities would be to go for the appropriation of private land, with the exception of household plots of 1 *hold* (0.58 hectare) as in the usual production cooperative, but also to retain the basic framework of the szakszövetkezet and not to compel its members to work in the socialist sector. The result of this would be to achieve the transformation of the economic role of the tanya and to put it almost on a par with a house in the village as a dwelling. But it would also leave individuals the option of remaining full-time peasant farmers and prospering as private producers, as have numerous village farmers up to now. It would not, of course, dispose of the worries of creating a privileged class; but in any case it would be clear that the tanya is no longer responsible and that the problem of the tanya has been transcended by the problem of the szakszövetkezet. If a class is now forming, the tanyas are not a prime cause, but have merely been a means of preserving continuity with the class divisions of the past.

The essential irony explored in this chapter will be pursued in the rest of this book in the context of the szakszövetkezet. Briefly, Tázlár was resettled late in the last century by the tanya movement and was an extreme example of the penetration of capitalist relations into Hungary. In the 1930s, despite 'full employment' on the land, the apparently small number of poor and landless peasants, and the limited impact of the outside market, the internal stratification of the peasantry was particularly marked. Tázlár thus provided an example of a certain simplistic socialist analysis of rural class relations which had its theoretical origins in Lenin's *The Development of Capitalism in Russia* and its practical apogee in Stalinist collectivisation. Hungary did not escape the pervasive influence of the Soviet model. The theoretical justifications of mass collectivisation here too were based upon an ideology of capitalist class division within the peasantry. Tázlár was strongly affected by policies based on this ideology in the 1950s. Later, however, this unambiguous product of capitalism, the tanya community, was excluded from mass collectivisation for obvious reasons of expediency and cost, when ideological considerations should have made it a prime target for transformation. Instead, Tázlár developed szakszövetkezets. These belong to a quite different socialist tradition, which had its clearest expression in the years of the New Economic Policy under Lenin, passed through Bukharin and long years of eclipse, and re-emerged after collectivisation in numerous socialist states in the guise of household plot incentives, and, in the case of Hungary, in close association with the spirit which has pervaded the entire national economy since the reform of the economic mechanism which was introduced in 1968.[4]

3 The transition to a socialist agriculture

In most Western countries the socialist debate on the peasantry and on the correct approach to the transformation of the countryside, to which brief reference was made at the end of Chapter 2, is known and widely understood only in the context of the Soviet experience. This chapter will review the comparable experience of Hungary. It is important that the reader should understand the course of events in Tázlár in the national context. Without this background it will be impossible to evaluate the detailed ethnography of the chapters which follow. There are important differences between the process of collectivisation in Tázlár and the transformation of other Hungarian rural communities, just as there are many differences between the national process in Hungary and the Soviet Model from which so much was taken. Perhaps overall the word 'transition' suggests the keynote for Hungary, if it is taken to imply a prolonged and gradual process, subjected to many political constraints, but ultimately designed to maximise the contribution of the agricultural sector to the development of the national economy in the phase of intensive industrialisation. It is instructive to compare how general issues of theory and practice have been tackled at both national and local levels and to consider the special features of the Hungarian path – without, however, nourishing too many illusions about the relevance of this path for other nations and for rural communities elsewhere.

I Land Reform and the origins of agricultural cooperatives 1945–56

Although Hungarian agriculture flourished through most of the Second World War, in the end it nevertheless suffered heavier losses than any other branch of the economy as a result of the slaughter of livestock in late 1944 and early 1945. Land Reform was a popular cause and a political necessity. It was carried through in the spring of 1945 in a highly decentralised and democratic manner by the formation of special committees in all the communities of the country. The main consequence was the destruction of the system of large estates and of the class of great property-owners, and, in their place, the consolidation of small and medium peasant holdings. In principle the reform covered only landholdings larger than 200 *hold* (112 hectares), but the tax system, labour market conditions and general political pressure further reduced the number of rich peasants in the years after 1945. Altogether almost

The transition to a socialist agriculture

35 per cent of agricultural land was affected by the Reform, including just under 30 per cent of the total ploughland. Of this area about two-thirds was distributed to those who put in claims for land and the rest was retained in various forms by public authorities, much of it going later to assist the foundation of State Farms and cooperatives. As a result of the Reform the proportion of small commodity-producers (defined as the owners of properties of between 1 and 25 *hold* (0.58 and 14 hectares)) in the agricultural population of the nation as a whole rose from 47.2 per cent in 1941 to 80.2 per cent in 1949. The proportion of the agrarian proletariat, those with less than 1 *hold* (0.58 hectare), fell from 45.8 per cent to 17 per cent over the same period, and the proportion of rich and 'capitalist' peasants fell from 7 per cent to 2.8 per cent (Berend, 1976, p. 31).

Thanks to a judicious range of measures taken by the State the agriculture based upon these radically altered property relations made considerable progress in the later 1940s. By 1949 both livestock levels and crop yields were approaching the pre-war levels. The government's levelling policy, however, resulted in the new peasantry being willing to market only limited surpluses, a consequence of higher peasant consumption, which was matched by a rise in working-class living standards during the years of the three-year plan 1947–9 (Berend, 1976, p. 91). Supply difficulties persisted despite the freeing of most agricultural prices and price controls that were favourable to agricultural products (Berend, 1976, p. 67). But even in the 1940s there were very strict compulsory-delivery obligations based primarily upon size of landholding, which together with changes in the tax system severely curtailed the production of the richer peasantry.

In Tázlár, given the general absence of large estates, Land Reform had a smaller impact than elsewhere and this is highly relevant to later developments. It did, however, result in the elimination of the previous landholding elite, as can be judged from a comparison of Table 3 with Table 2 (p. 6). Of the changes to be noted when comparing Tázlár in 1949 with the

Table 3 Land ownership 1949

					(area in *hold*)					
	0–1	1–3	3–5	5–10	10–15	15–20	20–25	25–50	50–100	100+	Total
No. of farmers	47	142	167	315	148	76	55	73	21	2	1,046

1 *hold* = 0.58 hectares (5,755 square metres)

Note: Figures include the farms of Harkakötöny, administratively separated from Tázlár in 1949.

34

pre-war community the most important reflect the general problems encountered by agricultural policy in the years after the Land Reform. The community was still predominantly agricultural. Of the total tanya population of 2,650 in 1949 no less than 2,553 are recorded as totally dependent for their living upon agriculture. Yet despite the small increase in the population living on the land, the sown area declined from 10,910 *hold* (6,110 hectares) in 1935 to 9,270 *hold* (5,191 hectares) in 1948. The shortfall can be entirely accounted for by the decline in the area of rye, barley and oats. There was no decline in the production of maize, but there was a significant change in the size of the farms which produced the crop, which underlines the importance of the Reform. Table 4 compares production in 1948 with three pre-war years. There was a rise in the production of the industrial crops sugar beet, tobacco and sunflowers, but this was for many a reluctant response to the system of compulsory deliveries.

Table 4 Maize area and farm size in Tázlár 1936–48

Year	Farm size (*hold*)					Total maize
	0–6	6–12	12–60	60–600	600+	area (*hold*)
1936	124	190	455	283	12	1,064
1937	294	342	672	282	40	1,630
1938	230	266	509	270	33	1,308
1948	875		473	63		1,411

1 *hold* = 0.58 hectares (5,755 square metres)

Faced with such difficulties and with similar problems in livestock production, the government began to take action on a new front from 1948 by encouraging the formation of agricultural cooperatives. The cooperatives, together with the large number of State Farms which were established between 1948 and 1952, brought a large productive area more directly within the sphere of influence of the State. On the other hand, the cooperatives also possessed from the outset an impeccably democratic structure, and this too was to be important in the long run. Membership was voluntary but tended to be sought by those of the former agrarian proletariat who had not adapted well to farming on their own. Control was effectively in the hands of the general assembly of all the members, though in practice there was frequent interference from outside, which began with the founding initiative and continued through a carefully recruited local leadership of Party sympathisers. Not all of the cooperatives were fully collective in their work organisation, and only the so-called 'third type' took the members' livestock as well as their land into collective exploitation. Remuneration, as in the Soviet Union, was based on the work-unit. But behind the impressive formal apparatus and the rules by which the cooperatives were supposed to function, in practice, as in the early years of cooperatives in the Soviet Union, they were very diverse. Thus despite a formal organisation into brigades it often happened that a cooperative with little machinery delegated the teams at its disposal and the responsibility for particular tasks to family units. Many cooperatives were dominated by a few families only. Machine tools, when they became available, were kept centrally and most often separately from the cooperative in machine stations, as in the Soviet Union.

In Tázlár the first agricultural cooperative was founded in 1949. It was called the *Red Csepel*, in memory of proletarian revolutionary activity in 1919. In 1951 a further six cooperatives were formed, which meant that in Tázlár in that year there were 142 cooperative members from 97 families, farming a total of 1,113 *hold* (623 hectares) of arable land and a total land area of 1,884 *hold* (1,055 hectares). There was no substantial increase in the membership of any cooperative after its formation, except later in the case of the *Red Csepel* through mergers. They were not, in fact, attractive to the bulk of the independent peasantry and it is not difficult to understand why. Many of those who joined were very politically-conscious former proletarians, but they were not the most practised farmers. They lacked much in the way of buildings and equipment, but what the government was able to make good here it could not remedy in the case of know-how and experience on the land. In any case it was difficult for richer peasants to join these cooperatives and there is at least one case in the district archives at Kiskőrös of an individual being expelled from a cooperative as a *kulák* (rich peasant).[1] It was not therefore surprising that only one or two of these cooperatives, which were all full collectives of the third type, remained economically viable and were able to pay out dividends to their members without regular recourse to outside subsidy.

The beginnings of the cooperative movement are important for the example they set and the spirit they created during these years when, organised on a local basis in a democratic way, they grappled with the tremendous difficulties facing them with the energy of pioneers. But they were not able to alleviate the government's problems with agricultural production and with the independent peasantry. A new phase of government policy began in the early 1950s, based upon anti-peasant policies and administrative methods involving greater government control. This policy affected the peasantry almost as severely in the case of cooperative members as in the case of those still farming independently. At best, the former were better placed to preserve at least the basic ration from appropriation, while, according to Berend, in 1952 two-thirds of all peasant families were left with insufficient corn for bread and future seed requirements (1976, p. 109). Cooperative members, like private farmers, conspired to conceal produce from government inspectors in order to have some food for consumption. Many farmers in Tázlár still have some bitter tales to tell from these years — of the land they were obliged to yield by extortionate tax demands, of their friend the former 'magistrate' who was several times taken away by police in the night, or of their own farcical journeys to distant markets in order to pay high prices for goods they would then hand over for a pittance at the local council. Many were obliged to seek work in industry and especially in the mines in order to keep their families. In consequence of this, as well as because of certain confiscations by the cooperatives, more land was lost to cultivation. The agrarian price 'scissors' widened dramatically in the early years of the 1950s, but for the great majority of the peasantry prices and markets, the central institutions under capitalism, were to a large extent replaced by a coercive relation with the socialist power.

The dark phase in which 'administrative methods' were applied to relations between town and countryside is now openly condemned by politicians and scholars alike in Hungary. But at the same time this regime initiated unprecedented industrial growth and secured the primacy of socialist enterprise in all major sectors of industry. The resemblances to Stalin's achievement in the Soviet Union are striking, even if Mátyás Rákosi was never politically strong enough to go for full collectivisation at this stage. What is the general connection between the political and economic attack upon the peasantry and the achievement of a 'crash' programme of industrialisation? The answer in economic terms must be that the use of coercion reduces peasant consumption by a quantity more than sufficient to compensate for the economic losses caused by the reluctance of the peasantry to produce, and thus the net contribution or surplus from the agricultural sector to the national economy and the needs of industry is positive. There *were* serious economic losses and the year 1952 was a disastrous year for agricultural production. But such an approach is exceptionally short-term and fails to take any account of the long-term consequences of large areas of land falling into disuse and of the costs to the industrial sector of the economy of repairing the damage done to agriculture before, during and after collectivisation. As recent debate on the Soviet experience has made clear both the long-term and the immediate economic rationale of the Stalin development plans are very doubtful (Millar, 1970; Ellman, 1975).

II *From 'counter-revolution' to mass collectivisation 1956–61*

The correction of administrative policies or 'leftist' deviation created further problems of a 'rightist' or 'revisionist' nature; and in the political struggle which led up to the 1956 uprising, agriculture, like the other sectors of the economy, suffered from the instability of central policy. The cooperative movement was particularly vulnerable, and suffered its first decisive check in 1953 with the dissolution of some 500 farms (Orbán, 1972, p. 132). In Tázlár the *Fight for Peace* was lost that year, although it had been founded only in 1951. But it was the more widespread withdrawals and preference for independent farming shown in 1956 which really exposed the weaknesses of the cooperatives. Although Orbán believes that there was some moral gain resulting from this shakeout which left a higher proportion of former proletarians and Party members amongst the remaining cooperative members, he does not conceal the new problems which arose, in part because of the poorer quality of the labour force (Orbán, 1972, p. 168). A confidential Party report of 1957 judged two-thirds of farming cooperatives to be 'weak' with those of most recent formation the weakest of all (Orbán, 1972, p. 169). Of the six remaining cooperatives in Tázlár before 1956 the three smallest, the *Comrade*, the *Progress* and the *Peace*, folded and almost all of their members returned to private farming. The other three continued separately until 1959, when they merged and retained the name of the largest, the *Red Csepel*. This remained chronically insolvent until it finally became the base of the State Farm's operations in Tázlár in 1961. Of all the early cooperatives in Tázlár, with the exception of the *Fight for Peace*, about which little is known as it functioned for only one year, only one, the *Second Congress* (named after the second congress of the Communist Party), succeeded in maintaining a consistent acreage of arable land throughout its existence, in spite of the fact that it lost 11 of its 34 members in 1956.

It is typical of the people of Tázlár that in the middle of the 1956 uprising, with only a few radios in the community and all communication services suspended, they responded to the exhortations and the news (brought from the capital by a stranger) by joking about the panic and confusion in the council offices and applying themselves to the final stages of the construction of the new Catholic church. Nor was there much sign in the rest of the country of any desire to return to the old division of property and to comply with the requests of some former rich peasants for the restitution of their land. There was no open expression of political opposition in the countryside (Orbán, 1972, p. 161).[2]

However, even if no major political concessions were made to the independent peasantry in 1956, the disturbances had many important consequences outside the cooperative movement. There were also some major changes in economic policy which were very well received in the countryside. The most important of these were the raising of agricultural prices and the abolition of compulsory deliveries from October 1956. The general result was a breathing-space for independent farming, and production more free from central controls than at any time since the beginning of the war. The number of private farmers rose almost to the level of 1949 with the return of some farmers from industry and the mines, and the adoption by others of farming as a secondary occupation. There was a general willingness to invest in farming, and a significant rise in the area of ploughland in 1957 and 1958. Moreover, although there was some increase in differentiation, especially in areas of intensive crop production, and although the former middle peasants benefited most from these policies, larger farms were by this stage unable to generate substantially higher incomes and on smaller farms income earned outside agriculture now tended to compensate for lower agricultural income (Orbán, 1972, p. 197).

There was thus at least temporary satisfaction with the considerable rise in peasant incomes and farm production which preceded the planning and implementation of mass collectivisation between 1958 and 1961. Politically, the ground was very carefully prepared for collectivisation, though the country was hardly prepared economically. The harvest had not been particularly successful in 1958 nor had the cooperative sector shown any great improvement in its performance. Within the Party the debate on collectivisation was won by the 'moderates' and therefore the resolution of December 1958 was explicitly gradualist and opposed to the use of force. Nevertheless, the first great wave of collectivisation in early 1959 was vital to the success of the policy, and when it was completed the cooperative and State Farm sectors together already controlled over 50 per cent of the ploughland of the country. By the summer of 1960 this had risen to 72 per cent, and a year later, in the final wave of mass collectivisation, a further 291,000 families joined cooperatives (Berend, 1976, p. 140), including the new cooperatives formed in Tázlár. This success owed much to the toleration of lower forms of cooperative on soils unsuited to collective exploitation. Flexibility was shown in the attitude to the leasing out of scattered vine plots in 1959 (Orbán, p. 221); and in the general policy towards the household plot a necessary compromise was struck with the peasantry – they were allowed to keep a limited stock of animals on the household plot and in practice only poorer animals were taken into the collective sector. Thus, although by 1961 land ownership was very firmly in the hands of the cooperatives and the State, the household plot sector on only 7.9 per cent of the land was still producing 24 per cent of the net agricultural product (quoted in Orbán, 1972, p. 247). All the vast problems in the material and technological development of the new cooperatives, as well as the social integration of their new membership alongside the former poor peasants, were resolved in some fashion in the years which followed, but the integration of 'private' production on the household plot has not evolved in the way foreseen by the policy-makers of 20 years ago, and is a theme which will be taken up again below.

With perhaps more irony than he really intended in view of the course of events in communities such as Tázlár, Sándor Orbán ends his book with the statement that collectivisation brought about the final *polgárosodás* (embourgeoisement) of the Hungarian peasantry (Orbán, 1972, p. 258). Presumably he intends the word in its 'developmental' sense and not with respect to bourgeois social relations. Before we consider the impact of collectivisation in Tázlár let us therefore note one further consequence of collectivisation upon the development of the national economy: between 1960 and 1963 there was a drop of 16 per cent in the numbers of those employed in agriculture and over the total period 1957–67 the agricultural labour-force declined by more than half a million (Berend, 1976, p. 141).

III Cooperative groups in Tázlár 1960–8

Mass collectivisation gave renewed impetus to the process of migration out of agriculture but its total impact was perhaps less radical than that of the first Five Year Plan. In the Soviet Union collectivisation had preceded the intensive phase of industrialisation. In Hungary, although the country was already much more developed than pre-revolutionary Russia, this sequence was reversed. It is the early 1950s, rather than the years of mass collectivisation, which merit Marx's description of '. . . one of those moments when great masses of men are suddenly and forcibly torn from their means of subsistence, and hurled as free and unattached proletarians on the labour market' (Marx, 1976, p. 876).

Hungarian agricultural policy was altogether more gradualist. In Tázlár the exodus from the land was still further staggered as a result of a Party resolution of October 1960, an essentially pragmatic measure typical of the willingness throughout the period of Kádár's leadership to compromise with the peasantry. This resolution encouraged the formation of 'simple cooperatives' in exceptional areas where collectivisation was liable to prove especially difficult, particularly in zones of poor soils and dispersed settlement and in communities where there was a high degree of intensive commodity production, e.g. in fruit and wine. Collectivisation in such areas would not only be expensive to finance, it would also risk doing serious damage to the production of the independent peasantry. Thus in Tázlár, towards the end of the national campaign, minimal ideological uniformity was attained by the formation of three 'production cooperative groups' in the last week of December 1960. After the usual short local campaign, consisting mainly of farm-to-farm visits by veteran urban 'educators', the vast majority of Tázlár farmers joined one or other of these groups and, with the exception of their vineyards and orchards and each with a nominal 1 *hold* (0.58 hectare) attached to their dwellings, signed their plots over to the group.

Many farmers claim today that they were reluctant to sign and did so only after three or more 'final' visits from the educators. Some claim to have been threatened with firearms. But, in private, given the general pattern throughout the country, where lands signed over to the cooperative were immediately adapted for large-scale, collective cultivation, the Tázlár farmers were reasonably contented with the basic organisation of the co-operative group. In practice they were not deprived of their land and not required to work in the *közös* (collective sector) although they could do so if they wished. Most land remained under private cultivation, with the proviso that a small percentage of the members' lands (originally 4 per cent was the figure specified) would be converted each year to collective cultivation. Members would be compensated for land appropriated, either with alternative plots in another area or by payments in cash or in kind.

They were expected to sell most of their farm production through the group, which would deduct a certain percentage as a levy to promote the development of the group and of the collective sector. There was also a small fee to be paid upon joining the group. Those who have defended the persistence of the simple cooperatives have stressed the virtual identity of its organisation at the centre and its management with that of a normal production cooperative, which in turn has strong similarities in its 'inner structure' to the Soviet *kolkhoz* (collective farm). The socialist nucleus gathers strength and expands its territory, but at the same time it develops its ties with the individual members, who themselves prosper as a result of the supplies and machinery services increasingly available to them through the group. Thus, according to the theory, an 'organic unity' is achieved and in the words of János Gyenis '. . . a many-sided programme of co-operation is worked out between the two farming types on the basis of mutual material interests' (Gyenis, 1971, p. 8).

In Tázlár the experiment did not succeed as planned in the 1960s. In the first place consolidation of plots did not proceed piecemeal annually as laid down. In the case of one group, the *Rákóczi*, the official figures actually show a contraction of the collective sector. The *Rákóczi* began operations in 1960 with 2115 *hold* (1,184 hectares), of which 364 *hold* (204 hectares) was collective, and of this only 129 *hold* (72 hectares) was arable soil. By 1969, probably as a result of the expansion of the State Farm, the total area of the collective sector had fallen to 320 *hold* (179 hectares). The small expansion that occurred in the other two groups over the same period was due mainly to the voluntary ceding of land by middle peasants, whose land-needs were indeed reduced by the services now provided by the cooperative group, and to migration. In the isolated cases where it was necessary to appropriate land from a reluctant farmer, he was adequately compensated elsewhere. The farmer might complain about the position or the quality of the new plot and frequently did not take up the option. But this indicates only that he no longer needed the acreage he owned, and he was often glad when the group gave him the chance to contract his area, while seeming to do so only under protest. The group was not perceived as a predatory threat by the mass of the peasantry.

The farmers elected the chairman of their group from amongst their own number. He was typically a well-respected farmer who continued private farming as best he was able alongside his official duties. Each group recruited a small permanent labour force, for the most part from amongst its poorer and less competent members, including some who had belonged to the earlier cooperatives. The administration, in temporary offices in the village, was small and the machine centres were rudimentary. The technical progress of these years nevertheless transformed the economy of most farms. It was during these years that chemical fertilisers first became widely available and the old threshing machines were replaced by modern combine harvesters. Yet these simple cooperatives were constantly criticised by their members. This was partly because of the poor economic performance of the collectivised sector, reviewed in Chapter 4. More fundamentally, there was never any effective link between the results of the group and the individual member's income. In the conditions in which the groups functioned, without substantial State support and for a long time with no technical or expert advice of any kind, individuals who remained outside the collective sector never had any incentive to become involved and to improve the collective sector's work. Some farmers were also conscious of inferiority in comparison with cooperative-group members, particularly with regard to social-security benefits and later to pension rights (Orosz, 1969). The State not only failed to make the collective sectors viable through the provision of investment funds, it also discriminated against cooperative-group members privately by denying them the price bonuses received by the members of full production cooperatives for their private production on the household plot. Tázlár farmers thus paid a heavy price for their temporary reprieve from collectivisation. They felt that they had signed over their property to the certainty of collectivisation in the long run, but had obtained few of the benefits and securities of cooperative membership in return.

The new order brought no major changes in the pattern of land use in the community. However, there was a large drop in the sown area in 1962 which affected almost all field crops and was only partially recovered in later years. The total area of private landholdings declined steadily, and, of greater importance for production, so did private animal stocks. At the same time there were signs in each cooperative group that some farmers were adapting more successfully than others to the new conditions and as a result of their transactions with the group were able both to raise farm production above the levels to which it had fallen and completely to overhaul the traditional organisation of the peasant farm. The implications of this transformation and of the parallel process of differentiation within the peasantry will be analysed below.

Comparisons of this type of simple cooperative with those of other countries and other historical periods can be very misleading. According to their practice in these years, the cooperative groups of Tázlár may seem not to differ much from many types of voluntary association of farmers found in generally more developed Western agricultures. In fact the differences are fundamental. The Tázlár cooperative groups are non-voluntary formations, and there is a presumption that they will eventually be converted to the nationally dominant *kolkhoz*-type. These points are equally significant in comparisons with those socialist states in Eastern Europe which have diverged more completely from the Soviet model. In many Polish and Yugoslav communities property relations and the general economic environment of peasant decision-taking may seem to resemble those of Tázlár. But Tázlár obtains its special interest precisely because it is not typical in the Hungarian national context. To some extent it has developed in the way that it has only in order to help continue an opposite trend in the

national economy. Following the reform of the economic mechanism
introduced in Hungary from January 1968 and the formal substitution in
the same year of three szakszövetkezets or 'specialist cooperatives' for the
production cooperative groups, Tázlár's deviation from the national model
became more pronounced in practice if not in ideology.

IV The formation of szakszövetkezets and the impact of economic reform

The change from cooperative group to szakszövetkezet in Tázlár was little
more than a change of name. Szakszövetkezets had also originated in the
last phase of mass collectivisation as another type of simple cooperative.
The difference was that while cooperative groups had been established in
the poorest tanya communities, szakszövetkezets had hitherto been located
in richer communities that were important for their fruit and wine production.
Thus Tázlár's neighbour formed the nation's first szakszövetkezet late in
1960. Soltvadkert's history since 1960 is in many ways an ideal type with
which to contrast that of Tázlár. Here too there was a general reluctance
to join the new cooperatives, and the experience of the 1950s and the
example of the earlier cooperatives had not been encouraging. However,
the initial fears allayed, the Soltvadkert farmers invested considerable
private resources in their szakszövetkezets. New collective vineyards were
begun almost at once, and growth was spectacular. As in Tázlár, the richer
farmers remained essentially private farmers. They were able to convert
their labour obligations to the szakszövetkezet to cash payments. Thanks
also to astute local leadership and to a larger measure of support from the
State than Tázlár received at this time, by the end of the 1960s the population of the community was expanding strongly and important foreign
visitors were being taken on tours of the szakszövetkezets, which were put
forward as an exemplary framework for the integration of collective and
private interests in a socialist agriculture.

The 1968 amendment to the 1967 law on agricultural cooperatives
left the szakszövetkezet as the only remaining independent type of simple
cooperative, but was unable to set Tázlár upon the miraculous path trodden
by Soltvadkert. There was no attempt now to establish greater conformity
with the production cooperatives, and the members of szakszövetkezets
who did not work in the collective sector remained underprivileged in their
access to welfare benefits. The ideology of a 'transitional type' was not
substantially amended, but szakszövetkezets were now to expect a long
future and it was explicitly recognised that wherever the collective sector
could be developed only at great cost to the State it would be preferable
to support the peasant farms of individual members for an indefinite
period (Gyenis, 1971, p. 109).

In mid-1969 there were 238 szakszövetkezets in the country. By 1976
this figure had fallen to 108, but this was mainly due to mergers and there
had been no comparable decline in the number of individual farms or in
the total area farmed within the szakszövetkezet sector. Obtaining precise

43

The transition to a socialist agriculture

data for this sector is often difficult. It figures as a section of the aggregate cooperative sector, but when this is broken down, as it commonly is, into 'collective' and 'household-plot' components, the szakszövetkezets can be wholly assigned to neither. The general agricultural census of 1972 provides the most helpful data.

From this it can be seen that 65,600 'private' szakszövetkezet farms comprised 15 per cent of the total productive area of small-farms, which may be thought of as the total 'private' sector, or, as we shall call it here, the 'small-farm sector'. About 50 per cent of this sector was made up of 782,000 household plot units belonging to families employed in production cooperatives, the remainder being mainly the auxiliary farms of industrial workers. Despite their small number, the szakszövetkezet farms contained 23 per cent of the small-farm vineyards and 37 per cent of the small-farm meadow area. Inside the szakszövetkezet sector only 12 per cent of the productive area is made up of vineyards, while the arable surface amounts to more than 66 per cent. The average age of szakszövetkezet farmers is high and in 1972, 31.8 per cent were over the age of 65. Of the total population in szakszövetkezet households 38.8 per cent are classified as active earners in agriculture and only 12.7 per cent as active earners in industry. Their land and livestock holdings are significantly higher than those of other small-plot farmers, and within their section of the small-farm sector there is a definite relation between the size of the holding and the level of animal-breeding. The average size of holding is 2.4 hectares, which compares with an average household plot size of 0.75 hectare. The animal stock begins to increase substantially above the 1.73 hectare mark, and only 15 per cent of cows are kept on less than 1.15 hectares. Vines are generally concentrated on the smaller farms. Large farms over 5 hectares are almost certain to be the property of those classified as active earners in agriculture. The effects of the size and the structure of the household are not of outstanding importance. Average household size is 2.75 persons. Five-person house-holders are more likely to have two breadwinners than one, but the presence of even three active earners causes virtually no change in the household's animal stock.

Szakszövetkezets are most highly concentrated in the Danube-Tisza interfluve and Bács-Kiskun has by far the highest proportion of szak-szövetkezet members (22.5 per cent of all its small-farmers in 1972). There were 31,693 private szakszövetkezet farms in the county in 1972, and of these the largest number, approximately 13,000, were to be found in Kiskőrös district. Within this district the szakszövetkezet dominates the small-farm sector more completely than anywhere else in the country. Of a total of over 10,000 hectares of small-farm vineyards in the district, more than 9,000 hectares belong to individual szakszövetkezet farmers. Tázlár is, however, the only community in the district which has no vine-yards in the socialised sector of the szakszövetkezet. Apart from the recent plantings by the State Farm the entire vine area in Tázlár (470 hectares in 1975) remains in private hands. The total small-farm productive area in Tázlár was 2,491 hectares in 1972. The rest of the community territory was approximately evenly divided between the State Farm and the Forest Farm on the one hand and the socialised sector of the szakszövetkezet on the other.

In recent Hungarian history the year 1968 is generally regarded as a watershed, principally because of the introduction on 1 January of that year of a wide-ranging reform of the economic mechanism. The links between this reform and the development of agriculture should not be exaggerated, but it has had a particular impact upon the szakszövetkezet sector and hence upon recent events in Tázlár.

The main aim of the reform was to achieve a new 'organic combination' of central planning and market relations. This entailed a large measure of decentralisation to enterprise-level, which included the agricultural co-operatives; these had been awarded enterprise status the previous year. In the extensive literature on the many variants of 'market socialism' there is a consensus that, despite running into serious problems in the 1970s, the Hungarian reform did have far-reaching social as well as economic effects. Essential to its success was a price reform which amounted to a qualitative change in the functioning of the price system. Whether there was any such qualitative change in the tools of agricultural policy is another matter, which neither Hungarian economists nor Western commentators have examined in detail. Csikós-Nagy contents himself with the observation (in Friss, 1969, p. 133) that '... price policy has become the main tool of control in agriculture'.

Qualitatively, this could only be interpreted as the continuation of the agricultural policies already practised at least since the Party's 'Agrarian Theses' of 1957. Quantitatively, however, there were now large increases in state purchasing prices and hence in the incentives given to the entire small-farm sector to raise its market production. It was now realised that the interest of the domestic consumer coincided with a major field of export demand, and that the output of many commodities could be substantially increased only in the small-farm sector. The performance of the total agricultural sector in the first five years after the economic reform contrasts favourably with the relative stagnation of the earlier 1960s, and very favourably indeed with the fate of agriculture in the years of the first Five Year Plan. The most impressive achievements were registered by the State Farms and by the socialised sectors of production cooperatives. There were also notable increases in the production of most branches of the small-farm sector, which had the additional merit of utilising no State investment funds. There was, however, a small decline in the first half of the 1970s in the value of produce marketed by the production cooperative members who owned household plots.

What the aggregated production statistics cannot reveal, but which must be reckoned against the positive achievements of the reform, are the disproportions and differential processes of development introduced by this sudden extension of the role of the market, and experienced in agriculture as in other sectors of the economy. The point can be made by comparing Tázlár with Soltvadkert. By 1968, after a number of amalgamations, the szakszövetkezets of Soltvadkert were as well placed to take advantage of the decentralisation of investment decisions as were their members to profit from the new higher purchasing prices. They were stimulated to combat the monopoly of the State buying agencies by investing in their own refining and bottling plants (Nagy-Pál and Apró, 1972, 135). Because the Tázlár szakszövetkezets were not in this fortunate position the prices offered to Tázlár members for their wine have remained consistently lower than those paid in Soltvadkert. Only the successful szakszövetkezets could compete as equal partners in the new environment. The measures of redistribution taken by the State during these years, mainly by the elimination of the tax burden upon all poorly endowed agricultural co-operatives, were quite insufficient to prevent the emergence of wide inter-community differentials.[3]

Thus the economic reform did more than extend to all branches of the economy a flexibility and an emphasis upon market-price relations which was already practised to a large extent in policies towards the small-farm sector in agriculture. The economic differentials, which it widened significantly almost everywhere, have had countless social and political ramifications. The new system has boosted a 'neo-bourgeois life' in the opinion of Ignótus, who goes on to claim that the reform induced a new respect for Mammon in all walks of life and, with some exaggeration, that 'A new era of *enrichissez-vous* has dawned in Hungary, reminiscent of the great upsurge of capitalist enterprise a hundred years ago . . .' (Ignótus, 1972, p. 279). It may come as no surprise to know that personal income differentials also widened appreciably in the years which followed the reform, and perhaps nowhere more so than in the szakszövetkezet community of Tázlár where, however weak the response of the socialised sector, many elements of the small-farm sector endeavoured to satisfy the demands made of them in small-commodity production, and reaped their private rewards accordingly.

V Recent trends in agricultural policy

There has been no major change in the direction of agricultural policy in the 1970s but it will be useful to emphasise a few points about the national context before proceeding to analyse the position in Tázlár.

As we have noted, total agricultural production was rising strongly and improvements were especially marked in the sphere of 'industrialised agriculture', i.e. in the socialised sectors. There were improvements in the yields of field crops, in the level of mechanisation, and in the supply of chemical fertilisers. However, there were also certain discouraging signs, including the stagnation or decline in animal stocks and contraction of several land-use types, including the vineyard area. In 1976 a poor harvest coincided with a sharp downturn in animal-breeding, especially in small-farm

pig-fattening, and the total value of agricultural production showed a
decline on the previous year for the first time since 1970.

Government policies are obliged to take into account the structural
composition of agricultural output, and the underlying problems of this
basic limitation on policy have intensified in the 1970s. It is in the production of field crops that heavy investment has enabled the socialised
sector to achieve its good results. In animal-breeding and in the production
of intensive commodities such as wine there remains much greater dependence on the small-farm sector. Thus, although there were respectable
increases in the stocks of pigs and cattle held by State Farms and by the
socialised sectors of production cooperatives between 1970 and 1976,
this was insufficient to compensate for the decline in the holdings of the
household-plot section of the small-farm sector over the same period.
In the case of pigs this decline was more than offset by the rest of the
small-farm sector, including of course the szakszövetkezets. The sector as
a whole continues to possess more than half of the total stock of pigs. In
the case of cattle there was a large decline in the household-plot sector,
but the preponderance of the socialist sector here ensured its greater
success in stabilising stocks and compensating for the decline in the small-
farm sector. The State has nevertheless made strenuous efforts in recent
years to stimulate small-farm dairy production.

Clearly there are important differences within the small-farm sector,
e.g. between, at one extreme, household-plot owners who now wish to
allocate less time to small commodity production or whose plots are
increasingly incorporated into the socialised sector and the benefits commuted to a cash payment, and at the other, the full-time farmers in szakszövetkezets.[4] The principal lever with which the State can hope to
influence the entire sector is that of price variation. The differences brought
about by collectivisation or resulting from different occupational patterns
do not alter this fundamental premise. In the case of pig-fattening, which
is perhaps unusually sensitive to the current price-level, there was a fall in
the total marketed from 726,000 tons in 1975 to 625,000 tons in 1976.
This was in spite of an increase in the basic state buying-prices for animals
and animal products of more than 25 per cent over the period 1970–6,
and an increase of 9 per cent between 1975 and 1976. The only answer
was to raise prices still higher, and eventually, at least in the szakszövetkezet
community of Tázlár, the response was satisfactory. The highest price increases of the 1970s have been awarded to the producers of wine. This
has not halted the decline in the vineyard area but it has increased the
proportion of wine which is sold on the market. Price signals therefore are
effective. The apparent decline in the willingness of household-plot
owners to produce may mean that still higher prices must be paid to other
sections of the small-farm sector in several important branches of production
where the socialised sector is unable to dominate. The more the smaller
part-time farmers drift away from agriculture, the greater will become the
role of the full-time private farmers of the szakszövetkezets. Already when

prices are raised all round, many szakszövetkezet farmers may gain a larger 'surplus' than other small-farmers because they are 'captive' producers who will market a certain quantity of produce in any case, irrespective of the price. When small-farmers respond very positively they will find the socialist sector of the szakszövetkezet ready to assist them to maximise their production by supplying them with feeds which are more efficiently produced in the socialised sector, and with machinery services. This is the trail which leads to the situation of Tázlár in the later 1970s. Underlying it is the structure of post-collectivisation agriculture and the fundamental problem that the transition to a large-scale mechanised agriculture is not equally simple in all branches of production. A related point concerning the detrimental impact of collectivisation upon factor combinations in agriculture is made by Kozlowski (1975, p. 427). It is a question of major structural weakness which in Hungary it has been the role of the small-farm sector in general and of the szakszövetkezets in particular to counteract.

There has been some controversy as to whether the policies of the economic reform have been consistently pursued, especially in the period since 1973. This is partly because of certain steps taken to curtail the spread of differentials after much adverse comment in the media, and partly because of measures forced upon the planners by international economic events. However, so far as agricultural policy is concerned, the stress must be upon its continuity, upon consistent strategies to complement high investment in the socialised sector. Kozlowski has criticised the capital privileges enjoyed by State-owned farms and their very high production costs (1975, p. 439). It is certain that the reform has increased inequalities within the socialised sector. On the other side, the continuing reliance upon the small-farm sector has been manifested above all in attempts to stimulate production through price policy. In this there has been no abandonment of earlier ideological positions, and indeed in Tázlár contradictory, moves have been made recently against key features of the szakszövetkezet. To what extent the farmers and szakszövetkezets of Tázlár have conformed to trends elsewhere and how they have responded to national agricultural policies will be the main subject of the next chapter.

4 The szakszövetkezet community – economy

In order to justify the definition of the community in terms of a single economic institution, the szakszövetkezet, the influence of that institution must be demonstrated in all areas of culture. This chapter begins the task where that influence has been most direct, with the economy. It concentrates on the changes in traditional farming brought about by the szakszövetkezet, but it also assesses the performance of agriculture's socialised sector and describes the impact of the employment opportunities which have arisen outside agriculture in recent years. Finally, the chapter analyses two levels of integration, each associated in a different way with the szakszövetkezet. The first, the transformation of the production processes of small-farms, has been a condition for the incorporation or integration at a higher level of traditional peasant economy into the modern socialist state. In Tázlár, as elsewhere in Hungary, the presence of a wage-labour component in many farming families is changing the character of small-farming as a full-time occupation.

I The socialised sector of the szakszövetkezet

The economic foundations of the cooperative groups founded in Tázlár at the end of 1960 were extremely weak. The major differences between them arose out of their location. In principle, each group farmed in one specific zone or zones and each farmer joined the group in the zone where the majority of his holdings lay. The groups were able to exchange plots to enable individuals to consolidate their holdings but such exchanges were liable to cause disputes. Sometimes the members of a family joined different groups in order to preserve their traditional holdings. Throughout its existence, the *Remény* (Hope), farming in the first and fourth zones, was the strongest and the most stable, whilst the *Kossuth* in the second zone and the *Rákóczi* in the third both suffered from leadership that was less secure, and experienced regular financial crises.

Theoretically the successors to the cooperatives of the 1950s, the new groups were not in fact able to attract the majority of their members to work on the lands inherited from the *Red Csepel*, and they also had difficulty in obtaining the machinery they needed to preserve the existing arable acreage of the socialised sector. The record of the *Red Csepel* was discouraging. The value of a work unit was very low and performance in stockbreeding was especially weak. In 1959, on a total land area of 1,370

49

hold (767 hectares), the cooperative had produced a total of 23 fattened pigs and kept 23 cows, which had a mean annual yield of only 938 litres of milk. Most of the land and buildings of the *Red Csepel* were taken over by the State Farm, which gradually moved out of stockbreeding altogether and switched instead to large-scale viticulture, to forestry, and to field-crop production that was susceptible to mechanisation, such as silo maize. It was the State Farm which accomplished what expansion there was in the socialised sector in the 1960s. Its workforce was larger than the collective workforce of the three new cooperative groups combined.

During the early 1960s each group was required to make substantial new investments. Between 1961 and 1964 a total of 138 *hold* (77 hectares) of orchards were planted in different zones using improved, modern methods. In the same years there was also new planting of vines and heavy investment in new livestock facilities and in machinery. The machinery was for deployment on members' individual farms as well as in the socialist sector, but, in practice, in the 1960s demand from the small-farm sector always exceeded the supply available. The major investments all failed, some of them within a very short period because of natural disasters, others because the fruit that was picked for a few years never reached the standards required for profitable sales. Today some of these orchards are still standing but they have long been neglected. Even the *Hope* lost one entire plantation of vines.

These failures all left their mark upon future developments and they had certain basic causes in common. Firstly, there was the absence of sound professional advice. More to the point, given that each new scheme relied upon local planning and local execution, many of the least successful projects were undertaken reluctantly in response to insistent outside prompting. Thus the attempt of the *Kossuth* to plant 30 *hold* (17 hectares) of apricots in 1964 was in part the result of pressure applied by the local Party secretary. Many of the leaders in each group had no enthusiasm for planting on a large scale and argued instead for the individuals' right to plant smaller areas, according to the techniques with which they were familiar. This was one reason why larger and genuinely collective projects failed. Voluntary investment schemes were seldom given the go-ahead when the decision was left entirely to the members. Yet the *Hope* farmers, for example, might have drawn considerable individual benefits from the development of irrigation channels in the second zone, a scheme which they turned down in the 1960s.

The acquisition of machinery proceeded much more rapidly than the expansion of the land area of the socialised sector. But the provision of services to the members remained inefficient, in part because of unnecessary duplication. Each group maintained separate offices and administrative staff, as well as separate storehouses and machinery centres. No group farmed very well in its socialised sector. At the end of the 1960s their maize yields were below the mean yield of the small-farm sector, which were in turn below the national average, at only 1,600 kilograms per hectare. Furthermore, by the end of the 1960s field-crop production was the only major productive activity of the new szakszövetkezets, the *Rákóczi* being the last to abandon the collective fattening of pigs in 1968. Worsening economic performance lay behind two thorough enquiries conducted into the *Kossuth* and the *Rákóczi* by the 'District Control Committee'[1] in 1969 and 1972. The need to improve efficiency and in particular to reduce machine overheads, was one of the main arguments put forward in support of mergers in the early 1970s. Eventually, despite considerable reluctance in all three szakszövetkezets, a single community-wide szakszövetkezet, the *Béke* (Peace), was founded in 1974.

Following the mergers, there was a marked increase in investment and also a considerable improvement in the quality of services provided to the members. This was to a large extent the personal achievement of the first szakszövetkezet chairman to represent the farming interests of the entire community. Further changes in the leadership following unification saw the arrival of a number of younger, qualified experts whose energy and know-how brought about an improvement in crop yields in the socialised sector in the mid-1970s. Attention was also focused on the poor pasture owned by the szakszövetkezet, mainly in areas remote from the main village. The investment by the *Hope* in a large sheep-fold had been one of the few durable achievements of the 1960s. The number of sheep rose sharply to reach almost 3,000 in 1977. Other initiatives taken by the new managerial leadership[2] had an adverse effect upon specific groups of members without bringing any lasting benefit to the socialist sector. The new leaders, on balance, worsened the image of the szakszövetkezet in the eyes of its members. The latter remained convinced that it was unduly bureaucratic and inefficient in farming the socialised sector. The leaders were unable to make work in the socialised sector more attractive to members. Indeed, in certain fields they now faced acute labour shortages. Rather than contract to work in a socialised sector which in their opinion did not qualify as an advanced socialist farm, many young workers with skilled-worker qualifications preferred to commute outside the community or to work irregularly in the 'private sector'.

A high proportion of those employed by the szakszövetkezet work only for very limited periods each year. For many of these, work in the socialised sector is only a subsidiary source of income, though one which may be very important for cash needs at particular times of the year, or for the assurance of later pension rights. In the national context of acute labour shortage neither skilled nor unskilled men have any difficulty in obtaining employment temporarily at any time of the year. The szakszövetkezet's workforce includes a few owners of substantial farms who reserve their main efforts, especially at peak periods, for their private farms. The number of members who work for short periods, when special jobs may be created for them, is at present small, but may well rise if collectivisation is carried through in such a way as to impose severe constraints upon small-farm production.

The szakszövetkezet community — economy

It should be made clear that there are major differences between the collective workforce in Tázlár and that of a typical production cooperative. Apart from the difference in size, there is the striking absence of females in the szakszövetkezet's manual labour force. This is because the men may be full members while continuing to farm individually on a full-time basis or to commute to work outside agriculture. There is no need for another family member to join the cooperative since ample land resources have been retained by the family and there is no need of a household plot allocation. The age-structure of the szakszövetkezet's collective workforce (though not that of its total membership) also differs from that of a typical production cooperative. Although it is difficult now to attract young workers, men in the generation now approaching retirement have generally preferred to take advantage of the opportunity to carry on full-time on their own farms. In consequence the average age of those working in the socialised sector may well be below the national average, but this is no indication of vitality and the problems in recruiting skilled labour will continue to grow in the near future.

Some workers in the socialised sector may not be members of the szakszövetkezet at all, but fall into a separate category of 'employees'. This group has only become prominent since mass collectivisation, as a result of the retirement of old members and the rise in the proportion of skilled workers. Both in a szakszövetkezet such as that of Tázlár and elsewhere on production cooperatives there is no longer any fundamental difference between these categories, and recently many employees have been encouraged to apply for full membership.

Levels of remuneration are determined, within wide limits, by the szakszövetkezet itself. In Tázlár, apart from the leaders, the general level is low. Annual bonuses remain of considerable importance, even in a poor szakszövetkezet such as that of Tázlár, which does not regularly make a profit. In addition to the main incentive, that of a guaranteed income, there are other features which may raise the attractiveness of the szakszövetkezet. Perks range from the car for the chairman to the provision of free working-clothing for the manual workers. Certain benefits in kind and the right to a household plot may apply to all those in employment.

The details of personal incomes paid out by the szakszövetkezet reveal a wide span of differentiation. Amongst those who worked over 200 days spread over ten or more months of the year, whom we may consider as being in full-time employment, the chairman received the highest salary in 1976 with 8,000 forints monthly (and a total of 315 days worked). Three other white-collar leaders earned significantly more than the monthly blue-collar average. The lowest wage was that of the office-cleaner with 16,748 forints for the whole year (314 days worked, and a total of 2,752 hours). Aggregated figures for the year will in most cases give a misleading picture of differences in wage-rates. Within the category of full-time, blue-collar workers there is wide seasonal variation in earnings. A good tractor-driver may treble his normal wage in the high season, especially if he is good enough to be assigned to a combine harvester. Most of the workforce are paid at an hourly rate, which may be readily altered by the leadership. The system is not universally popular, but there is no demand for, nor any likelihood of, a return to a 'work-unit' system (cf. Russian *trudoden*) and the present complaints would not easily be solved by any alternative system of remuneration. The real problem is the higher level of pay which prevails in the communities to the west, and the higher rates which can be earned within Tázlár, e.g. by a few private tractor-owners. The hourly rates of the unskilled are very low and turnover in this category is predictably high. In 1976–7 virtually no 'labourers' *(gyalogmunkás)* as such were employed by the szakszövetkezet, although there were several unskilled workers attached to the construction brigade.

White-collar workers, with the exception of the engineer and the crop-production leader, all work in the main offices, which are situated in the centre of the village, about 300 metres from the machinery centre. They have fixed monthly salaries and fewer possibilities to work overtime, but exceptional effort and good results may be rewarded with substantial bonuses. The atmosphere in the offices is relaxed, except when outside visitors are present or when committee meetings are taking place in the chairman's room. The wages clerk and junior officials may have to take work home with them in order to meet deadlines, but there are no large bonuses for them. Their salaries are lower than those of many blue-collar workers, but their status as office-workers may be higher. There is no difficulty in filling posts at this level, but, at the top level of the leadership, salaries well above the average have not been enough to tempt qualified agronomists, accountants and engineers to settle in Tázlár.

Outside the offices the social conditions of labour remain primitive. There is no common room or canteen at the machinery centre, and practically no heating. But for the presence nearby of a house where home-distilled *pálinka* is readily available, attendance might be somewhat down on many winter mornings, when work is supposed to commence well before light. For years there has been talk of the need for showers at the centre, but none have yet been installed. The chairman had the construction brigade devote its main energies in 1978 to renovating and sprucing up the exterior of the main offices.

Coffee is available in the offices, the heating is good and a pleasant conviviality has been maintained by a nucleus of female accountants and clerks, who have provided essential personnel continuity in recent years. Their relations with the young managers who led the szakszövetkezet from 1975 until 1977 were very good. Namedays were regularly marked by office collections, present-giving and parties. At the same time a personality conflict between the chairman and the financial manager was always present in the background during these years, and had some effect both upon the working of the administration and on discipline below.

Although more than 100 persons were employed by the szakszövetkezet in 1976, including just over 50 who could be classified as 'full-time', the white-collar group in the main offices, with a total of just over a dozen, is in fact the largest group to work regularly together throughout the year (separated only by office doors). The blue-collar workforce lacks any cohesive organisation. The construction brigade has been highly unstable since its inception. The only other relatively homogeneous group is that of the tractor drivers, but they have little *esprit de corps* and, apart from seldom working together, must vie with each other in the knowledge that their wage rates are individually assessed by the leadership. In daily contact at the machinery centre are a number of mechanics, electricians, lathe-workers, flour-millers, etc. There are also several drivers and others whose work is mainly solitary, such as the 'field inspectors', whose job is to protect the interests and property of the szakszövetkezet over the entire community, perhaps against the encroachments of members themselves, and on occasion to dispose of the produce of the socialised sector to the members. Finally, there are other employees who need never attend the machinery centre, and who may have their pay packets brought out to them in the fields. József Hazai earned 10,500 forints in 1976 for looking after the szakszövetkezet hogs throughout the year, while the shepherd Imre Nagy in the same year worked longer hours than any white-collar leader (3,330), all of them spent alone, some 3 miles (4.5 kilometres) or more from the village centre.

Work discipline in the socialised sector of the szakszövetkezet is inconsistent but generally lax. It is admitted as lax by many of the workers themselves. Punctuality in reporting for work and in returning promptly from lunch may be carefully observed, while serious infringements of the regulations, especially those concerning the consumption of alcohol, sometimes pass unnoticed. The nationwide labour shortage forces the szakszövetkezet to employ a few individuals to whom it would not otherwise be willing to offer jobs. Though discipline weakened because of instability in the leadership in 1977, there are certain problems which are always recurring, such as workers' obtaining private access to szakszövetkezet machinery, or the habits of some tractor-drivers who fail to log their journeys in advance, as stipulated by the rules. Behind such details lie still-unresolved difficulties, experienced equally by the State Farm and generally by all large units in the countryside, of creating an industrial-type factory hierarchy and enforcing the discipline of industrial labour where all labour is now in short supply and where formerly the ultimate source of authority over the economic unit was the patriarchal head of a peasant household. It was not easy for any cooperative leaders, and especially for the young, professional managers, to strike the right attitudes towards the labour force, and neither is it easy for young skilled workers to give orders to men who may be their seniors not only in years but also according to certain status perceptions that have retained their force. In 1977 during the leadership crisis two members of the elected executive committee of the szakszövetkezet were hired to fill key posts in the offices and in the machinery centre. One of the reasons for the success of this unusual step was the fact that each individual concerned had considerable prestige because of his age and general social standing in the community, independently of his new szakszövetkezet office.

A special case on the payroll of the szakszövetkezet in 1976 was that of three families of melon-growers. For the purposes of payroll statistics they were assumed to have worked 2,500 hours each, spread evenly over all the months of the year, and to have earned a monthly wage which approximated the national average. Although not fully part of the socialised sector and not subject to its labour discipline, they fell clearly outside traditional small-farming practice. They demonstrated a uniquely close cooperation with the szakszövetkezet, which differs from the general integration of small-farmers to be discussed below.

The melon-growers hailed from a region on the northern edge of the Great Plain which has long specialised in this branch of production. Each year they leave their permanent homes in early spring and settle for more than half the year in temporary accommodation — either in huts dug down into the soil for maximum coolness, or in wooden chalet-type dwellings. The melon-fields, which may be 16 *hold* (9 hectares) or larger, constitute part of the socialised sector of the szakszövetkezet, which negotiates a contract with each family. According to those concluded in 1976 and 1977, the szakszövetkezet made available high-quality land, undertook deep-ploughing, assisted with fertilisers and with water supplies during the drought of 1977, and supplied the transportation for final marketing, mostly to Budapest. All other tasks were performed by the families, each one a distinct economic unit (though there was systematic cooperation between two of them in 1977). However successful the outcome, the greater part of the final revenue accrues to them. They are paid advances by the szakszövetkezet to help cover the costs of various outlays during the production process. Whereas the ordinary farmer in Tázlár who wants to grow a few melons simply sows a seed, these families hired day-labourers to assist in the planting of carefully nurtured seedlings. It was the first time this culture had been introduced on a large scale for the market in Tázlár. The families had practised their speciality in many areas of the Plain, but as the risks involved are high on both sides they seldom stay very long in one place. Their first year in Tázlár, 1976, was highly suc-cessful for all concerned, but in 1977 the glut on the national market kept prices very low, possibly below what the szakszövetkezet needed to cover costs. Whether because of this failure, or because of the departure of the chairman who had first invited the families to come to Tázlár, only one family negotiated a fresh contract in 1978.

In the national context, sharecropping, of which this may be seen as a particular form, is now accepted as a means for the integration of socialised and small-farm sectors in agriculture. Its general effect can be compared with the integration that is achieved in most production cooperatives via the household plot. The main difference would seem to be that the individual retains greater control over his own labour process through household-plot arrangements, although in many modern, highly mechanised, production cooperatives this is no longer the case.[3] In Tázlár there are very few household plots and these are held for the most part by white-collar employees who are eligible because they have no private landholdings in the community. The szakszövetkezet performs the basic machine services on these plots, for which it charges the same prices as it charges its other members, and it may see some return in animal produce marketed. From another point of view, the generally larger holdings of all individual members of the szakszövetkezet can be regarded as household plots, which are integrated to varying degrees into the socialised sector. Sharecropping, on land that has already been 'collectivised' by the szakszövetkezet (i.e. taken into the socialised sector), has not yet been explored as an alternative.

There are two obvious reasons for the failure to promote sharecropping schemes in Tázlár. The first is the strength of the current household plot organisation, when this is taken to denote all small-farming pursued, however loosely, in the framework of the szakszövetkezet. Sharecropping is superfluous in the szakszövetkezet community because its essential result, the utilisation of marginal peasant labour for production in labour-intensive branches, is accomplished by other means, based on the more complete survival of the traditional family farm. Secondly, the strength of the szakszövetkezet and its present level of mechanisation is not sufficient to enable it to cultivate large tracts of former arable land already in collective ownership. Granted more favourable labour supply conditions it would still be necessary to increase significantly the capital base of the szakszövetkezet before any large sharecropping schemes could be put before the members. A third possible objection is that Tázlár farmers might at that point object to being told what they must cooperate to produce, and they might respond, as in the 1950s, by a general contraction of output. Thus, up to 1978 there have been only limited ad hoc arrangements to sell produce from the socialised sector, such as lucerne, to members willing to pay a given sum and to go out to the fields and collect it themselves; but these scarcely qualify as sharecropping schemes.

There is already considerable leasing to small-farmers of former arable land now used as pasture, especially by the State Farm in the third zone. If this is not to become a major trend in future and if the proportion of arable land is to be maintained, then it may become necessary to consider sharecropping as the most appropriate means for achieving integration. This would presuppose an advanced szakszövetkezet context in which the majority of holdings were collectivised, machinery was more plentiful and, displaced from their present privileged extra-large household plots, sufficient peasant labour resources were still available in the community. The typical household plot arrangement with its limit of 1 *hold* (0.58 hectare) – plus in most cases the plot on which the house itself stands – would be less appropriate in Tázlár because of the poor quality of the land and the demonstrable fact that most families utilise more than this area to maintain their present levels of production (see section IV below).

The socialised sector of the szakszövetkezet

Such arguments have already been cautiously advanced by certain elected executive committee leaders of the szakszövetkezet. But when the new young managers in 1975 collectivised the large areas of reeds around the two major lakes they refused a sharecropping compromise with the previous owners and instead, offering minimal compensation, they made over the entire area to an outside contractor, who moved in and cut the reeds swiftly and efficiently with modern methods. This pursuit of quick profits is easier to defend in the case of a product where the labour-saving gains from mechanisation were considerable. The problem is to redeploy that labour in branches where it is still needed, and the leaders have not yet appreciated the adverse consequences of intensifying collectivisation without at the same time exploring all opportunities to maintain production in the small-farm sector. Fishing, which has stagnated at very low levels in recent years, is another specialised activity which might be greatly expanded by a well-planned incentive structure. It should be possible in other branches as well to involve individual farmers while leaving the ownership of resources and full control over the process of production firmly in the hands of the leaders of the socialised sector.

The szakszövetkezet envisages no immediate move in this direction, with the exception of one ambitious scheme to raise funds from individual members for the foundation of a new large-scale vineyard, which would involve the members in the most labour-intensive stages of production in return for a major share of the profit. It is intended greatly to extend collectivisation in every zone, including the high-quality area near to the village which is of the greatest importance for small-farmers based in the village. There are also plans for a joint venture in vines with the State Farm, which has almost two decades experience in the field. The other main line of development in the szakszövetkezet's blueprint for the 1980s is the improvement of the quality of the outlying pasture and the further expansion of sheep-rearing (rising to an estimated 7,640 head of sheep by 1980). With a new leadership from 1977 bringing some much-needed stability to all levels of the organisation, there seems a good chance that all of these targets will be met.

However, there is still a crucial need to maintain a large area of arable land and as yet the small-farm sector remains indispensable to stockbreeding. Geographers and soil scientists have argued that it is particularly important on the Danube-Tisza interfluve, in conditions such as those which prevail in Tázlár, that a large quantity of organic fertiliser be used regularly on the land. In the similar geographical conditions of Kiskőrös, Berényi has stressed the need to develop stockbreeding based on the intensive utilisation of arables, meadows and pastures, in addition to the expansion of vineyards and orchards (1971, p. 131). For local ecological reasons and because of more general imperatives arising out of the structure of post-collectivisation agriculture in the national context, it is desirable that the socialised sector of the szakszövetkezet should make greater efforts to reproduce the balance of the traditional farming economy. This need not restrict the extension

57

of collectivisation and is not inconsistent with a sharp increase in the labour force and the capital strength of the socialised sector, but it does inevitably entail continued reliance upon the small-farm sector.

II The main characteristics of small-farming

According to the classification of Beluszky (1976, p. 49) Tázlár must be rated today a rural settlement of type A_2, 'villages of a decisive agrarian character without definite secondary functions'. In type A_3 'villages predominantly of agricultural character' the proportion of all earners active in agriculture is greater than 82 per cent, and although at the last national census of 1970 87.3 per cent of all active earners in Tázlár performed some agricultural work, this proportion has since declined (though relatively few enterprises have disappeared).[4] Farms and landholdings may still be inherited and most enterprises have been able to survive (though sometimes in a very attenuated form) the entry of one or more family members into full-time wage-labour, and occasionally even the migration of the entire family. From a total of around 760 households, 19 of which could be subdivided into two economic units, it was possible to identify 400 units which sold some produce through the szakszövetkezet in each of the years 1975, 1976 and 1977. The mean annual value of produce marketed by these units fell from 33,565 forints in 1975 to 29,800 forints in 1976, but then rose sharply to 55,052 forints in 1977. These units owned on average 18,411 square metres of arable land, 13,063 square metres of pasture and 6,209 square metres of vineyard. Of course not all of them were active in all branches of production. The figures for 1977 show that 372 units fattened pigs, 349 sold grapes or wine (or, in a small number of cases, a little fruit only), and only 230 units were active in the third major branch of production, dairy farming. Table 5 shows that only a minority of these units can be regarded as consistent substantial producers. Only 199 units marketed produce in excess of 15,000 forints in each of the three years examined, 95 consistently exceeded 30,000 forints, and only 40 were invariably above the 50,000-forint mark. Of the 400, a total of 179 were to be found in the main village and the rest divided between the four tanya zones, including the upper hamlet.[5]

A preliminary outline of the agricultural cycle for small-farms must emphasise the continuity with the traditional farming economy. In the records of the former Catholic elementary school a document has survived from 1933, which casts useful light on how peak-period labour needs were satisfied. Signed by the chief clerk (*fő jegyző*), it is entitled 'Community Testimonial' and part of it reads as follows:

... we officially declare that the larger agricultural tasks commence here at the beginning of May and continue through until the end of October.
    MAY: hoeing potatoes, maize, turnips and vines; tying the vines;
    JUNE: picking potatoes; hoeing maize; cutting and collecting hay; beginning the harvest; spraying;

The main characteristics of small-farming

Table 5 Small-farm aggregate production 1975–7

	No. of units	Mean value of production ('000s of fts)	No. of units in village	No. with arable holdings	No. trans-acting with szak-szövetkezet (all 3 years)	Mean value of trans-actions (fts)
Total units marketing produce 1975–77	400	118	179	340	270	9,662
Total marketing over 15,000 fts annually	199	174	89	175	162	11,335
Total marketing over 30,000 fts annually	95	233	45	85	85	12,721
Total marketing over 50,000 fts annually	40	299	15	37	35	14,962
Total marketing all 3 products* annually	54	207	20	52	52	12,293

*Pigs, milk, and wine and fruit

SEPTEMBER: digging potatoes; picking beans; picking maize; ploughing and sowing; harvesting grapes;

OCTOBER: picking maize; ploughing and sowing; harvesting grapes;

. . . We hereby certify that the 4,016 inhabitants of our community, excluding a handful of artisans and traders, teachers and officials, are occupied entirely in agriculture and in this occupation have an unavoidable need of particularly the older schoolchildren during the months of May, June, July, August, September and October.

Prónayfalva, 1933. Chief Clerk/Magistrate

Compulsory education in the 1930s was only six grades, so that 'older schoolchildren' referred at best to 14-year-olds. Today the inventory of tasks needs little amendment. The vines are now opened earlier than indicated in this testimonial, certainly during the first half of April. Spraying is not confined to one month only, but is now repeated systematically by all larger wine-producers, until August if necessary. A few of the jobs listed would in most small enterprises no longer be performed by the family but by the szakszövetkezet. This applies most notably to the harvesting and ploughing, but also possibly to all sowing, harrowing and cutting of natural grasses as well. Yet a preference for traditional methods lingers in some households. At the same time the general reduction in the size of the

59

household presents formidable problems in the case of all those tasks which cannot easily be performed using large-scale techniques. Prime examples would be the tying and the final picking of grapes. The holidays of the schoolchildren still begin in time for the early summer peak in June, but they must return to school in early September. Their only involvement in agriculture in autumn is likely to be with a school party drafted to assist on a State Farm, most often as fruit-pickers.

Small-farming has adapted to changing conditions in a great variety of ways. This variety can be explored by considering the degree of specialisation of the producer and the extent of his dependence upon the supplies and services of the szakszövetkezet. Between 1975 and 1977 only 54 economic units marketed produce in all three sectors in all three years, and only 270 units made regular use of szakszövetkezet services. There are considerable differences between the production processes in the major branches. The size and the composition of the household affect not only the decision of what to produce but also the techniques employed, the use, if any, of hired labour, and participation in mutual-aid groups. These questions will be examined in greater detail below, in the section on the integration of small-farming.

Although the cultivation of vines dates back to the beginning of mass resettlement, and although many of the early settlers established large vineyards, the risks involved in this branch of production were too great to permit the emergence of a group of exclusive specialists. But by the 1930s a small number of richer farmers had specialised to some degree on the basis of well-developed trading outlets in Soltvadkert. The greater part of the wine area was widely spread over a large number of small plots, and it is possible that in this period the greater part of production did not regularly reach the outside market. The varieties planted were always those most popular in the region, but compared to its western neighbours Tázlár had inferior cellar facilities and, when comprehensively surveyed in the 1960s, it had an older vine stock and a higher proportion in ineradicable decay (Szigetvári, 1968). This must be attributed in part to socialist policies, which, though leaving vineyards in private ownership at the time of mass collectivisation, have never ruled out the possibility of their ultimate collectivisation. The freedom to invest privately has been restricted since the 1950s, although the theoretical prohibition of unauthorised private planting has not been strictly enforced and some of the best vines observable in Tázlár today are the results of such 'black' investment. The trading of small vineyards was officially suspended in 1977. It is still, in practice, possible to dispose of a good-quality vineyard, but demand is not strong and in fact vineyards in reasonably good condition have been abandoned as their owners have migrated, or in response to one particularly bad harvest.

Some indication of the decline is given by the szakszövetkezet production statistics (see Table 6). The harvest of 1976 was so bad that some farmers did not bother to tend their vines at all that year. This is shown by the

Table 6 Production trends in the three branches of small-farming 1975 – 7

	1975	1976	1977
Total no. of pig-fatteners	324	279	372
Mean value of pigs marketed (fts)	19,463	19,532	28,717
Total no. of dairy farmers	237	248	230
Mean value of milk marketed (fts)	9,412	17,204	22,733
Total no. of wine and fruit farmers	376	307	349
Mean value of wine and fruit marketed (fts)	16,171	9,557	23,263

limited extent of the recovery in 1977, even though that was a very good year (as indicated by the jump in the mean value of the wine and grapes marketed). In a considerable number of households wine is the only commodity marketed. This is largely because a number of aged and pensioner families have abandoned the constant fatigue of stockbreeding but retained a small vineyard near the farm. In 1977 the mean age of the head of a wine-producing enterprise was almost 60. The mean in 1976 was 56, still above the average for all enterprises, but an indication that the younger men were better able to cope with the damage caused by late frosts. The number of 'specialist' units (those who marketed exclusively one commodity) was 110 in 1975, fell only to 97 in 1976, but declined further to 80 in 1977. It is characteristic of the specialist wine producers that they have relatively little demand for the services of the szakszövetkezet. In 1977, 48 of them did not transact at all, while the average of the remaining 32 was below that of most other enterprises (see Table 7). Curiously, the mean vineyard area of these 'specialists' was below the mean for the total 400 regularly-producing enterprises, and their production was consistently lower than that of the total of wine-producing units. The small scale of this specialist production in Tázlár contrasts with the large-scale profit-maximising specialisation in wine which is common in some of Tázlár's neighbours, particularly in Soltvadkert and Kiskőrös. The maximising specialist is not yet common in Tázlár, but, as will be shown below, his future cannot entirely be discounted.

Table 7 *Breakdown by branches of production, showing specialist producers, 1977*

	No. of units	Mean value of production ('000s fts)	Mean age of head of unit	No. of units in village	No. of units transacting	Mean value of trans- actions (fts)
Pig-fattening units, 1977	372	29	53.2	192	293	2,655
Units marketing only pigs, 1977	79	22	51.1	57	38	2,033
Dairy-farming units, 1977	230	23	53.9	66	202	2,585
Units marketing only milk, 1977	20	17	56.1	3	16	1,022
Fruit- and wine-producing units 1977	349	23	55.0	158	265	2,575
Units marketing only fruit and wine, 1977	80	18	59.2	27	32	1,284

These results can be explained by the regional context and by the nature of the labour process in this branch of production. It is the branch which has been least affected by the szakszövetkezet. At best, the socialised sector may supply fertilisers and chemicals for spraying, and arrange final transportation for sale. At present no szakszövetkezet machinery is deployed in vineyards. The entire production process remains under family control. In recent years it has become common informally to share power-sprayers or to hire the services of the owners of large motorised pumps, a costly way in which to ease the major labour burden. Remaining labour demands are seasonally highly concentrated, and only with great difficulty can they be carried out by one person. Tying and picking require large bands of labour which the modern household is unable to provide. In consequence, certain new strategies have been devised, based on new patterns of co-operation and renewed exploitation of hired labour, which enable peak shortages to be overcome. The secular trend has been, nevertheless, one of steady contraction in the small-farm vine area and, given the labour difficulties, it is hard to see how this can be reversed, except by large investment by the szakszövetkezet in collective vineyards.

Dairy production has also experienced a downward trend in the whole of the post-war period, but in recent years government policies designed to stimulate milk output have begun to take effect. The number of producers has remained roughly constant, and the total size of the small-farm herd has been stabilised at around the 500 mark (compared with 1,463 head in 1935 for the territory which included Harka-Kötöny, 752 in 1966 and 732 as recently as 1972). The mean value of production rose consistently between 1975 and 1977, although there was no significant rise in the buying prices for milk in these years. The statistics implied a mean production of some 4,000 litres of milk per enterprise in 1977 but in fact the variance in output (and hence also in earnings) was much greater than in the other major branches of production. The government's success is attributable partly to large grants which have both attracted new and able producers and encouraged existing producers to increase their stock, and partly to the efforts of the szakszövetkezet in making fodder available at reasonable prices and in guaranteeing the daily collection of milk from even the most remote tanyas (including some tanyas actually located outside the boundaries of the community).

Relatively few households specialise in milk production (see Table 7). The larger number of specialist units in 1976 (56, compared with 33 in 1975 and 20 in 1977) may be related to the poor wine production of that year. In 1977 the mean value of the production of the 20 specialists was below the mean for all milk producers, while their age was above the mean, indicating again that specialisation does not arise from any tendency of dynamic elements to maximise, but is associated with the limited ambitions of older households. The mean pasture area of the specialists greatly exceeds the mean for the 400 enterprises, while their arable area shows no significant difference. A majority of them made some demand on the services of the szakszövetkezet, but the mean value of their transactions was again well below the average for all producing units.

These results must be explained by the influence of national and local policies and again by the requirements, especially the labour demands, of the production process itself. Although the expansion which has taken place since 1975 cannot be associated with exclusive specialisation, it is probable that many smaller enterprises have abandoned dairy production and that larger and younger units have taken their place. The latter were encouraged by the new subsidies to diversify into dairy farming, or to take it up again after their stables had long been out of use. The statistics show that some enterprises soon reached previously unknown high levels of output. Leading the way in 1977 with a herd of eight cows, almost double that of his nearest competitor, was Lajos Égető, a resident of the village, but one who still made some use of his family's tanya, as well as making very heavy demands upon the services of the szakszövetkezet. His milk production rose from a value of 29,830 forints in 1975 to 119,327 forints in 1976 and 277,293 forints in 1977. Over the three years he paid out a total of more than 75,000 forints to the szakszövetkezet, including large sums for supplies of straw and fodder. Moreover, in 1977 he also marketed wine to the value of 89,500 forints and pigs to the value of 125,450 forints. In achieving this extraordinary output he was assisted only by his wife on a full-time basis: a son and daughter-in-law resident at home helped out occasionally, but they had full-time jobs outside the community and young children to look after. To mark his industry Lajos Égető was honoured with the title 'Excellent Agricultural Worker' in 1976 and took a day off to be feted at the ministry.

Many other farmers have tried to take advantage of the economies of scale in dairy production. Milk marketing is now simpler than at any time in the past. For a period before the Second World War only cream found a market outlet in Soltvadkert. Later a cooperative purchased milk as well, but as late as the 1960s when milk was dispatched daily to Kalocsa, both the total output from the community and the yield per dairy cow were very low. The labour demands are quite different from those associated with vines. Not even the largest producers have yet mechanised milking, which remains at least a once-daily chore. The assurance of supplies at the szakszövetkezet makes for greater evenness of output over the year, though there is still some decline in winter. The major agricultural task associated with dairy production is the cutting of hay, and most Tázlár farmers still rely upon large stockpiles of natural grasses for the winter. Cows can, however, be given over to the szakszövetkezet for organised grazing on collective pasture from May until October, when they do not therefore impede other tasks on the land or any outside occupation. Milk producers' generally low value of transactions suggests that few exploit fully the possibility to purchase winter fodder.

The risks involved in keeping cows, the occasional delay and expense of obtaining veterinary services from Soltvadkert, and the monotony of the work are the major drawbacks in dairy farming. On the other hand, this branch of production leaves much control with the head of the enterprise himself. He is able to choose when to buy and sell animals (within limits, if he has accepted the recent subsidies), he decides whether he wants the trouble and the additional risk of raising calves, whether to purchase extra supplies and attempt to increase the yield, or to continue relying solely upon his own rough pasture, etc. Dairy production is common in aged households and with solitaries where often only a single cow is kept, and it fulfils an important role in subsistence. But it is also increasingly attractive to modernising *'paysans évolués'*[6] such as Lajos Égető, who appear to make careful calculations to maximise their revenue or their profitability. It does not require the application of large resources at any one time and so the problems caused by the decline in the size of the household are not relevant here.

Pig-fattening is the third major branch of the small-farm sector. It is the one which has expanded most dynamically in the szakszövetkezet period. It is not a new activity, but the number of enterprises which fatten pigs for the market has actually risen in recent years. Major changes have taken place in the speed with which piglets can be fattened and, associated with new techniques, in the sensitivity of production to market prices.

In the pre-szakszövetkezet past the marketing of animals required their time-consuming transportation to Soltvadkert, Kiskunhalas, or even further afield. Many farmers still attend major markets (*vásár*) outside the community, and twice annually a large animal market is organised in Tázlár itself. These markets have survived throughout the socialist period and their popularity is undiminished. However, their trading role today is insignificant compared to the simple procedures now in operation for direct marketing to the State through the szakszövetkezet. The member only has to contract to sell a certain number of pigs at guaranteed prices, report to the szakszövetkezet offices when he judges they have reached the specified weight, and then at a given time deliver the animals to a weighing point just outside the main village. From there they are picked up by lorry and taken to abattoirs in remote towns. In addition to the producer, three persons are involved in the final stage: the household-plot agronomist from the szakszövetkezet, the representative of the State meat enterprise, and the vet who has to certify the condition of the pigs.

The statistics reveal interesting trends in pig-fattening over the period 1975–7, though it must be noted that prices rose appreciably at the end of 1976 and the figures therefore exaggerate the increase in output in 1977. In 1976 the mean value of production was maintained, but by only 279 producers, causing a decline in total production. In 1977, following the impact of the price increases, 372 pig-producers marketed a mean value of 28,717 forints, which implied some eight or nine animals each (no larger than the size of an average litter). The upward trend showed no sign of abating in 1978. Indeed, supply was so great at the traditional early summer peak (many farmers preferring not to keep animals during the hottest months), that the szakszövetkezet experienced great difficulty in disposing of all the animals which the farmers wished to sell.

The number of farmers who marketed only pigs rose steadily from 57 in 1975 to 67 in 1976 and 79 in 1977. In 1975 and 1976 their production was only slightly below the mean for all pig-producing enterprises, but they were left straggling in the expansion of 1977. Once again the expansion cannot be explained by a trend to exclusive specialisation. However, the age of the specialist pig-fatteners is well below the mean. Their land-holdings are also well below the mean for the 400 enterprises, both for arable land and for pasture. Of the 79 specialists in 1977, 27 possessed no arable land of their own and 53 had no pasture. The value of their transactions with the szakszövetkezet is inconsistent, but with the exception of 1977 (when there was a drop in the value of transactions for most enterprises) a large majority of the specialists did make some purchases or demand some services. In each of the three years examined, almost three-quarters of the specialist pig-fatteners lived in the main village. This was the exact inverse of the distribution of the specialist milk producers, and amongst the wine specialists also a consistent majority live out on tanyas. Finally, we may note provisionally the much greater probability of finding sources of income extraneous to small-farming amongst the specialist pig-fatteners than amongst the specialists of either of the other branches, or in the 400 enterprises taken together. The implications of this result will be analysed below in Section IV on the integration of small-farming.

Relating these results, as before, to distinctive features of the labour process involved, it can be stated at once that the recent popularity of pig-fattening owes much to its negligible capital requirements. Even if they lack suitable stables and have no equipment for the processing and storing of wine, few Tázlár dwellings lack some old outhouse which can serve as a sty. The labour demands are smaller than those of dairy production, do not require that time be spent in the fields and are perfectly consistent with regular wage-labour. At the same time, reliance upon the szakszövet-kezet is far from general and amongst pig-producers as a whole there are many who still fatten pigs without any recourse to the szakszövetkezet for either grains or concentrates.

Pig-farmers can set their own production targets. Some families rear only one litter each year to guarantee a cash supply during periods when other sources of cash are inadequate. It is not essential to keep a sow, for piglets may be readily bought on the market, or from neighbours reluctant to rear a large litter. Some larger producers do, however, keep as many as four breeding-sows. Several keep their own hogs as well, although this practice is attacked by the leaders of the szakszövetkezet, who prefer members to make use of the special breeds of hog which it keeps centrally and on a few strategically situated tanyas.

For many enterprises today, pig-fattening is little more than an extra household chore, the timing and the intensity of which is regulated by current financial circumstances or by the need to prepare for a major life-cycle event such as a *lakódalom* (wedding reception). The constraints of traditional peasant farming do not apply any longer in this branch. This is reflected in the differentials which have appeared between the tanyas and the central village. Although tanya pig-production has followed the same market trends as village production, in mean value it has lagged consistently behind, despite the larger landholdings of tanya-resident farmers and the smaller proportion of tanya pig-producing households active outside small-farming in wage labour.

In addition to pig-fattening, there are today a number of subsidiary branches of production which similarly exist outside the traditional frame of reference of the peasant farm and its associated organisation of labour, and which also operate outside the szakszövetkezet. There are a few indi-vidual specialists, such as beekeepers, where if the specialisation is full-time it is pursued in a more or less profit-maximising manner, and if it is not full-time then it is regarded more as a hobby or at most as an important source of supplementary income. There is also a wide range of activities in what can be summed up as market gardening. This too has become for a few a full-time 'business-like' activity. More than one farmer has ex-perimented with greenhouses to produce early lettuce and tomatoes. Another has estimated profits of some 30,000 forints from intensive paprika production on a land area smaller than 3,000 square metres. But in general, market gardening complements the main production of the farm. It is an exclusively female domain on most full-time farms, and often it is the wife alone who carries the produce, fruit or vegetables, to Soltvadkert for sale. Like pig-fattening, market gardening can also be pursued alongside a regular wage-labour job. If the marketing opportunities for small-garden produce were improved, there is little doubt that many more households in the village and on tanyas would expand their gardening beyond what most of them currently undertake for subsistence needs.

Before the detailed examination of how the production of the small-farm sector is integrated by the szakszövetkezet and how total agricultural activity is related to the occupational structure and to ever-expanding labour opportunities outside small-farming, the next section will examine this 'public' labour market, which we have so far seen only in the socialised sector of the szakszövetkezet.

III The employment market outside the szakszövetkezet

There is no unemployment in Hungary.[7] Old-age pensions have only recently been introduced for szakszövetkezet farmers, and the general level of welfare benefits is low although it has risen substantially since 1968. In any case, farmers do not receive their pensions until the age of 70. Hence there is a constraint upon most households to participate in the labour market. If this is conceived of as being composed of two parts, 'public' and 'private', corresponding to a distinction between factory-type wage-labour and what is known in the West as self-employment, then it should immediately be made clear that a discussion of small-farming by no means exhausts the private sector. In many cases households and individuals are found active in both sectors.

The public sector includes, besides the socialised sector of the szakszövetkezet, additional wage-labour employment in agriculture through the State Farm and the Forest Farm. It also includes industrial wage-labour in nearby towns, which involves daily commuting, and similar employment further afield, in which case the return to the Tázlár home may be highly irregular. Within the village, the major opportunities for work in the public sector are offered by the spinning factory, the school and the council offices, and the shops and the *bisztró* (bar, cafe) which are controlled by the Consumers' Cooperative.

In contrast, the private sector is inevitably more of a catch-all, residual category. It includes a small section of the peasantry which engages in subsistence production only and has no need for regular inflows of cash. It includes also the wage-labourers hired seasonally by the private builders in the village, whose attitudes to work may approximate to those of the factory labourer. There is also an important group of skilled self-employed to whom we may refer collectively as 'artisans', although many have withdrawn from their traditional specialisations and now devote more of their

67

energy to small-farming. Like wage-labourers, they may become members of the szakszövetkezet. Hungarian law does not prevent a man from joining more than one cooperative, but in cases where certain welfare benefits could be compromised, another family member might maintain the link with the szakszövetkezet. However from the point of view of the leadership of the szakszövetkezet today it is of no importance who the member might be, or how many persons might join from the same family. The leadership was willing to accept produce for sale on virtually the same terms from all small-farmers, members and non-members alike.

Some of those who procure a livelihood in the private sector alone are directly involved with agriculture without themselves being farm owners and without marketing any produce. However, the diffuse problems of hiring private labour on the land, the means by which a few families earn enough to maintain themselves throughout the year without undertaking any regular wage-labour in the public sector, will be separately discussed below. There are also artisans, controllers of their own labour, who have prospered through the supply of special services to small-farmers, services which the socialised sector has been either unable or unwilling to provide, or for which it has charged higher prices or offered unreliable quality. Indirectly, the business of all artisans has depended upon incomes generated in small-farming.

It is difficult to draw the line in the private sector between the day-labourer who has invested in some simple spraying equipment and is willing to use it for a fee in the vineyards of his neighbours, and the specialist owners of motorised pumping vehicles which they place at the service of the entire community for rather higher fees. A good example of current practice in the private sector is that of Attila Kertész, the most energetic and successful of the private tractor-owners. Tractors, especially modern multi-purpose machines, are hard to come by privately in Hungary (there is a belief in Tázlár that across the border in Yugoslavia they are freely available), but it is possible to purchase old machines that have been discarded by the socialised sector. This loophole has enabled skilled mechanics in communities such as Tázlár, where the large size of small-farm holdings gives the tractor its great value, to establish lucrative, but quite above-board, businesses. Attila Kertész likes to refurbish one complete tractor each winter, which he then re-sells privately for a large profit. He retains another machine which he operates himself or with the help of an assistant throughout the agricultural season. Demand is sometimes so great that the tractor may be delegated to the assistant, who commutes to work in a nearby town, for late-evening or night work. He then obtains one-quarter of the fee, the remaining three-quarters going to the owner. Attila Kertész is a member of both the szakszövetkezet and of the Consumers' Cooperative. As the son of a well-to-do family he has inherited a medium-sized vineyard, on which the members of his family supply the necessary labour with the regular help of hired labourers. He cooperates informally with other public-sector tractor-drivers, such as employees of the State Farm, or with anyone who can help him with parts and with the supply of fuel. Theoretically, like the members who sell their produce, he too must pay a 10 per cent levy to the szakszövetkezet on all his private contracting work. This is his major tax liability and one which is inherently difficult to enforce. He is popular with many small-farmers because he saves them from having to wait for the szakszövetkezet, and his efficiency leaves no grounds for complaint.

One way of classifying the very heterogeneous self-employed is by the size of their small-farm production. In recent years some older craftsmen have become almost indistinguishable from the full-time farming members of the szakszövetkezet. This has not always been a voluntary decision. In the case of smiths and wheelwrights, technological changes have forced several individuals to devote more time to farming, but most keep their workshops and are happy to accept the occasional commission. Comparable transitions have enabled a few of the private traders and shopkeepers supplanted by the Consumers' Cooperative to maintain their independence. They may conserve vestiges of their traditional occupation over a long period. Others have shown no hesitation in moving out of a declining craft. Demand for the services of the village cobbler and tailor have slumped, but both men have prospered in private farming.

Not all trades have gone into decline and a few new ones have flourished recently. There has been a shortage of electricians, in part because one of them has worked full-time in the socialised sector of the szakszövetkezet and the others have worked irregularly in the public sector outside the community. The chimney-sweep has migrated to Soltvadkert, but has retained his old monopoly. New hairdressers' have opened. Large numbers of women embroider at home for the Kiskunhalas hand-industry cooperative. other home-workers make attractive wicker chairs for a similar cooperative, and there are plenty of part-time seamstresses who work at home to individual commissions. There is a deficiency in carpenters and a great need for a repairer of television sets. Some deficiencies can be met by non-qualified, semi-skilled labour; for example, some of the seamstresses fall into the category of amateurs. But the practice is best demonstrated in the building-trade, where there has been a long boom in private house-building and the limitations of a March to November season have made it hard for the qualified gang-leaders to keep up with demand. Hence, although they continue to compete in the rates they charge and in the speed and quality of their work, they have ceased to object when smaller jobs are undertaken by semi-skilled competitors. The latter may be very popular with customers because of their lower rates and because they are often immediately available. In 1977 a young builder, freshly qualified and without experience, had no difficulty in forming a small gang and carrying out small jobs such as building outhouses and garages. He was not, though, able to obtain a licence from the council offices and was therefore forced have prospered in private farming.

to pay a premium for the signature of one his authorised rivals when the final result was subject to official inspection. The total number of part-time specialisations is very large. About a quarter of village households have some regular source of private-sector earnings outside small-farming and outside labouring. Specialisations in this sense can be established without formal training and, as in the case of the home-workers, they can have no economic function in the community apart from increasing the inflow of cash. Individuals can make money from lending machinery, but they also hire out dining-sets, or the entire marquee, tables and lighting required for a *lakódalom*. As with the tractor-driver, the hirer generally obtains the services of the owner of the goods as well as the goods themselves. The owner of the marquee also acts as a professional master-of-ceremonies throughout the *lakódalom*. The same is true when transportation (either mechanical or horse-drawn) is demanded and supplied. In a small community an individual's ability and willingness to provide an original service or to undercut a State-endorsed supplier quickly becomes common knowledge. The same applies in the local trading of certain small commodities, such as paprika, and in illicit spirit distribution. There is some tendency for children to adopt the specialisations of their parents or of other relatives. Custom, however, depends upon the personality of the specialist and the loyalty he can attract as an individual. When one barber recently retired and his son set up a new establishment in his own home, not all of the old clientele moved over to the younger man. The latter was proud of his qualification and of having trained outside the community. He denied that being his father's son had conferred any business advantage.

Specialisations, as the term is used here, range from those of the private tractor-owners and the builders, who may pay more in tax in a few months than most households expect to earn in a year, to that of the lady employed for very low wages by the Catholic Church to tend the cemetery. Some posts, such as that of the representative of the State undertakers, are more honorary and prestigious. Others are remunerative but are highly demanding only in emergencies, such as that of the *vizes* (water-man), who is responsible for the public wells and the piped-water system developed in the 1960s. The unifying characteristic of all these specialisations is their compatibility with the running of a small-farm. Potentially, the farm can be quite large when the specialisation does not make heavy and regular demands upon the labour of the individual. Even where the incentives to full-time specialisation are greatest, in the building-trade, the individuals have maintained szakszövetkezet membership (though perhaps more to enable them to draw upon particular machine services than to facilitate their production of agricultural commodities), and they at least keep gardens for subsistence requirements.

Almost all of the specialists are resident in either the main village or the upper hamlet. The same opportunities, with the exception of that for female home-working, do not exist for tanya-dwellers. It is not difficult for the latter to become chairmen of szakszövetkezet committees, and many of them have become regular commuters. But only in a few exceptional cases have central functions been devolved to outlying tanyas, e.g. by the szakszövetkezet (in the case of its pedigree hogs), or by the soda-water producer (one of the older and most coveted of specialisations). There is also one energetic tanya-resident tradeswoman who buys up small produce, mainly from village households, and employs a chauffeur to assist in distant urban marketing. A case might also be made for regarding the distillers of illicit spirit as enterprising tanya specialists.

It is common in many Hungarian villages nowadays that a proportion of young persons who qualify as skilled workers fail to take up employment which would make use of their skills (cf. Zsigmond, 1978, p. 168). Young people have been tempted by highly-paid work in the unskilled urban labour market, particularly in the construction industry. In Tázlár it generally takes some years of apprenticeship before one is able to establish oneself as an artisan with an assured income in the private sector outside small-farming. It is therefore common to find that intelligent youths dissatisfied with farming are openly cynical about the benefits of study, and reject both subordination to older craftsmen and employment in the low-wage socialised sector of the szakszövetkezet. Such youths have in Tázlár many more opportunities in the private sector, inside and outside agriculture, which have reduced the proportion of commuters. In Tázlár intensive day-labouring brings in the largest sums, and the house-building boom has created similar opportunities outside agriculture. Not only unskilled labourers, but also the skilled and semi-skilled can earn large sums through private contracts and by working long hours in summer. Because Tázlár prices are slightly below those of the rich neighbours to the west, the Tázlár gangs are also much in demand outside their native community.

The 'public sector' of the labour market is the sector in which individuals are subjected to a factory-type labour discipline and deprived of control over their labour time, unlike the full-time small-farmers, the 'specialists', and the other participants in the private sector who retain this control. In Tázlár the public sector has three main divisions. These are (i) wage-labour within the community, (ii) daily commuting, (iii) long distance commuting.

The opportunities for wage-labour within the community are limited. The State has two large monthly payrolls, one for all the staff of the school, the other for the administration at the council offices, plus a few specialists such as the doctor, the midwife and the policeman. The Consumers' Co-operative employs a number of girls in the self-service shop, the kitchen staff and waitresses in the *bisztró*, and a few other shopkeepers, including a part-time butcher. One individual runs a small collection point for eggs, occasionally rabbits, and other small items of household production. An outlet for building materials is also maintained and employs one individual full-time.

71

The szakszövetkezet community — economy

The Tázlár division of the Kiskőrös State Farm is based just outside the village on a large, former *kulák* (rich peasant) tanya. Its main activities are concentrated in the third zone on the two large vineyards which spill over into neighbouring Bócsa. It also has some mechanised maize production, some forest, and a considerable area of poor pasture, much of which is now rented out to small-farmers, as the State Farm keeps no animals in Tázlár. Because so much of the production is mechanised, a fair proportion of the workforce have skilled-worker qualifications. The leader of the Tázlár division is not a native of the community, but was building a house in the village in 1978. He is a well-qualified agricultural engineer. The technology commanded by the State Farm includes spraying by helicopter, and its maize production likewise contrasts with the labour-intensive methods of the small-farm sector. State Farm employees are less likely than other public-sector employees to market small commodities through the szakszövetkezet, although some have retained szakszövetkezet membership. The leader of the division himself sells a small quantity of grapes annually through the szakszövetkezet.

The Forest Farm is also managed from outside the community, but the greater part of its workforce, mostly drivers and a substantial body of unskilled labour, both male and female, is locally recruited. The Forest Farm has no headquarters in the village but has a tanya base deep in the forest. Each day the workers are picked up and driven by van towards the fourth zone and Kötöny. Forestry has greatly expanded in many areas of the Danube-Tisza interfluve during the socialist period, as part of complex strategies to improve land utilisation: it is likely that in Tázlár both the area and the numbers employed in forestry will continue to increase. Little private use is made of forests, nor do any large woods remain in private ownership. But certain public sector employees are able to turn their rights to timber on small plots of *illetmény föld* (bonus plot) to commercial advantage, and the trees are also important to the private beekeepers.

Also in the south of the fourth zone and in Kötöny, scattered across the forest, the last decade has witnessed a series of moderately successful oil and gas explorations. The oil has proved disappointing compared with results elsewhere on the Great Plain, but drilling for natural gas continues and plans exist to pipe supplies to the towns of the region and beyond. The drilling centre is manned on a three-shift system by 12 Tázlár men, most of whom have received only minimal technical training. Control is exercised from the more successful drilling bases at Szank, some 10 kilometres distant. This workforce is a well-satisfied one. Although the pay is not high the work is not demanding and leaves plenty of time for other activities. Most of these men belong to households which are active small-commodity producers through the szakszövetkezet.

The largest source of local wage-labour is also non-agricultural. This is the spinning factory which was opened by the Kiskunhalas hand-industry cooperative in the centre of the village in 1971. The importance of this factory lay in the openings which it brought for initially unskilled female labour. Of the 150 or so persons active full-time in the other major sectors of the local public labour market (i.e. in the socialised sector of the szakszövetkezet, the State and Forest Farms and the oil- and gas-drilling enterprise), the great majority is male. In the spinning factory, of a total workforce of about 50, approximately four-fifths are female. Only a few machinery maintenance engineers, loaders in the yard, and the director are male. It is usual now for school-leavers who are to be employed in the spinning factory to attend classes in Kiskunhalas and to perform a variety of training tasks before they qualify for full wages. In any case, because of the demanding nature of the work, beginners cannot often earn as much as more experienced women. Payment is by a piece-rate system; the local director is in sole charge of recruitment and the system is such that it is easy for him to assess performance individually. Wages and quarterly plan-fulfilment targets are fixed in Kiskunhalas, and it often happens that full weekends must be worked when the deadline is imminent.

Almost 150 women applied for jobs in the spinning factory when it opened, but of those originally taken on, only 8 remained in 1977. In that year more than three-quarters of the women were under 30. Turnover remained high, despite a 50 per cent pay increase between 1975 and 1977 (the increase was accompanied by reductions in bonuses, and raised average monthly earnings to only the 2,400-forint mark). Women are

5. Inside the spinning factory

slowly becoming less willing to take on the night-shift work, and there are plans to construct a new factory in which night-shift work will be phased out. Many women still find the factory the most suitable employment in the first years of their marriage. Seventeen former employees were receiving the child-care allowance in 1977, and the director estimated that fewer than half of those who benefited from these allowances actually returned in the long run to their old employment.

A thin line divides the community-based workers from the daily commuters. There are, for example, some employees of the State Farm who commute daily to the Farm's machinery and stockbreeding centres in Kiskőrös, while other employees of the same Farm reside temporarily at their workplace and return home at only five- or six-day intervals (not necessarily at weekends). Larger numbers of workers take the bus which leaves from the village centre at dawn for the light industries of Kiskunhalas. They return on the same bus in mid-afternoon. Kiskunhalas is not a major industrial centre, but it is the last major station on the railway line to Belgrade and has benefited from several large national investments in recent years. Residence in Kiskunhalas is not greatly desired by many of the people of Tázlár, partly because of its high gypsy population. But when a large textile factory opened for the first time in 1977 and advertised for unskilled labour, both males and females of all ages showed tremendous interest. The greatest expansion in the 1970s has been in local commuting by females. Workers of both sexes change jobs with a frequency that has disturbed the authorities, but the general labour shortage encourages their fickleness.[8]

Rather greater stability was shown by many of the long-distance commuters. There were about 70 of these in 1977 and they were predominantly male. Some Tázlár men have worked for decades with the same Budapest construction firm, or the same oil enterprise beyond the Tisza. Many received their first taste of industrial work in the 1950s in the mining industry. Some of the earlier commuters moved to the towns at the first opportunity, and there are still fresh departures each year. But although there are some for whom long-distance commuting is merely the necessary preliminary to final migration, for many older men with families in Tázlár it remains a temporary strategy designed to bring in extra income, sometimes only in the years when the children are growing up. It may be prolonged afterwards, perhaps in order to establish pension rights, but urban residence is never seriously considered. The patterns of return vary considerably. All buses to and from Tázlár are always crowded at weekends. There are families who live for only short periods in the community and spend most of the year in modern workers' hostels. These families are unlikely to produce agricultural commodities in Tázlár, and unlikely to maintain even tenuous links with the community when they have obtained a flat in the town. Another extreme has been represented in recent years by a few youths who have spent up to three years in the German Democratic Republic as guest workers. While there they improved their skilled-worker qualifications, saved substantial sums in Deutschmarks, and upon completion of their contracts at least some have resettled in Tázlár. The total number of households with one or more members employed full-time in the public sector as we have defined it is 348. In a further 19 households an individual specialisation verges on being 'full-time'. Of the total number of households which thus have regular sources of income outside small-farming, only 108 failed to market any produce whatsoever in the period 1975−7, and a high proportion, about 46 per cent, marketed some produce in all three years. This is one empirical estimate of the 'worker-peasant' population. It is more usual to exclude 'artisan' households from the definition, since the duality in their case is traditional and full control over all production is retained within the family based enterprise. Worker-peasant households are then defined as households where at least one individual has no direct control over a part of his labour which is expended outside small-farming. Occupational pluralism influences the division of labour at a household level, particularly in the case of the long-distance commuters. Farmwork has often become the responsibility of the commuter's wife, or of an elder family member, and the worker or workers help out only at special periods. The greater proportion of males employed in the public sector has contributed to the feminisation of agricultural work.

The existence of a large worker-peasantry is a major consequence of Hungarian industrialisation strategy, and of post-collectivisation agricultural policies in particular.[9] Infrastructure improvement and urbanisation have been consistently neglected, and every effort has been made to maintain small-commodity production in the households of rural commuters. Almost 50 per cent of Hungary's industrial workers still lived in villages in 1977, and approximately the same proportion of households were active in small-farming. The number of 'mixed' households may be smaller in szakszövetkezet communities than elsewhere because of their exceptional incentives to full-time small-farming. In 1977 there were in fact 275 regular commodity-producing households in Tázlár without any source of income from outside small-farming. Nevertheless, especially amongst younger persons, there is no strong desire to remain full-time in small-farming. The relatively poor communications of Tázlár make the social consequences of commuting as bad as anywhere else in the country. In the long term it must be expected that further migration to the towns will diminish the extent of small-farming.

There are, however, sociologists who have tended to argue that many worker-peasants are content with their 'dual economy' and have no desire to migrate.[10] Only a substantial improvement in the urban housing supply can put this argument to the test. There are a few families in Tázlár for whom commodity production in agriculture is at present a remunerative by-product of rural residence, but one which they say they would gladly forgo; in a small number of cases activity is limited strictly to subsistence needs. But in the short term, the transition to an industrial pattern of employment in both industry and agriculture has made occupational pluralism indispensable to the government. Despite consequent social problems in the community and the economic problems created by the fickleness of the worker-peasant labour force, one can expect a rise in the number of worker-peasant households at the expense of homogeneous 'full-time farms', and no overall decline in the number of small-farm commodity-producing enterprises. The labour shortage shows no sign of alleviating, and the State will continue to offer high-price incentives to the small-farm sector. The szakszövetkezet community will remain well placed to exploit this conjuncture.

IV The integration of small-farming

The main features of small-farm production and of the employment market inside and outside agriculture should now be clear, but there has been some abstraction in the analysis so far. The characteristics of the major branches of production were outlined with the help of the statistics for exclusive specialists in each branch, although such specialisation is exceptional and most enterprises have at least some activity in more than one branch of farming. There has been no discussion of how artisans are able to reconcile their dual activities within the private sector, nor has there been any indication of how full-time labour in the public sector is rendered compatible with particular patterns of small-farm production. Even full-time jobs prescribe some holiday entitlement, and even where labour discipline is most strict, in the spinning factory, absenteeism is conspicuous at agricultural peaks. This section will concentrate on the integration of small-farming which has taken place in the context of, but not always through the agency of, the szakszövetkezet. It extends to the enterprises which have retained traditional homogeneity and practise small-farming as their exclusive full-time occupation, as well as to the farms of worker-peasant households. The differences between these two broad categories, the likely future of full-time small-farming in the szakszövetkezet community and the implications of the present situation in Tázlár for theoretical attempts to understand the organisation of 'peasant economy' are points taken up in Section V.

It has been shown that the production process in each major branch of farming is susceptible to differing degrees of integration, and leads enterprises into varying degrees of dependence upon the szakszövetkezet for inputs and services. It appears from Tables 5 and 7 that there is relatively little variation in levels of transactions with the szakszövetkezet. Either this is a highly imperfect measure of integration, or some other feature such as the size of the household or the subjective preferences of the farmer outweighs the objective requirements of the production process. Some farmers demand services which are not related to their production (e.g. transportation of building materials). Others purchase essential inputs from the socialised sectors of farms outside the community, and certain other transactions are also excluded from the accounts (see note 5 to this chapter). Nevertheless, a large and increasing proportion of producers in all branches, on tanyas and in the village, do obtain services from the szakszövetkezet, and the larger the enterprise the greater the level of transactions is likely to be. Some contact with the szakszövetkezet and advantage from simplified marketing is necessarily established by everyone who sells produce, if only once a year in disposing of the grape harvest. The transformation of traditional farm organisation is the precondition for what may be termed the limited 'social integration' of most households and enterprise types to be found in Tázlár today.

Sándor Horváth is a tanya farmer and an exceptional example today of an individual who is preoccupied with minimising cash outlays to the szakszövetkezet. His major cash expenditure is the rent which he pays to the State Farm for the pasture which is grazed by the most substantial privately-owned flock of sheep in the community today. His relatively autonomous farm organisation is made possible by the large size of his family labour force: in 1976 he had five sons (aged between 11 and 19) still resident at home. Other households are similarly reluctant to pay out cash for services which were traditionally performed on the farm by the family. Resistance to technological innovation is often defended by the people of Tázlár with the proposition that only time-hallowed methods

6. Sándor Horváth ploughing with his oxen

are appropriate to the special ecology of the community, and that modern ideas which may succeed elsewhere are inapplicable on the soft sand. Such attitudes have hindered the expansion of szakszövetkezet services. However, Sándor Horváth is now the only farmer who keeps oxen, and even he turns to the szakszövetkezet for harvesting. The szakszövetkezet has altered the production process of most farmers, most decisively in replacing the former privately-owned threshing machines and the large bands needed

7. Harvesting rye by hand

to operate them by Soviet-built combine harvesters which require only one skilled operator. Threshing is perhaps the only activity which is now performed exclusively by the szakszövetkezet. The shortage of combines causes a few farmers to harvest by hand if the machine is not available in their zone when they judge their crop to be ready (Plate 7), but all will turn to the szakszövetkezet later for threshing. Older farmers frequently complain about the quality of the combines and the quantity of straw which is wasted.

The relationship between the total output of a farm and the value of its service transactions with the szakszövetkezet is not a strong one. The elected members of the executive committee are amongst the heaviest demanders of services, thereby putting into practice the ideology which governs the relationship between the socialised sector and the members. We have seen (p. 63) how men such as Lajos Égető may strain the servicing capacity of the szakszövetkezet and may be constrained to make supplementary purchases elsewhere. Ambitious individuals willing to contract high levels of output may be able to obtain special terms and substantial advances of inputs. Although larger producers may have certain advantages, in principle the szakszövetkezet tries to offer maximum support to any individual who wishes to expand his farm production. Its primary goal is the overall maximisation of output. It may also make available extra land at a low rent, in the unusual case of a producer anxious to expand by

8. Harvesting with a combine harvester

traditional self-reliant methods and lacking the necessary land resources. For the same reason it is generous with the size of the household plots which it allocates to its own workforce. Since the early 1960s, the szakszövetkezet has gradually extended the range of its machine services.

It is the main source of tractor power and, building upon the former tractor station which became the machinery centre of the socialised sector, has, in the 1970s, generally satisfied local demand for the most essential of services, except at isolated peaks. New tractors are not freely available on the market, and only those of the szakszövetkezet have road licences which enable them to travel outside the community (e.g. in transporting supplies). Smaller items, such as sprayers, mini-tractors, or multi-purpose mechanised carts, which can be purchased by individuals on the market, are not supplied by the szakszövetkezet, even though in practice few small-farmers are able to buy them. At the other end of the machinery scale there are also deficiencies. The szakszövetkezet no longer possesses up-to-date harvesting technology. In 1977, Tázlár was unable to bale waste straw economically, relative to price levels elsewhere in the region. Although the straw was necessary for expanding dairy production, and although bales were much the most convenient form, the treasurer was adamant that the szakszövetkezet should not provide the service. The eventual compromise, worked out after executive committee members had voiced the interests of the members, was to raise the price so high that very few farmers were willing to pay it; several sought cheaper supplies in other communities. There was an overall decline in services provided in 1977, partly as a result of the instability within the leadership.

Supplies of fertilisers are also criticised by many of the members, though in the opinion of the leaders the stocks at present available are not used in sufficient quantities on most small-farm landholdings. The szakszövetkezet has also become a vital supplier of fodder and feeds to the whole spectrum of small-farmers, i.e. to full-time farmers eager to maximise farm output as well as to part-time farmers anxious just for a little extra cash, most frequently through pig-fattening. The main storehouse of the szakszövetkezet at the machinery centre opens regularly like a shop, and normally stocks a wide variety of feeds and concentrates. For some purchases a chit is required from the szakszövetkezet offices which authorises the purchase on the basis of a contract to market future produce. The 'shop' was accepted somewhat cautiously when it opened in 1972, but in recent years the increase in trade has been spectacular. Purchases are made in cash and are not recorded individually: hence they do not appear in the statistics. Some of the feed which is sold to members, particularly barley and rye, originates from inside the socialised sector of the szakszövetkezet. However, because of the limited storage and processing capacity much local crop production leaves the community and crop 'imports' are separately managed. Tázlár is now, perhaps surprisingly, a substantial net importer of animal feeds. In other words, in the 1970s the economy of the community had reached a stage where the level of animal-breeding in the small-farm sector was not being sustained by crop production within the community, or within the local socialised sector, but required substantial net imports from the national farm economy. Many members have frequent occasion to visit the main offices of the szakszövetkezet. The leader most frequently consulted is the 'household-plot agronomist'. Not only is his advice commonly sought on technical questions, but the major part of his job consists in liaising with small-farmers in arranging for the marketing of their produce. He is also responsible for organising summer grazing, travels most frequently amongst the tanyas, reports on farmers' topical grievances, ensures that they are informed of subsidies available to them, and may deliver public lecture programmes in winter. With the marketing of dairy and wine produce the practical difficulties are small, although members continually find fault with the tests for fat content, on the basis of which payment is made to milk producers. The agronomist has more serious problems in harmonising the supply and demand of fattened pigs, which is not well regulated by the system of advance contracting. Farmers are advised to give considerable notice of intended sale. Then, if one or two animals in a litter fall outside the prescribed weight limits, the farmer may have to waste time later,

9. Buying supplies at the szakszövetkezet stores. The 1950s slogans are still visible on the wall

accept lower prices, or even (e.g. in the case of old animals which are rejected by the vet, or by the representative of the purchasing enterprise) be obliged to resort to 'forced slaughter' at a very low price. Cash payments to the producer are normally made on the day of the sale in the case of pigs and wine, and mid-way through the following month for the month's production in the case of milk.

Apart from reporting to the household-plot agronomist and the cashier, members may have diverse business at the offices. The chairman and the financial manager are rarely approached. There is also a full-time clerk of landholdings, who handles occasional boundary disputes and inheritance settlements, arranges for the ceding of holdings to the szakszövetkezet, and has the impossible job of maintaining up-to-date records of land ownership and land use, in association with the tax inspectors at the council offices. The Reformed Church pastor was in charge of social security and pensions inquiries in 1977, and was regularly consulted by members about continual minor modifications of the benefit system. Other personnel, including agronomists, accountants and secretaries, may be sought out on specific issues. The extremely fluid staff situation in 1976–7 makes it impossible to generalise about individual spheres of responsibility in the leadership of the szakszövetkezet. In 1978, after one year under a new chairman, it was felt by some members and junior staff that power had remained too highly personalised and that there was no significant delegation of responsibility by the chairman to his new financial manager, his new chief agronomist, or to any other leaders. With one or two exceptions, notably that of the household plot agronomist, there was no close contact between these white-collar leaders, several of whom lived outside the community, and the mass of the members. As a general source of information for small-farmers on all matters relating to farming, the szakszövetkezet offices are perhaps less important and less efficient than the council offices.

There is, then, some interdependence of socialised and small-farm sectors in Tázlár. Integration of some form affects virtually all enterprises. The balance of feed imports into the community is a good illustration of the general productive role of the small-farm sector. Yet the szakszövetkezet is not merely one type among others in the small-farm sector. The owners of household plots have access to similar supplies to aid their animal-breeding. Integration has not been a uniform process there either, as some household-plot owners make much heavier demands upon the production cooperative and market more commodities than others. We cannot assume that all the szakszövetkezet farmers are fully integrated in the same way; this would imply that, if feed imports from the socialised sector outside were guaranteed and prices manipulated to give some kind of 'reasonable return' similar to that earned today, then the excessive landholdings of the szakszövetkezet farmers (everything above the household plot norm of 0.58 hectare) could be creamed off without damaging the will to produce. The basic problem is that in Tázlár willingness to produce may still depend

Table 8 Mean landholdings of various small-farm units 1975–7

	Total no. of units	No. of units owning arable land	Mean area of arable (square metres)	No. of units owning pasture	Mean area of pasture (square metres)
All units owning land	546	521	16,103	314	11,575
All units marketing produce, 1975–7	400	340	18,411	221	13,063
Units marketing produce valued over 15,000 fts 1975–7	199	175	21,274	122	14,449
Units marketing produce valued over 30,000 fts 1975–7	95	85	23,394	66	14,319
Units marketing produce values over 50,000 fts 1975–7	40	37	23,431	29	15,314
Pig-fattening units, 1977	372	305	18,302	192	12,500
Milk-producing units, 1977	230	201	21,514	154	13,858

upon substantial on-farm crop production and hence on the retention of a private farm substantially larger than the area of the household plot.

Table 8 shows that there is a significant rise in arable landholdings as the level of production of the enterprise increases, and that even in the lowest category, that of landowners who were not regular producers between 1975 and 1977, the area is substantially in excess of the household plot norm. The table also suggests that the appropriation of private pasture could be highly detrimental to milk production. The table is complemented by the highly seasonal pattern of sales at the feed-shop, which consistently peaks in early summer and declines dramatically from early autumn as many households resort once again to their own crop output. It is therefore a mistake to exaggerate the extent and the uniformity of szakszövetkezet economic integration. 'Full integration' in the sense hypothesised above may never become generalised.

Within the total number of small-farm enterprises a basic distinction was drawn above between 'full-time farms', where no member of the household has any source of regular income from outside small-farming, and 'mixed' or 'worker-peasant' households where there is at least one such regular outside earner. In Table 9 it can be seen that of a total of 498 units which marketed some produce through the szakszövetkezet in 1977, 275 could be classified as full-time farms. The table brings out some of the differences which previous analysis would lead us to expect. Many more full-time farms are located outside the main village, there is a large difference in the mean age of the head of the unit, and there are notable differences also in each major branch of production. Only in wine production does the output of full-time farms tend to exceed that of worker-peasant farms, yet the larger average value of total production of the former is proof of their greater diversification. This is in line with what we should expect from the earlier analysis of production branches. The incidence of outside earners is lowest in the branch which is least integrated by the szakszövetkezet and where the labour demands of the small-farm enterprise are highest. In specialist wine-producing units in 1977 the mean

Table 9 Full-time and worker-peasant farms 1977

	No. of units	No. in main village	Mean age of head of unit	Total produce	Pig products	Milk products	Wine products
					Mean value (fts)		
Full-time farms	275	101	59.8	49,148	26,590	21,641	24,485
Worker-peasant farms	223	133	47.8	47,150	31,087	24,595	27,396
All farms	498	234	54.4	48,254	28,718	22,732	23,263

incidence of outside employment was 0.56, in pig-fattening it was 0.94, and in milk production it was in between at 0.75. Pig-fattening is the branch most easily carried on by the worker-peasant household: indeed, a further distinction may be made and pig-fattening recognised as compatible with a homogeneous worker-peasant household in which *all* adults are active earners outside small farming.

But perhaps the more surprising feature of Table 9 is the final similarity of mean aggregate production in the two broad groups of worker-peasant and full-time farm households. It is difficult to find a reason in the earlier analysis of the different branches of production why average milk production in those worker-peasant farms which market milk should exceed the full-time farm average. Many milk producers are tanya-residents who are not easily able to commute daily, and they generally need at least one individual full-time on the farm, if only because of the need to guard a valuable animal. The landholdings of the full-time farms exceed those of worker-peasant farms, but not by a large amount (18,924 square metres compared to 16,616 square metres in arable land, 13,032 square metres compared to 11,086 square metres in pasture). The proportion of full-time farmers who transact with the szakszövetkezet is slightly lower than the proportion for worker-peasants, but again there is no significant difference in the mean level of transactions. There is still clearly an 'autonomous' element within the worker-peasant group as well as amongst the full-time farmers.

Further problems arise when we try to see which group has very large enterprises and whether the full spectrum of enterprises can be found in both. The mean incidence of outside employment is 0.63 in the 400 enterprises which marketed commodities in each year between 1975 and 1977. It falls slightly as the production level is increased, but in the top group, the 40 units which marketed over 50,000 forints-worth of produce in each of the three years examined, the mean incidence rises again to 0.6. In those units which marketed produce in all three branches in all three years, the incidence of outside employment is very low (only 0.3), but the total mean value of production of this group of enterprises was not especially high (see Table 7). Large enterprises clearly exist amongst both full-time farms and worker-peasant households. It is noteworthy in Table 8 that while the mean area of landholdings rises with production at first, there is no rise in the top group, those producing 50,000 forints-worth of goods in each year. The mean value of this group's transactions with the szakszövetkezet is however almost 50 per cent higher than the 400-enterprise mean (Table 5).

It is possible that the differentiation which needs to be explained requires a more sophisticated classification of enterprises. A number of analysts of peasant economies have taken demographic variables as major factors which underlie farm production.[11] Yet it is by no means clear which variables should be considered in the case of Tázlár. Is the size of the household, or the number of active earners, or the number of earners active full-time on small-farms of greatest importance? It is conceivable that the number of active earners might give the best explanation of pig production, while the number of those in full-time small-farming might give the best explanation of milk production, and total size of household including pensioners and children the best explanation of wine and fruit production. Rather than develop these interesting possibilities here, and experiment as some writers have done with 'standard labour units', where the labour of outside earners is converted as a certain fraction of that of a full-time farmer, only a general account will be given of the continued importance of the family unit and the size of the household in production, as well as of the means through which most worker-peasant households may still reach potentially high levels of output.

There is first of all a consistent but weak relation between the aggregate production of regular commodity-producing units between 1975 and 1977 and the size of their households. Mean household size for all 400 units was 3.1 persons. This rose to 3.2 in the group producing over 15,000 forints in goods annually, 3.4 in those producing over 30,000 forints and 3.7 in those producing over 50,000 forints. Clearly, the size of the household is an insufficient explanation for the level of production achieved. It is significant that those units which produced all three commodities in all three years, which as has been noted have the lowest incidence of outside sources of income, also have the lowest mean household size.

Household size is included as a variable in Table 10, which explores the effect of the number of full-time earners in small-farming upon the production of the unit, its holdings in arable land, and its transactions with the szakszövetkezet, for each of the two basic groups. It is apparent that only 40 worker-peasant households lack a full-time adult non-pensioner, active in small-farming, and that a substantial proportion has more than one such individual. Production increases significantly in both groups as the number of earners in small-farming rises from one to two. It is noteworthy that mean total production in the 65 worker-peasant households with two or more full-time farmers is very similar to the mean for two-farmer full-time farms, though there is a large difference in the mean size of household in all categories. Only a small proportion of households have a third full-time farmer. His presence creates no substantial rise in the mean production of worker-peasant households, and actually results in a large fall in the mean production of full-time farms. This fall occurs in spite of the fact that full-time farms with three earners have substantially higher transactions with the szakszövetkezet than other full-time farms. It is interesting to observe the level of transactions rising with the number of farm workers in the case of full-time farms, but declining in the case of worker-peasant farms. Arable landholdings increase predictably in both groups. The table does not give the details of specific production branches, but the greater diversification of full-time farms is apparent in all categories: worker-peasant enterprises attain consistently higher production in pig-fattening and in milk, while only in fruit and wine do the full-time farms show larger mean output.

These results imply that simple 'demographic differentiation' cannot

Table 10 *The effect of household full-time labour supply 1977*

	No. of units	No. in main village	Mean age of head	Mean value of total production (fts)	Mean size of household	Mean size of arable landholdings (square metres)	Mean value of transactions (fts)
1 *Worker-peasant enterprises*							
All units	223	133	47.8	47,150	3.85	16,616	2,600
Units with 1 or more full-time adults in farming	183	100	48.9	50,623	3.98	16,265	2,505
Units with 2 or more full-time adults in farming	65	27	53.1	61,325	4.59	20,428	2,489
Units with 3 or more full-time adults in farming	15	5	53.7	62,791	5.73	22,738	2,070
2 *Full-time farm enterprises*							
All units	275	101	59.8	49,148	2.48	18,924	2,292
All units minus those headed by pensioners	221	71	57.8	54,633	2.62	20,020	2,414
Units with 2 or more full-time adults in farming	154	46	54.0	62,768	2.96	21,538	2,506
Units with 3 or more full-time adults in farming	24	3	54.8	52,769	3.96	24,833	3,161

account for the range of differentiation in production, nor for the differences between the two major types of enterprise. Other explanations must be sought for the decline in full-time farm production when a third earner is introduced, and for the decline in worker-peasant enterprises' transactions with the szakszövetkezet as the number of full-time farmers in their households is increased. The effect of the number of individual worker-peasants also introduces puzzles into the analysis. Sixty-six enterprises had two individuals in full-time employment outside small-farming, and the average production of these enterprises was only 36,719 forints – more than 10,000 forints down on the average for all worker-peasant enterprises. Yet 15 enterprises had three outside earners, and their mean production in 1977 was over 40,000 forints.

Without attempting more complex explanations from the manipulation of statistics it will be more profitable to look next at some basic differences between the two major types, which greatly influence the organisation of the enterprise, but are not necessarily decisive in the determination of its level of output. We must bear in mind from Table 10 that whereas a majority of worker-peasant enterprises has only one individual adult active in small-farming full-time, the majority of full-time enterprises has two or more such individuals. This naturally has an important effect on the organisation of the farm. The larger size of worker-peasant households is an obvious advantage to them at peak periods. However, they have few other advantages compared to full-time enterprises, which have been able to adapt to the constraints of a smaller household size by making some traditional features of peasant economy become significant in szakszövetkezet conditions.

Labour-hiring is a traditional practice in Tázlár which has been significantly rehabilitated in the szakszövetkezet period. The hiring of labour, usually on a daily basis, for the payment of a previously agreed sum known as the *napszám*, is one way in which farmers can solve the problems caused at peak periods by labour scarcity. Chapter 2 commented on the importance of the labour market in the pre-war farming economy, but there is no suggestion that current activity is on the same scale. The widespread system of permanent farm-servants (*cseléds*) disappeared at the end of the 1940s, and the possibilities for even occasional labour-hiring were greatly reduced in the 1950s. Today only a very few households make permanent use of outside labour through what amounts almost to a *cseléd* relationship – and the latter-day *cseléd* may drive a car of his own and is not likely to reside at his place of work. Larger producers more commonly seek to devise a means of guaranteeing a supply of non-family labour for peak periods. Some of the dependency relations which have resulted have retained the old paternalist tinge, e.g. when a large wine-producer makes alcohol available cheaply throughout the year in return for work in the vineyard when required. Conditions and bargaining power having changed so fundamentally on both sides, only the financial incentive is effective in most cases today. There is no longer the pretence, as there was in the 1930s, that labour-hiring was a form of charity to the underprivileged.

For farmers who cannot meet their labour needs in any other way it is now a calculated necessity. Many tanya farmers, especially those in the first and second zones with large vineyards, estimate that they need over 100 days of hired labour on their farms every year. Their major complaint is not the rise in the *napszám* (which stood at around 250 forints in 1978 and was considerably higher in the richer communities to the west), but the quality of the workforce and the basic availability of any men or women to undertake casual labour at peak periods.[12]

The supply of *napszám* labour has almost completely dried up in the main village. In outlying tanya areas, which is where more of the full-time farms are located, the situation is more favourable to larger producers. Old men approaching retirement are reluctant to commute and prefer a quiet life at home with subsistence farming eked out by work for prosperous neighbours. A few of those who now spend a part of each year as casual labourers are men who once belonged to the earlier cooperatives but find it is now to their advantage to work privately rather than in the socialised sector of the szakszövetkezet. For some women in tanya areas, work as day-labourers is the only means of gaining access to cash resources. In addition to those for whom the *napszám* is the basic source of income there are also those with full-time wage-labour jobs or with their own small farms who can be tempted by the large cash sums to work at weekends. There are also seasonal immigrants to Tázlár from less privileged communities in the region, though perhaps not so many as commute regularly from Tázlár at peak periods to obtain the higher wage-rates in neighbouring communities to the west.

The work of the day-labourer is prescribed by unwritten rules which hark back to days when the hirer had more power than he has today. The labourer would arrive at dawn, spend the entire day in the fields, and if he was given food at all it would not necessarily be the same as that consumed by the hirer's family. Today the hours worked are still long (although in their anxiety to obtain labour some hirers make it possible to work for less than the minimal ten hours at proportionally reduced rates), but the labourer cannot now be sent away if he arrives late: at the most he may forfeit his first glass of *pálinka*. Throughout the day it is now the duty of the farmer to ply his labourers with good food and drink, for stinginess will make it impossible for him to recruit on any future occasion.

Labour-hiring functions not so much as an alternative to greater reliance upon the szakszövetkezet as a necessary addition to such services where family labour resources are most deficient, notably in those branches where production remains unalterably labour-intensive. The government now supplements high-price incentives to the small-farm sector by turning a blind eye to the widespread buying and selling of labour power. Effectively it has rejected the former socialist insistence upon the non-exploitative character of the family farm. The scope given the small-farm sector in Tázlár has made the mitigation of labour scarcity more imperative than elsewhere. The same underlying problem has been accentuated even here by continued outmigration, but there have also been other approaches to a solution.

The second archetypal feature which has been adapted to meet szakszövetkezet conditions is a more novel phenomenon in Tázlár. In the pre-war period, cooperation between tanya farmers on the basis of mutual aid was inhibited by the conditions of settlement and the diversity of the settlers, and was rendered less urgent by the large labour resources available within the kin group. Informants stressed the *unequal* character of a great deal of the exchange that did take place, most commonly the exchange of labour by dwarf-holders for labour plus tools or the services of draught animals, and for such exchanges there were commonly agreed conversion ratios. While older farmers are more likely to hire labour, in the socialist period labour shortage has induced some members of the younger generation of farmers to begin cooperating with each other and even to purchase jointly essential tools and horses and carts. In some cases the informal work-group is still formed within kin-groups. In many other cases simple dyadic partnerships have replaced kin-based groups, often when the latter have declined through emigration, but sometimes when close kin are still resident in the community and active in farming, Such partnerships are informal understandings between friends about the order in which respective maize plots will be tackled and no fixed rules prescribe how many members of one family will turn out to assist on the other family's plots. The attractions of cooperation are considerable for the young and able-bodied, especially for tanya farmers who wish to save up for village housing. Labour scarcity is mitigated at production peaks without the expenditure of large sums either to the szakszövetkezet (for substitute supplies) or to hired labourers.

Compared with labour-hiring, informal mutual aid is poorly developed, and cash payments of one sort or another find their way into many 'informal' transactions. Some farmers have tried to combat labour scarcity by increased investment in labour-saving machinery, but while some may exploit such machines on their neighbours' farms for gain, the climate of competition and emulation restricts such 'unequal exchange'. In one revealing case in the first zone, a young farmer was unable to benefit from machinery purchased by his neighbour, because the latter was unwilling to accept payment in cash. In return for the use of his machinery he was anxious to obtain some labour services from the younger man, but the latter preferred to continue with time-consuming techniques on his own plots, rather than perform any services for a neighbour who was not willing to offer labour in return.

The reluctance or inability to repay labour services in the same currency, the equally great reluctance to pay out large sums to hired labourers, and the difficulty in supervising the work of any outside labourers, are three reasons why worker-peasant households are unable to make full use of the outlined strategies for combating labour shortage. In spite of their larger households and their smaller landholdings it must not be thought that they do not experience shortage. They may be more successful than full-time farms in mobilising labour resources from outside the nuclear family. They may time their own holidays to coincide with the major tasks on the land, and they too will strive to exploit the labour of elderly relations and of children. But worker-peasant households, though they may cooperate from necessity in other fields such as private house-building where the need for large labour groups is unavoidable, are less likely to cooperate with other households in major agricultural tasks and are less likely to produce at levels which strain the labour resources of the simple family household. Where they do produce at high levels they are likely to have large resources of labour in the family and to be highly dependent on the szakszövetkezet. In fact there are few very large producers amongst the worker-peasants. Their mean value of production is close to that of the full-time farm enterprises only because of the greater variance within the latter and the high proportion of aged and 'marginal' households (cf. the greater polarity of the tanya population noted in Chapter 2: this is where most of the full-time farms are to be found).

All production in the small-farm sector is ultimately labour-intensive. Demographic variables impose limits upon the enterprise, which can be countered in a number of ways: by specialisation in the least labour-intensive branch of production, by private capitalisation, by hiring labour or cooperating with other households, or by greater dependence upon the szakszövetkezet. Possibly more significant than a distinction between full-time farms and worker-peasant farms, another distinction based on the subjective preferences of households might be drawn between, on the one hand, those farms which seek to attain optimal combinations of the above strategies in a desire to maximise their production and, on the other hand, those which accept the constraints imposed by the supply of labour and limit their aspirations to maintaining something like the traditional level of farm output, with the help of szakszövetkezet machinery. The latter are averse to cooperation, private mechanisation and the expenditure of cash in any phase of the production process, either to the szakszövetkezet or to hired labourers. They do not aim at any maximisation of output or profit – indeed their farms are integrated unities of production and consumption to which any application of a concept of profit is inappropriate (cf. Chayanov, 1966, p. 4).

The word 'maximise' has been introduced loosely without a specification of what it is that some households may seek to maximise, but it may be assumed there is a general consistency between the maximisation of output and the maximisation of net income. Maximisers are not necessarily more integrated technically into the szakszövetkezet. Non-maximisers tend to transact at very low levels, if at all, and amongst the full-time farms today there are some who are farmers 'by default'. They may be described as 'satisficers' and in their reluctance to develop the production functions of their farms and to separate them out from the consumer functions, they remain closer to classical models of the family farm.[13]

Satisficers can be identified amongst both full-time and worker-peasant enterprises, but in the latter farm activity is better conceived as part of an overall income-maximising strategy or as a secondary, hobby-type activity with certain leisure attributes. The full-time satisficing individual is a more traditional, conservative 'peasant type' who has no concept of leisure. He has not realised the potential either to free himself from full-time farming or to improve the efficiency of his labour allocation on the farm in conjunction with the szakszövetkezet. The satisficer has been integrated only to the extent that he accepts compensation from the szakszövetkezet for the reduction in the family labour supply and the possible migration of his own children. His attitude to his own labour is one of self-exploitation, i.e. an absolute commitment to the farm as both productive enterprise and household consumer unit. He executes most tasks personally in conjunction with his immediate family. He has not responded to all the efforts that have been made by the government to stimulate small-farming. Unexpected, urgent requirements for cash are more likely to be met through casual work in the service of a maximising neighbour than by an expansion of his own production to unfamiliar levels.

These ideal types must naturally be treated cautiously. The transformation from satisficer to maximiser may be made with surprising rapidity, since the basis of the distinction is in subjective attitudes and not in wealth or capital requirements. However doubtful the future of the satisficing type at the moment, he still outnumbers the maximiser amongst the full-time farmers. In spite of the 'subjective' definition offered, it is possible to approach satisficing and maximising elements within the full-time farm enterprises by careful demographic selection. Table 11 illustrates the production of two possible sub-groups. Similarly, within the worker-peasant farms there are wide differences between the farming activity of those still engaged in saving up for or actually building houses and those beyond this stage in the developmental cycle. The greater integration of the maximisers has been manifested in their response to government price incentives, may result in greater technical integration into the szakszövetkezet, but also has entailed features to which the government is strongly opposed, such as labour-hiring, and has led to wide disparities in income within the farming population. The numbers of full-time maximisers are reduced by the uncertainty attached to full-time farming as an occupation, and the strong disaffection of the young. Most recently the farming activities of worker-peasant households have also been threatened by talk of the appropriation of private land resources, including vineyards, from households where no individual is employed full-time in agriculture. The previous pattern of integration here too is likely to be modified in the 1980s.

This section has examined major differences between full-time and worker-peasant farms. Although all have been effected to some degree by

Table 11 *Full-time farms 1977 – possible sub-groups of 'maximisers' and 'satisficers'*

	No. of units	No. in main village	Mean age of head of unit	Mean size of household	Mean value of total produce (fts)	No. of units transacting with szakszövetkezet	Mean value of transactions (fts)
Maximisers[1]	33	7	43.1	4.0	89,469	33	3,826
Satisficers[2]	104	41	69.9	1.9	29,721	46	580

1 Maximisers: defined as those units active in 1977, with no source of income from outside small-farming, where the age of the head of the unit is less than 55, where there are one or more children either living at home or in further education, and where the level of transactions with the szakszövetkezet was greater than 2,000 forints.
2 Satisficers: defined as those units active in 1977, with no source of income from outside small-farming, where the age of the head of the unit is greater than 55, where there are no children at home or in further education, and where the level of transactions with the szakszövetkezet was less than 1,000 forints.

the framework imposed by the szakszövetkezet, some farms have shown a much more positive response to the incentives of the government to 'integrate'. The patterns of integration are diverse. Many full-time farmers maintain high levels of output through reliance of labour-hiring or co-operation rather than through outlays to the szakszövetkezet. But if not all maximisers are well-integrated in the way the government would prefer, many satisficers are hardly integrated at all, despite the routine services which they may obtain annually from the szakszövetkezet. The worker-peasants as a group are more integrated by definition into the national economy, but there is little uniformity in this category either, and the mean overall level of their transactions with the szakszövetkezet is still low. From these bare bones of a typology of enterprises let us move from integration to the obverse of the coin and examine the continued 'marginality' of all szakszövetkezet farmers.

V The marginality of szakszövetkezet farmers

Marginality is a term to be handled with care. The small-farm sector has been treated officially as 'marginal' in the agricultural development of Hungary, but we know in fact that it performs essential functions which the socialised sector is unable to perform. Within the small-farm sector the szakszövetkezets might be dismissed as of marginal importance, in view of their small number, yet they make a contribution to production out of all proportion to their number. Tázlár itself might be regarded as an atypical, late-settlement community on the margins of Hungarian society. And the entire economic development of post-feudalist Hungary may with some justification be viewed as 'marginal' to the expansion of capitalism in Western Europe over a long historical period (cf. Berend & Ránki, 1974b, Part 1).

Marginality has also been actively utilised or implied as a concept in numerous theories of peasant economy and explanations of peasant behaviour. The marginality of the peasantry as a class caused Lenin, even while analysing the process of their incorporation into national capitalist markets, to hold out little hope of their participating in revolutionary transformation of the capitalist system. The same marginality was the basis for the creation by Chayanov and the neo-populist school in Russia of a theory of a fully autonomous domain of peasant family economy (Chayanov, 1966, Part 1). There are, however, signs, especially in his later writings, that Chayanov was well aware of the role and the position of the peasantry in the national society. He fought to spare the peasantry from political attack and condemnation to the margins of socialist society under Stalin.[14]

Marginality can be seen as associated with exploitative, possibly coercive, relations with extraneous forces. It can also be seen as the key to the internal functioning of peasant economy, or rather to the organisation of each of its units, the family-labour farms. It has been common since Chayanov to describe the attitude of the head of the farm to his own and to his family's labour as one of self-exploitation (Galeski, 1972; Franklin, 1969; etc.). Because of the unity of the farm as a producing and consuming entity, there is no calculation of return on labour, but instead a total commitment which makes the application of bourgeois 'maximising' assumptions as irrelevant from the perspective of the family as the application of Marxian concepts of 'under-production'. The Polish rural economist Jerzy Tepicht has developed Chayanov's thought in this connection (Tepicht, 1973, pp. 15–46).

Tepicht's basic position is to contrast the peasant labour process with that which is typical of industrial conditions, and to emphasise in this way the special relation between peasant labour and its remuneration. Unlike industrial labour, the traditional peasant labour process cannot be conceived as an undifferentiated continuum. It consists rather of two qualitatively different parts, each of which may be schematically connected with a different part of the production process. One of these parts is crudely to be associated with crop production, which is highly conducive to industrial working methods, i.e. to mechanisation and also to collectivisation. The other part may be thought of as the 'irreducible peasant component', and it corresponds in a general way with livestock production. Because of its heavy and irregular labour demands it cannot easily be industrialised. These labour demands can be conceived as bearing upon the 'marginal' labour time of the family, i.e. as falling over and above the activities of 'normal working time', which on an integrated farm is the time allocated to crop production. In the pristine condition of the farm ('natural economy') there is no means of distinguishing between the two components of the labour process and their schematically complementary labour-time requirements. Hence it is unrealistic to speak of aggregate under-employment in the countryside since this is an economic concept which can be applied only to one part of peasant time allocation, 'normal working time'. But in modern, industrialising economies Tepicht is opposed to subjective 'leisure-preference' explanations of peasant behaviour, and he too stresses the isolation of the peasantry as a class as the precondition for the outside exploitation of the marginal and normal labour time of largely non-transferable labour resources.

On the basis of his division of farm output and of labour inputs into these two ideal-type components, Tepicht proposes a general redefinition of a 'peasant mode of production' in the socialist states of Eastern Europe. The sectoral complementarity which was formerly achieved at the level of the family farm is now organised community-wide through the production cooperative (*kolkhoz*) and nationwide through the interdependence of socialised and small-farm sectors. The production cooperative is conceived as reproducing the integration of the family farm. The 'normal labour time' of the old labour process has been replaced by a highly mechanised socialised sector, which is liable in addition to claim most of the farm's former landholdings. But the small-farmers will be left the facilities to enable them to continue small commodity production, and particularly to specialise in livestock. It is thus a mistake (though one frequently committed by the people of Tázlár), to contrast the performance of the small-farmers with that of the socialised sector, since to do this is to miss what the ideology has been proclaiming all along: their structural complementarity. Tepicht sums up this system as '. . . peasant economy multiplied by 'n', where 'n' signifies the number of individual farms incorporated in a production cooperative. Agglomerated, without being essentially transformed' (Tepicht 1973, p. 69).

How appropriate is this model to the conditions of the loose servicing and marketing cooperative in Hungary, the szakszövetkezet? We have already looked in some detail at integration and we might first of all wish to emphasise the nationwide level at which integration now takes place. In the szakszövetkezet, in contrast to more typical production cooperatives, the relative weakness of the socialised sector requires imports from the national farm economy to satisfy the input demands of small-farmers. But more rigorous specification of the model is necessary if Tepicht's basic distinction between complementary components of production can be related to the types of enterprise we have seen active in Tázlár in the later 1970s.

The reformulation of 'peasant economy' at the level of the production cooperative implies that individual farms are no longer integrated units of production. They produce primarily in one sphere, that of animal-breeding, corresponding to the 'marginal labour time' of the old production process. Yet by now the break-up of the old production process at farm level has been accompanied by a general breaking down of rural isolation and an expansion of opportunities in the outside labour market. The notional distinction between the two types of labour time has become effective as the sphere to which 'normal labour time' was applied has been generally removed from peasant control and taken outside the sphere of 'peasant economy'. 'Normal' labour power has become effectively transferable and in the case of the worker-peasants has been displaced from small-farming. The marginal labour time of the worker-peasant is, however, still devoted to small-commodity production in agriculture. This marginality is no longer the same as the former isolated marginality of the peasantry as a class of captive producers. But, as a result of the government's inability to dispense with the products of the small-farm sector, the worker is still encouraged to allocate a *part* of his labour power to a *part* of agricultural production. Since this latter part is the traditional labour-intensive component of family farm output and since the labour power applied is the irreducible marginal labour of the producer (which in a fully industrialised context would be his 'free-time'), Tepicht still considers it useful to speak of a peasant mode of production in the present stage of development in Eastern Europe.

At this point there are immediate complications in the case of the szakszövetkezet. The worker-peasant may be of overriding importance in the national context, but he does not yet dominate here. The 'vertical integration' of many worker-peasant enterprises is far from complete and in most households there remain one or more individuals who allocate all of their labour power (i.e. 'normal' as well as 'marginal') to small-farm production.

In addition there are those whom we have classified as 'maximisers' and 'satisficers' who may dispense with vertical integration through cooperating horizontally amongst themselves, hiring labour, or even through continued reliance upon the family alone to meet traditional labour requirements in a traditional manner.

Let us take the 'maximisers' first, and include with them the majority of worker-peasant households, in which some individuals still devote their total labour resources to farmwork. Again, we need no precise definition of the maximiser.[15] It is superfluous here to detect 'capitalist' tendencies and ambitions amongst all the maximising farmers of Tázlár. The term can be applied loosely to all those who market larger quantities of produce than would be possible for them without some integration into the szakszövetkezet or which was achieved by the traditional family farm. It should not include those for whom the szakszövetkezet merely substitutes the former land and labour inputs. 'Maximisers' may thus have quite low levels of production, if the supply of family labour is very small, and they need not strictly be maximising the product of either their 'normal' or their 'marginal' labour time. For many maximisers, total labour power is still applied to a wide range of productive tasks, i.e. not only to the marginal component, which we have seen to be the tendency for the worker-peasants. This sub-group of maximisers is peculiar to the szakszövetkezet. The genuine 'integrated maximisers' are those who apply their total labour power to only that part of production in which the socialised sector is less productive. On a larger scale they resemble the pattern of the worker-peasants and that of other small-farmers, such as the members of production cooperatives who do not have the opportunity to work full-time in small-commodity production. As with the more traditional maximisers (and we have seen that there is a whole spectrum which ranges from almost complete dependence on the szakszövetkezet to farm autonomy through maximum reliance on traditional methods of production), no matter how well integrated the *paysan évolué* it is impossible to distinguish between the 'normal' and the 'marginal' components of his labour time on the full-time farm. 'Self-exploitation' remains a characteristic of the family farm enterprise in advanced capitalist agricultures, although only a few Tázlár farmers, those most heavily dependent upon hired labour, could be said to be developing in a capitalist direction. Full-time farming is on the wane even in the nationally non-collectivised agricultures of Poland and Yugoslavia,[16] and in Hungary the szakszövetkezet is the only sector in which this type may have a future.

The trend of the 1970s has been towards an increased reliance upon the szakszövetkezet, and within the maximisers there has been a greater tendency to increase production in branches where the benefits of vertical integration are high and increasingly to forgo the back-up activities of inefficient small-scale crop production. The 'satisficers', however, remain a group apart. They are the conservatives who have adhered to the production levels determined by the traditional productive forces. In 1977 there were 111 units amongst full-time farms whose value of production marketed was under 30,000 forints, compared with an average for the group of almost 50,000 forints. Only 59 of these units transacted with the szakszövetkezet, and they averaged only 1,407 forints in value, compared with the group average of 2,292 forints. The average age of the heads of these units was 64.6 years, compared with 59.8 for the group and 54 for all households. The satisficers have not been integrated in the national context. In their case marginality is comparable to that of the old peasantry, isolated as a class. This group too is peculiar to the szakszövetkezet community. No doubt they would not have welcomed the establishment of a production cooperative in Tázlár, any more than the maximisers would have welcomed this. Nevertheless, against the achievements of the szakszövetkezet in stimulating high levels of production amongst older, former well-to-do farmers and amongst younger worker-peasants must be weighed the stagnation and in many cases the deprivation which has afflicted the satisficers.

Again we return to the special characteristics of the szakszövetkezet. The Hungarian government has in general attempted to make the fullest use of marginal labour power in small-farming, as part of its overall economic policy and as the necessary consequence of the timing of collectivisation and the establishment of an 'industrialised agriculture' post-collectivisation. Only in the szakszövetkezet, however, has an integrated labour process and the unity of the family farm as both enterprise and unit of domestic consumption been preserved. On the positive side, from the point of view of the government, this exceptional type has induced a number of maximisers to make conscious decisions to remain full-time farmers and to maintain high levels of commodity production in small-farming, albeit not always with the recommended degree of integration into the szakszövetkezet. On the negative side, besides the undesirable traces of 'capitalism' primarily in the extent of labour-hiring, a large group has forgone all the opportunities and, though many have sought out wage-labour occupations in diverse spheres and the number of worker-peasant households is continually rising, these might have drawn greater benefits from the formation of a production cooperative in place of szakszövetkezets. Although the details will depend upon the government's resolution in the final carrying through of collectivisation and success in persuading maximisers to accept more complete vertical integration, the number of full-time farms may still be expected to decline and Tázlár will then increasingly approximate to the pattern of production cooperatives typical in the country as a whole. In the meantime only the szakszövetkezet farmers have not been fully converted to a nationally uniform, industrial-type labour process, and we can reflect on the contrasting types of marginality which they represent.

The alcohol market – a special case?

Given the exceptionally long hours worked by the worker-peasants and by most of the maximisers, and given the abject conditions of many of the satisficers, who have simply been passed-by by modernisation, it is arguable that in the end every group in the szakszövetkezet community has been in some way 'exploited' by government policies over the last two decades. This question will be raised again in Chapter 7.

VI The alcohol market – a special case?

The ideology of complementarity of socialised and small-farming sectors is most applicable to field-crop production and animal-breeding. A somewhat different marginality is at issue in the case of fruit and wine production, where it is generally admitted that the technical bases for the integration of the small-farm sector are but feebly developed. Here the production of the small-farm sector is no less crucial than in other branches, and indeed this was the major economic reason advanced for the stabilisation of a dense tanya network in the region of the Danube-Tisza interfluve (Lettrich, 1969, p. 160). No significant grass-roots modification of the production process has taken place (although the quality of the product marketed has fallen, for reasons we shall come to below), but government policies at national level have influenced producers indirectly through the price system. The government thus has considerable power to manipulate production levels in this branch, but the nature of the small-farm production process is such here that undiscriminating policies to maximise output have had highly deleterious social consequences.

Alcohol consumption is traditionally high in Hungary and certain controls over this market were developed by pre-capitalist forms of the State. In recent years, following the reform of the economic mechanism in 1968, there has been a substantial rise in domestic consumption and also in wine exports. In order to satisfy rising demand the government, in addition to promoting large-scale vineyards in the socialised sector, has also been concerned to halt the decline in the vine area of the small-farms. In addition to the stabilisation of a tanya network, the prevalence of the szakszövetkezet in the Danube-Tisza interfluve is also due in part to the importance attached to this policy, an importance outweighing that of uniform collectivisation.

The government's recent dilemma results not only from the contradiction with collectivisation policy. For many obvious social reasons the government has wished to restrain alcohol consumption. It has been particularly concerned to restrain the illicit production and distribution of *pálinka*. Despite a multitide of campaigns in the media and despite the rise of beer as a staple alcoholic intoxicant in recent decades in both towns and countryside, the government's campaign for restraint has met with little success. This can be attributed in part to the conflict between its general welfare goals and its underlying economic purpose of maximising the wine output of small-farmers. In the spirit sector of the market the government is at least able to attempt to enforce its monopoly of production by the penal taxation of small producers. Very few individuals in Tázlár have sought the right to produce legally in recent years. But, as the sociographer Tibor Zám has forcefully argued (1974), the government has undermined its own monopoly in the spirit sector through the subsidy of a commodity which is generally used in the wine sector to increase output and alcoholic strength. The commodity which links illicit spirit production to small-farm wine production is sugar. It is the major input which must be purchased for *pálinka* production, while if the regulations which technically prohibit its use in wine production were to be strictly enforced, then yields in the small-farm sector would fall so low that vineyards would be abandoned by maximising and satisficing enterprises alike. Zám is able to present elaborate estimates of the ratio in which sugar is now divided in the szakszövetkezet communities of Bács-Kiskun county between the technically illegal but tacitly encouraged adulteration of wine and the high-risk but high-profit spirit sector.

Wine was a new commodity in Tázlár at the time of mass resettlement in the last quarter of the nineteenth century, although there is evidence for the more ancient cultivation of vines in neighbouring Soltvadkert (Nagy-Pál and Apró 1972, pp. 9–12) and we have noted in the introduction that the Wattay family used to sell wine and spirit, some of it produced in the region, at the Tázlár *csárda* in the eighteenth century. But wines have never

10. Drinking inside the *bisztró*

become as important in Tázlár as in Soltvadkert. According to an official estimate for 1965, total production in grapes and in wine amounted to 28.4 per cent of the total value of the agricultural production of the community, rising to 35.3 per cent with the inclusion of fruit (in the so-called *két-szintes* ('two-level') system fruit trees are planted within the rows of vines; the system is no longer used but remains dominant in the small-farm vineyards). The corresponding figures for Soltvadkert are 51.7 per cent and 59.8 per cent, and the rest of the district falls somewhere in between (all figures given in Szigetvári, 1968). As we have seen, since 1965 the area of vines in the small-farm sector has declined to reach only 736 *hold* (412 hectares) in 1977. Even this figure includes many vineyards that are no longer fully productive. In 1968 Szigetvári noted a higher than average proportion of 'weak' and 'disappearing' vines in Tázlár, though their age structure was close to the average for the district (only 15.7 per cent under 13 years old; 54.3 per cent over 25 years old). Since the 1960s there has been a virtual ban on new planting in the private sector, such that at best farmers have been able to replace non-productive vines within existing vineyards. Tázlár had consistently below-average yields in the years of the 1960s which Szigetvári examined in detail, and this had not changed in the mid-1970s. Zám has estimated that a minimal yield for small-farm vineyards, one giving a small return on labour, would be in the region of 3,000 kilograms per *hold* or 5,215 kilograms per hectare (1974a, p. 33). Between 1963 and 1967 Tázlár's yields varied between 1,670 kilograms per hectare in 1965 and 4,050 kilograms per hectare in 1964, compared with district averages for those years of 3,025 kilograms per hectare and 6,100 kilograms per hectare (Szigetvári 1968). Tázlár's small vineyards produced 4,020 kilograms per hectare in 1975, compared with 6,880 kilograms per hectare in Soltvadkert and 9,550 kilograms per hectare in the most successful of the Kiskőrös szakszövetkezets. One of the reasons offered by the leaders of the szakszövetkezet in Tázlár for the relatively poor performance of their members is the age and the conservatism of many of the producers and their unwillingness to modernise their techniques (i.e. amongst other factors, to use sugar). Cellar storage capacity in Tázlár is mainly private, stood at only 5,300 hectolitres in 1967 and probably has not risen substantially since. Even the larger producers have not invested in cellar equipment and in the means of transportation on the same scale as the successful wine producers of Soltvadkert and Kiskőrös, and they may therefore be constrained to earlier sale and realisation of the produce in fruit or *must* form.

The current importance of the larger producers is apparent from Table 12. Amongst the 94 producers who sold over 60,000 forints-worth of wine through the szakszövetkezet in the period 1975 to 1977 there were 35 who topped the 100,000-forint level, and 21 who were over the 20,000-forint level in each of the three years separately. At the other extreme there is the large number of satisficing units, including many pensioner families, where this is now the only commodity marketed. In the past the average

Table 12 Small-farm wine-producers 1975–7

	Total units	Units in main village	Mean age of head of unit	Mean area of vines (square metres)	Mean annual value of produce in other branches (fts)
Units marketing wine up to a total value of 20,000 forints	213	81	55.5	4,920	14,999
Units marketing wine over total value of 20,000 fts and below 60,000 fts	154	74	55.0	5,536	21,980
Units marketing wine over a total value of 60,000 fts	94	48	54.0	9,228	33,105

vineyard area and wine production in Tázlár was probably higher than elsewhere in the district, and in 1967, which was a good year, the difference between mean production in Tázlár and the district mean was much smaller than the difference in yields. However, the available statistics, especially when based on the farmers' own tax returns, are notoriously unreliable in this branch of production. Large vineyards under the control of a single maximising farmer may be nominally held by scattered urban relatives. Because of this and because tax is still paid on some vineyards in very bad condition, there is only a weak relation between the size of vineyards and the quantity of wine produced from them. Some cynics in the community would attribute this result entirely to the new adulteration techniques, which enable some farmers to produce very large quantities from very small areas of vines. No wine was produced at all by 106 nominal owners of vineyards.

The table shows that the larger producers of wine tend to maintain above-average levels of production in other branches. Large specialist producers constitute only a very small group in Tázlár compared with neighbouring communities to the west. Nevertheless, similar social consequences can be observed. It is this branch of production which has greatest need of large work-groups and therefore makes greater use of labour-hiring practices when production is expanded. Policies to stimulate output in other, more integrated branches of small-farming do not necessarily have this effect.

It was pointed out in Chapter 3 that it is in this branch that the rise in State buying prices has been greatest in the 1970s and that there has been a considerable rise in the proportion of output which is officially marketed. At the same time it can be argued that policies designed to stimulate production, which have had some polarising impact upon traditional producers, have also weakened the government's control over distribution and marketing. Theoretically each producer is entitled to an annual personal allowance of 250 litres (the so-called *fejadag*). He must declare his total produce to the tax inspectors at the council offices a short time after the harvest, and he must pay a tax of 8 forints per litre on the quantity which he retains in excess of his personal allowance. It is one junior tax inspector's job to proceed from cellar to cellar in late autumn checking the validity of the declarations, and large numbers of minor frauds are invariably discovered. In fact, all producers have virtually unlimited scope for deception. Even if we do not question the integrity of the solitary responsible tax inspector, it is not especially difficult to conceal barrels, temporarily bury them or move them elsewhere. The potential rewards are large, for the wine retained can be sold privately for considerably more than the official purchasing price, but still undercutting the price per litre in the shops. Indeed, even after paying the tax some entrepreneurial producers calculate that higher profits can be made through private sale (which is not then illegal in small quantities) than through sale through the szakszövetkezet, because the official mark-up, in an attempt to limit consumption, is so high. The incentive to private marketing exists only in this branch of production: in the case of milk the subsidy is such that the price in the shop (admittedly for a milk low in fat content) is 1 forint less than the basic buying price. Some larger producers regularly sell large quantities of wine privately and have developed excellent trading connections outside the region. The most frequent customers are those who seek large supplies for a *lakódalom*. Others maintain retail outlets on urban housing estates, e.g. in Budapest. One of the more unlikely trading networks was that linking one of the pillars of the Reformed Church in Tázlár to Catholic presbyteries throughout the non-wine-producing areas of Transdanubia. Some producers are always willing to measure any small quantity informally for kinsmen or neighbours.

It is commonly the larger wine producers who are most active in the production and the distribution of *pálinka*. The technology required in production is exceedingly simple – many prosperous families produced for their own needs in the past and still have fruit readily available in their vineyards. Because of the characteristic smell it is more dangerous to distil in the main village, but on certain tanyas at certain times of the year the equipment may be in use virtually round the clock. In the event of discovery, following a raid by outside excise officials (there is no internal law-enforcement procedure), very heavy fines are imposed (e.g. 10,000 forints upon a Tázlár farmer discovered in 1976). However, despite the newspaper publicity and derogatory portrayal of the unlucky individual, there are grounds for supposing that some larger producers have the capacity to protect themselves at least against the possibility of being reported by the internal authorities. The distribution of *pálinka* from private houses in the main village and elsewhere is the most open secret. In some respects this is a specialisation like many others, which serves to bring in a little extra income. For example, in the upper hamlet, where in one row *pálinka* is available at almost every other house, the doors are found open at all reasonable hours and custom depends upon the quality of the product and often upon some personal tie with the producer. The personal *tekintély* (prestige) of the producer is likewise important in the establishment of trading connections outside the community, even with institutional customers such as the police or the army.

There are also private outlets in the village today for both wine and spirits. Here the sellers are only middlemen who obtain their supplies from direct producers who are often still resident on tanyas. Where turnover is higher there may be a willingness to sell, by the glass or by the bottle, even to strangers. Alcoholics thus have private shops to which they can turn for spirit even when the *bisztró* is closed, and where they can be more certain of obtaining service as long as their money lasts. The traditional family still (e.g. that of the old man who lives near the bus-stop and serves the frozen commuters at dawn in winter when the *bisztró* is not open) was never used in such an undiscriminating manner. One or two producers are prepared to justify the production of *pálinka* as one activity in which private enterprise is rewarded by large profits, as just compensation for the taxes that farmers must pay and the hard work that goes into other branches of production. Many others who once produced small quantities primarily for family consumption have recoiled from the numerous accidents which have occurred over the years during and as a result of production (commonly, when the producers are unable to refrain from immediate consumption), and question the morality of the present sales network and the high profits made by a few. There remain many who prefer the quality of the best home-made *pálinka* to the standardised tastes of the shop brands. But it should be clear that it is neither the flavour of the drink nor the sociability of the landlord that attracts customers to the current major sales outlets: it is a straightforward price differential. As with wine but more emphatically, *pálinka* prices can undercut the shop and still remain high enough to give a very large return to the producer.

By now it should be apparent in what sense the branch of fruit and wine production constitutes a special case. In the first place the small-farm's production process has not been significantly altered during the period of the szakszövetkezet. Integration of the production process has developed in richer communities such as Soltvadkert where the socialised sector has invested in its own processing plant and has been able to offer higher prices for the produce of its members. In Tázlár, effectively, there is only the purchasing agency of the State, which dictates the prices paid by the szakszövetkezet to its members. These prices have still been high enough to encourage a section of the population, those who have inherited the best vineyards (in other words the traditionally prosperous sections of the peasantry), to expand their production in this branch. They have done so in the way that prosperous families expanded their production in the past and the only way possible in view of the production process: they have made heavy use of hired labour. The means chosen by the government to stimulate wine production in the small-farm sector have had further undesirable consequences because of high alcohol consumption in the community and the links between the wine and the spirit sectors of the alcohol market. The apparently high degree of price responsiveness of small-farmers in this branch has been achieved at the cost of frustrating government control over the black market production of *pálinka*, has increased the scale of tax evasion, and has encouraged the black market distribution of both *pálinka* and wine. A rise in the shop prices of alcoholic beverages, such as that announced in July 1978, may do more to encourage black market activity than to discourage consumption. Market principles have even penetrated the informal household sales of spirits within the community, breaching traditional norms (e.g. in serving an alcoholic against the wishes of his family), but following predictably from the decision to rely on untramelled markets and material incentives to remedy the structural deficiencies of the agricultural sector.

5 The szakszövetkezet community – politics

Having analysed in some detail the economy of the szakszövetkezet community in Tázlár the next step is to consider its influence upon other fields of culture. In this chapter on 'politics' it will become clear that events and individuals have in practice been considerably manipulated from outside Tázlár. This was traditionally so from the beginning of mass resettlement, and it follows now from the theoretical premises of democratic centralism that the community must be studied in a larger context. Therefore it is appropriate to consider the evolution of local government and administration in the same chapter, together with forces more 'internal' to the community, notably those founded upon religious belief. It will be seen that the szakszövetkezet itself, though invested with important 'centralist' functions from outside, has also developed an 'internal' representative role in the expression of the political opinions and demands of the people of Tázlár. We have seen how the szakszövetkezet has facilitated the strategies of individuals in the economic sphere, where it has impeded the emergence of that economic 'community' which is necessarily created by the productive cooperative. Here we shall see that it has been a vehicle for the expression of political unity and an effective community-wide, collective strategy of opposition to the policies of outside forces.

I The traditional system of local government

The revolution of 1848 and the liberation of the serfs did not eliminate feudal elements from many Hungarian institutions and practices. Certain tithe payments continued for several decades and it has been estimated that some 53 per cent of all land remained with the noble owners of large estates (Berend and Ránki, 1974, p. 31). Continuity with the feudal past and with the centralist traditions of the Hapsburg state was also preserved by the system of local government which developed in the later nineteenth century. All self-governing communities, the category to which Tázlár belonged from 1872, had an array of officials, notably the 'magistrate', the 'notary', and their assistants or deputies. These individuals held much power in the community, being responsible for law and order, tax collection, the administration of community-owned land, road-building and the control of spirit sales, to name but a few of their activities. But they were also directly subordinate to the administration at district level. Tázlár was at this period part of a large district whose centre was Solt. There was also a 'body of representatives', which was, however, only in part representative of the population of the community; half its membership was comprised of the so-called *virilistas*, the largest landowners in the community whose right to representation was automatic (although few of the absentee landowners made use of this right). Without major modification, except temporarily during the revolutionary chaos of 1919 when the clerk was dismissed by the local *direktorium*, this system and its feudal characteristics survived until the beginning of the socialist period, and was not formally replaced by the present structure of councils until autumn 1950.

While it may be true, as Horváth has argued (1965, p. 318), that in the national context the political and administrative organisation of the community had by the end of the nineteenth century become quite detached from peasant control and could not further the goal of local self-government, there are a few special points to note in connection with the tanya settlements of Tázlár. The county archives (BKML, Prónayfalva) offer much useful information on the local government practice of the period. In the very first decade of the community's existence it appears that the majority of the representatives came from one family. Later the number of representatives was increased, and we can see from the archives that each of the 12 *virilistas* of 1887 owned over 500 *hold* (288 hectares) of land, and that they included one or two members of the upper nobility. By the end of the pre-war period this had all changed and the largest taxpayers were merely richer members of the local peasantry or successful local merchants. The main office-holders were also for the most part the educated sons of richer local families. This does not alter their practical subordination to forces outside the community and there is no disputing the fact that, although the elective posts were actively competed for in the inter-war period, the mass of the populace had no voice in local government. There was, however, no dominant noble family and there was more scope for the articulation of middle-peasant interests than in many communities where the social relations of feudalism had been better preserved, particularly in regions dominated by large estates.

There is not a great deal to say about the early activity of the local administration. Although we have emphasised in the discussion of the tanya problems the ineffectual nature of public control in the early decades of resettlement, there are nevertheless constant references in the archives to the welfare undertakings of the council, usually couched as the paternal responsibility of the magistrate or of some other official. The most ambitious relief works culminated with the State-financed street-building programme of the 1930s, designed specifically to aid poorer families. But an early copy of the rules for the local officials charges the magistrate with the alleviation of distress (and, incidentally, the midwife with a special duty to watch the unmarried pregnant, and to report all cases of abortion and infanticide). It is far from clear how much help poor families did receive from the council. In several years the payment of the officials' salaries was by far the largest item in the budget. Some welfare assistance was provided indirectly. The doctor, for example, according to his contract with the council, was obliged to treat the needy without request for payment. Later, certainly following the impact of the economic crisis in the 1930s, there was close cooperation with the Catholic church in welfare relief, and according to the local church records 40 to 50 families were fully supported during the winter of 1931–2.

Apart from its role as the local agent of State welfare policies, the administration was active in many other spheres. At the beginning of resettlement it was directly involved in the agricultural cycle, being charged with the job of officially proclaiming the day on which the grape harvest should begin (BKML Prónayfalva, n.d.). It offered employment to a few, e.g. in addition to the prestigious white-collar jobs, employment in road-building, or as a forester or summer herdsman. It also constituted an important forum for the voicing of opinion on political issues at all levels, ranging from heated debate on the number of postmen needed to make all the tanya deliveries to unanimous protest at the 'mutilation' of Hungary following the first world war (BKML Prónayfalva 1933 and 1919).

II Local government and administration since 1950

It is as well to begin a consideration of socialist local administration by outlining the 'pure theory' of democratic centralism, which has its origins in the organisational principles developed by Lenin for the Communist Party in Russia (Lenin, 1902). The essential concept then and now is one of 'dual subordination', each tier in the apparatus of either the Party or the State being subject both to its members or its local constituency, and to the decisions taken at any level further up the hierarchy. Western social scientists have found the theory of little use in understanding contemporary reality, but have sometimes attempted to gauge the political climate in communist states by isolating two components, basically a 'democratic' component which is implied by responsiveness to members or to the electorate and a 'centralist' component which is the command-pattern of all political hierarchies. Recent studies have found the origins of this theory in Rousseau and conceived the hierarchies as information-systems in which the essential task is the channelling of issues and information upwards; it is no longer the case in most socialist states that all important decisions are issued as commands from the top of the hierarchy, as is assumed to have been the norm in Stalin's time (cf. Piekalkiewicz, 1975; Taras, 1975).

Since our concern is with the very lowest tier of State administration and local government there is no need here to take account of 'decentralisation' to other levels, e.g. to provincial level, and the scope that is now afforded a large variety of interest-groups above the level of the community (see e.g. Hough (1969), or Lane and Kolankiewicz (1973), for a wealth of material on other socialist states). It is probably not only in Hungary that the rural community has benefited least from the general post-Stalinist reaffirmation of the 'democratic' component. The basic council structure remains as it was when it was established in the 1950s, with a permanent staff subordinate to the elected council and the executive committee of that council on the one hand, and on the other to the next level of the administrative hierarchy, which is the district centred on Kiskőrös. The chairman, the key figure, is both an elected member and chairman of the council's executive committee, and also a full-time official on the payroll of the State, together with the other staff at the offices, clerks and tax-collectors, whose work he oversees daily. According to the theory, the executive committee of the local council is subordinate to the entire council, and at the same time to the executives of higher councils at district or county level. The specialist administrative bodies are subordinate to the local executive committee, but also to the corresponding specialist bodies at higher levels. Executive committees of councils have no power to oppose the instructions of superior specialist administrative bodies, although technically they have a right to 'object' to them. Thus the possibility for a unique vertical chain of command is clear. In practice the functioning of the system depends greatly upon the individual at the centre of both the elected organ and the administration, the council chairman.

The authority of the present chairman, Pál Trsztyinski, is very great indeed, and is commonly acknowledged even by his enemies. The councils elected in the 1950s were initially large, 50-member organs, revolutionary 'soviets' according to the ideology, but in practice a subordinate part of the larger State bureaucracy which was brought to bear most heavily upon the independent peasantry during the period of the first Five Year Plan. Although a few individual council members became important as 'brokers', especially in the implementation of the compulsory-delivery system, the composition of the council was not representative of the mass of the peasantry and it was helpless to protect their interests. The turnover of officials, almost invariably strangers to the community appointed at district level, was also extremely high. The chairman's job changed hands six times in as many years after 1950. Since 1957 however, Trsztyinszki, who is of Kiskőrös Slovak descent, has retained office. He maintains firm control, and this, in combination with the general precepts of administration, has restricted the council's ability to mobilise or express the views of the population in general. In addition to heading the council and the local administration, Trsztyinszki is also the community's representative on the county council and is the one man invariably consulted on all decisions affecting Tázlár which are taken in Kecskemét or Kiskőrös. The entire functioning of the council is commonly perceived as manipulated by him in concert with outside forces. This is enough to earn him a measure of respect, although there are many who criticise his intellectual abilities. He has remained for most purposes a social stranger in the community, living in a house which is adjacent to the offices and owned by the council.

The actions of the council chairman and the administrative bodies are effective in a number of fields. Apart from its general task of 'coordination' in all spheres, there has been direct intervention in the szakszövetkezets, which, as we have seen, has not always had the desired effect. The council chairman makes regular public speeches on socialist holidays and addresses the community of farmers at szakszövetkezet open meetings. He may play a leading role in resolving crises, such as that which developed in the leadership of the szakszövetkezet in 1977 (see section VI).

The administration no longer has any direct economic functions, and employs no manual workers apart from cleaning-ladies. However it does exercise considerable influence over the running of the school, the nursery and the culture house, since the finances of all these are channelled through the administration. It also has an enlarged role in welfare policy. Although assistance given to individuals is only a small portion of the annual budget of the community, ensuring its optimal distribution is the major task of one employee at the offices. There is careful monitoring of households where children may be 'endangered' and of old people in need of attention. The administration has the power to remove persons in both categories to State institutions and this commonly takes place against the will of the individual or of the parents concerned. Special allowances have been paid out in recent years for winter fuel, and children have been given clothing. Nine persons were drawing regular cash grants from the council in 1978, but the allocation of such funds is not always undisputed. A gypsy family was refused support after an appeal, on the grounds that they were capable of procuring a livelihood from the cultivation of the land which they possessed (see chapter 6, Section II).

Much has been made in recent years of attempts to encourage local self-government (*az önkormányzati jelleg*) in Hungarian rural communities (cf. Dányi, 1976, pp. 288–9). In Tázlár they carry little conviction. The full-time salaried chairman and his permanent staff, numbering seven in 1977, although charged only with the implementation of the decisions of the council, in practice exert great influence over its executive committee and indeed over the infrequent sittings of the full council. Despite successive reductions in the size of the council it remains, with 28 members, too large to permit frank discussion of the kind that is occasionally possible within the 12-member executive committee of the szakszövetkezet. Meetings tend to be dominated by the chairman and a select group of floor speakers, usually committee chairmen or officials or invited speakers from outside, who deliver prepared speeches which they have discussed beforehand with the chairman. Many members sit in a silent group towards the rear of the chamber as if in a classroom. They feel that the effect of any real decentralisation of power to the community would only be further to strengthen the personal resources of the chairman, who is at present subject to many checks from outside the community.

Such a development is unlikely. Despite some theoretical control over taxes raised locally through the so-called 'community development fund', in practice the improvements in public utilities carried out so far have always relied upon considerable State grants, and this dependence becomes

ever more pronounced. Local budgets have, nevertheless, continued to
rise. There is a staff of three in the local tax office which is responsible
for all tax collection in the community and works under close supervision
from Kiskőrös. But the Hungarian tax system in general has not responded
to the jump in personal incomes which has occurred through a great
variety of causes since 1968, and in Tázlár the large incomes earned by
many over the last decade have not been tapped for community development purposes. Even in self-managing Yugoslavia, control over the local
budget is still the means by which considerable power is exercised from
the centre (Pusic, 1975, p. 143).

If many members of the council are apparently resigned to a ceremonial
role, they are nevertheless chosen very carefully. Each individual represents
one small constituency, either a street in the village or a particular tanya
area. The composition is very heterogeneous, but biased towards the
village intelligentsia, and strongly biased against women. As in the case of
the executive committee of the szakszövetkezet there is no attempt to
nominate exclusively Party sympathisers, but outspoken critics could not
expect nomination. The organisation of elections and the drawing up of
lists of candidates is the task of the Patriotic People's Front, an otherwise 'purely ritualistic organisation' (Ignótus, 1973, p. 273). In practice
it is the members of the Party and the chairman who have the last word.
Although there has been at least one case when a nominee was rejected
by the electorate (which is possible by scratching out the name on the
ballot paper), this is a surprisingly rare occurrence given the size of the
constituency and the scope for collusion between electors. There are
procedures for the recall of members and new members may be elected at
by-elections in the course of the four-year duration of the council. Thus
in 1977, after one council member had left his wife and eloped with a
young teacher, and a member of the council's much more prestigious
executive committee had committed suicide, the new secretary of the Party
cell was elected to fill both posts, despite the drawback of not being a
resident of the community.

Anyone may accept nomination. Since few people believe that the
council has much power anyway, one is not compromised by participation
in a 'talking-shop'. And on the positive side there is the possibility that
one day a councillor might use his meagre resources to voice a specific
request or perhaps a personal complaint, either publicly or privately with
the chairman. Points made by farmer councillors are generally highly
specific and, if they warrant action of some kind, can be dealt with by
the chairman within the community. Some members intercede regularly
on behalf of individuals, one recurring issue in the 1970s being the extension
of electrification in the tanya areas. As in the 1950s certain councillors
play important roles in mediating between farmers and the representatives
of State power. However, it would be an exaggeration to see the office of
local councillor as creating some institutional 'middleman' or any kind of
systemic regulator either in the 1950s or today. The office cannot create

or enhance personal resources, it can only be a useful vehicle for their deployment. Many councillors are respected citizens, influential because of their general standing in the community, and only a competitive election might further raise their legitimacy. As councillors they are obliged to participate in maintaining the illusion of an elaborate mechanism of social control under the patriarchal aegis of the chairman. Each year, according to the familiar principles, they must present formal reports, not only to their constituents, giving an account of the activities and achievements of the council, but also 'upwards' to the chairman, outlining their agitation work, and hopefully their successes in raising the consciousness of their constituents.

It is difficult to gauge the incidence of the upward channelling of information from Tázlár to Kiskőrös. Some people assume that Trsztyinski must be a man of authority at the district centre, simply by virtue of his length of service. But there is no evidence that he has been able to influence the lines of policy which emanate from Kiskőrös and Kecskemét, nor even the manner and timing of their implementation in the community. This is certainly the feeling of most people in Tázlár, whose own contacts with officials from outside are limited to szakszövetkezet open meetings. The evidence of Szegő (quoted by Triska, 1976, pp. 165–6) shows that few Hungarians believe that their 'deputies' have much influence upon county council decisions. More interestingly, few of the deputies interviewed would accept the conceptual possibility of conflicts of interest between communities. Their own model, and it must be assumed that of most council chairmen, is of an indivisible polity which they identify with the State apparatus. It is the prevalence of these notions, and the strict subordination of the salaried local bureaucracy, which establish the continuity with the traditional system of local government, cause the council structure to be widely regarded as no more than the local manifestation of State power, and prevent its developing as a representative and responsible political forum in which the mass of the population might usefully participate.

III The Hungarian Socialist Workers' Party

Whatever the defects in the council structure it is significant that when Trsztyinszki wants to underscore a point, e.g. at a meeting of the szakszövetkezet executive committee, he will say that he is speaking in the name of the council, even though he is also the pillar of the local Party organisation. In practice the elective council seems to embody the greater legitimacy. Few studies have been made of the role of the Party at the local level. In theory one knows only that, like the council, the Party is expected to influence and coordinate all other community institutions, including economic enterprises and agricultural cooperatives. The Party is always well represented on the council, but Party members can claim unambiguous priority only on 'political questions'.

The Party has never had a large membership in Tázlár. Today it has only a few dozen members. Its meetings are infrequent, and gone are the days of the 1950s when, as many villagers recall, the Party occupied a large headquarters outside the council offices and introduced such novelties as communal news analysis during work breaks in the fields. Many of its leaders in the past and today have been strangers to the community, including immigrants of urban origin in the 1940s. Very few of the pre-1948 members (in 1948 following complex tactical manoeuvres and political pressure the social-democrats merged with the communists to form the Hungarian Workers' Party) can be found in the community today. Perhaps because of the course followed here by the cooperative movement, and also because of the absence in Tázlár of a clearly-defined landless proletariat in the pre-socialist period, there was no committed native political nucleus which could assume a guiding role in the village through the Party. This latter pattern was common in other Hungarian communities, where a stratum of veteran communists has consistently maintained its prominence in both cooperatives and councils (e.g. Sárkány's observations on Varsány, the village studied by the ethnographers of the Academy in Northern Hungary, 1978, p. 102). In Tázlár council chairman Trsztyinszki qualifies by his social origin, as a good example of a communist of this type.

A large proportion of the members today are white-collar workers, teachers and clerks, who are often encouraged to apply for membership by their superiors and to believe that at whatever level it will improve their prospects for career advancement. Members of the early cooperatives were also encouraged to display their political commitment by joining the Party. In addition, there is a significant proportion of self-employed tradesmen, including the richest building contractors, who may hope to draw attention away from their essentially private and highly remunerative trades by the demonstration of their political orthodoxy. In common with other cells all over the country the Tázlár branch has become increasingly less of a workers' party. It was rather embarrassing that the senior secretary in the local administration had to wait almost a year before she could gain admission to the Party, because the cell was unable to tolerate any further deterioration of its worker/intellectual ratio. In the country as a whole there was a heavy decline in the ratio of workers in the 1960s, from 59 per cent in 1962 to 38 per cent in 1970, and the switch to a classification based on social origin rather than current employment obviously does not offer a long-term solution to this problem for the Party (Keefe *et al.*, 1973, p. 158).

In the Kádár period there has been no attempt to broaden substantially the mass-base of the Party. At the grass roots it has retained much of its elitist exclusivity. It makes certain demands of its members, of which the cessation of Church attendance and the exclusion from the life-cycle rituals still dominated by the Church are the most serious in a rural community. However, there is no difficulty nowadays in relatives of the Party member preserving their religious afiliation. Increasingly, Party members themselves can be seen in church on important occasions. Prominent members of the Reformed Church in particular have retained Party membership. Much now depends upon the will of the individual. Party membership is widely regarded as instrumental in the planning of one's career or as a genuine but vague declaration of 'progressive' views in the realm of politics, rather than as a fundamental statement about ultimate beliefs. The headmistress of the school, who arrived in the 1940s as a Reformed Church teacher and part-time cantor, is one Party member who still feels inhibited from openly expressing her religious convictions, but pays regular visits to the pastor's house (he is her next-door neighbour) and is widely reputed to have paid her Church dues in secret over many years.

In recent years the Party has become almost inconspicuous. The secretary for some years was a quietly-spoken female teacher, who was invariably upstaged by district Party representatives at all the more important meetings. Meetings are not generally advertised, but may be awaited with great interest when price increases are rumoured. It is said that turnout is highest whenever such an item appears on the agenda and that Party members are followed over to the shop when the meeting is over! An 'open day' is organised annually, but little effort is made to attract a crowd. Political education has been left almost entirely to Trsztyinszki, who makes the traditional speeches on May Day, 7 November (the anniversary of the Soviet October Revolution), and other holidays, but only to captive audiences from the school.

The extent of positive intervention by the local Party in the affairs of the szakszövetkezets, as opposed to a quietist presence which is always maintained, depends a great deal upon the personality of the secretary. There was a period in the 1960s and early 1970s when a local secretary intervened regularly, for example in siding with an executive in criticism of the szakszövetkezet chairman. He could always invoke threats of inquiries from outside in the name of the Party. It is customary also for all long-term development plans for both the community and the szakszövetkezets to be carefully discussed by the Party before they are officially placed before other bodies for adoption.

I was informed by members that debate at Party meetings could be lively, although as the numbers are small and turnover not high the personalities are all well known to each other and differences of opinion all too predictable. I was not able to attend any meetings myself, despite being the subject of discussion at several. On rare occasions votes are taken and a unified front is then presented behind the result, in strict accordance with Leninist theory.

Two other bodies are closely associated with the Party. The Patriotic People's Front is active only at election time. The Party youth wing, KISZ has functioned more spasmodically in recent years, mainly owing to problems with its leadership, but also because few young people live and work in the community beyond school age. After a number of small scandals involving salaried leaders, the culture house was entrusted part-time to an older housewife who performed her task conscientiously but had little rapport with the young. Although for a time a youth club continued to meet within the culture house, by 1978 this had disbanded. It is therefore scarcely surprising that the composition and the total activity of the Party in Tázlár are viewed with contempt by some of the people who live in the village. These include a few commuter workers and others who have obtained few of the material benefits available through small-farming in the szakszövetkezet community, as well as at least one Party member. Thus while the Party is still viewed with suspicion by the mass of the peasantry, which makes no distinction between national and local spheres, there are a few Tázlár residents who despise the torpor and the 'conservatism' of this cell and its failure to take more initiative in community affairs. An overdue attempt to rectify this situation began in 1977 with the re-establishment of the Party cell within the major economic institution of the community, the szakszövetkezet, and the appointment of its household agronomist, a popular man in the community although a resident of Kiskőrös, as a full-time salaried secretary. Previously an older member had been delegated as an unpaid Party functionary in the szak-szövetkezet. Henceforth Tázlár was to conform to the pattern of almost all production cooperatives, where the full-time Party secretary is a ubiqui-tous figure in the leadership, a freelance and a troubleshooter who has the power to intervene everywhere and is accountable ultimately only within the Party. The choice of a popular individual should help to galvanise the Tázlár cell out of its previous lassitude. It is difficult to predict whether the new secretary or anyone else is capable of altering general perceptions of the Party or even of winning the support of the nucleus of long-standing Party members for schemes of reform proposed from outside the com-munity. There are elements in the Party today with a strong interest in the maintenance of the current szakszövetkezet status quo. Because of the importance of the small-farming sector in the economy it is hard to conceive how the local Party could begin to organise and express mass public opinion and aspirations on any major issues.

IV The Church

The inclusion of a discussion of the Church in a chapter on 'politics' calls for preliminary justification. In fact relations between the State and the Catholic Church have created many problems in the socialist period, which in the national context were resolved partially by the 1964 accord with the Vatican, and more completely following the departure of Cardinal Mindszenty from the American Embassy in Budapest in 1971. The Church has taken up many liberal causes and at the higher levels followed a very conciliatory policy, even offering support for the government on such issues as the basic desirability of collectivisation. However at the grass roots, and especially in rural communities, many of the old conflicts still linger. In the absence of any other mass-membership organisations in the modern community, it is important that we consider the functioning of the Church and whether its organisation has much social and political significance today.

In the history of Tázlár religious belief and denominational differentiation were of immense importance. Numerous small sects flourished in the early decades of resettlement and there are many records of sectarian conflict. However, the major Churches were not slow in attempting to institutionalise religion. In this they were considerably aided by their virtual monopoly of public education. The Catholics had been the more numerous since mass resettlement began, but at the end of the last century the Protestant minority in Tázlár was still the third-largest in the lower Solt district, after Soltvadkert and Kiskőrös. Recently it has declined and today comprises less than one-fifth of the total community population. Everyone but a handful of white-collar communist families has an affiliation to some denomination, and is anxious that his children should grow up with the same affiliation. The most scandalous memory from the 1919 Revolution is of the man who espoused atheism in the centre of the village and argued that man was descended from monkeys. In the inter-war period the Church regained and strengthened its position throughout Hungarian society, feeding on troubled economic conditions. In Tázlár we have already noted close collaboration between Church and State in welfare policy. The Church was also of great importance socially. A place on the church council was the coveted ambition of many well-to-do farmers, in both Catholic and Reformed Churches. There were separate prayer societies to which families of similar social standing could affiliate, and separate committees, e.g. that responsible for education, which offered responsibilities and prestige to a few. There was also a mass-membership Catholic circle which involved much larger numbers in a wide variety of activities both inside and outside the sphere of religion.

The Church has seen its wider role in the community drastically curtailed in the socialist period. Yet in the case of Tázlár it is only in the socialist period that the 'institutionalisation' of religion has been carried to its conclusion. Both Catholic and Protestant Churches have now realised longstanding ambitions to erect new centres of worship in the village, the Catholics succeeding laboriously, mainly through voluntary effort, in the 1950s, and the Reformed Church erecting its chapel in the mid-1960s. The Protestants remain divided into *Reformed Church* (Calvinist) and minority *Lutheran* components, but both use the new chapel and are served by the same Reformed Church pastor who also administers scattered Protestant families over a vast area of the former *puszta* to the east, in the communities of Bodoglár and Bugac. The Catholic parish on the other hand corresponds to the secular community boundaries, with the exception of the extreme settlement cluster at Kötöny, which is now attached to Kiskunhalas. There is also a small Baptist chapel, still regularly attended by some half-dozen families, with different visiting preachers each month.

Although there is abundant evidence of secularisation in the modern community, most conspicuously in the decline in regular church attendance, it is not a simple matter to relate this to underlying loss of religious conviction and to the impact of State policies. We are not concerned here with the great importance which faith may have for some people who no longer display it in the traditional manner, i.e. with its private importance. In public, in everyday life, the reconciliation of religious and secular demands is continually creating extraordinary conflicts and anomalies. Most families have to make some compromises, and the details of specific compromises form one of the mainstays of local gossip and comment in the community. The problems arise because in many recurring situations, notably the rituals of the life-cycle, no effective secular alternatives have yet been devised. It is likely that the families of even Party members will prefer to call in a priest rather than have the Party secretary officiate in the cemetery. Similarly a majority of families scorn the naming ceremony which occasionally takes place at the council offices in lieu of a church baptism. Weddings create the greatest difficulties, highlight the differences between generations, and provide the clearest public occasion for the demonstration of religious convictions. According to the law the civil ceremony in the council offices is obligatory and the religious ceremony optional. Nowadays there are plenty of couples, especially those who have already worked away from the community, or whose remote tanya families have no history of regular church attendance, who opt only for the civil ceremony. This itself has become something of a rite, the Hun-garians having shared the Soviet concern with the elaboration of secular ceremony in the effort to replace religion. The council chairman or senior secretary, draped in the colours of the national flag, makes weighty speeches to the accompaniment of taped music in the council chamber. However, especially when a large *lakodalom* is planned, there are often strong family pressures to proceed to the church. Some guests may slip away from the procession before the church, but others will join it only there. All will unite later for the festivities of the *lakodalom*. Another solution, if the couple do not hail from the same village, is to hold the civil ceremony in one community and the religious ceremony in the other, perhaps even a considerable time later, when the couple are living together or when they decide they wish to have their children baptised. In such cases there may be two *lakodaloms*. But if there is to be only one it is more likely to follow the religious wedding. To dispense altogether with a religious wedding may result in family reluctance to mount a *lakodalom* and could be financially very expensive for the new couple. It may also be noted that some couples, often with only tenuous links with the community, satisfy family pressures by returning for quasi-secret church weddings which they are reluctant to go through with in a town, either because of their careers or because of the over-zealous insistence of a local priest on regular church attendance and religious education in preparation for the sacrament.

Marriages can thus create delicate problems for ordinary families in the socialist community. A more serious matter, long seen as a kind of litmus test by Church and State alike in their strategies to maintain family affiliation, is that of religious instruction in the schools. The Roman Catholic priest deploys all his considerable oratorical skills each year in order to persuade Catholic parents to sign the special form which may enable their children to enrol in the classes conducted inside the school by the priest himself. Enrolment is not guaranteed because the list is then carefully scrutinised by the secular authorities and the names of children who ought not to receive religious instruction may be withdrawn. In any case many parents are naturally reluctant to commit themselves publicly by signing the list at the council offices. Some have contrived 'accidentally' to miss the times stipulated. Others enrol their children in the lower grades, but see no point in continuing beyond the sacrament of confirmation, especially if the child hopes to go on for further studies. The total percentage of children attending was 76 per cent in 1957, but has fallen since to under 50 per cent. The priest, of course, rails against this system, which allows him to enter the school, but then to reach only a declining percentage of the pupils, and to find that even these may be reluctant listeners, as the instruction falls outside normal lesson time. In contrast the pastor has adopted a low profile and throws the decision wholly onto families by making attendance voluntary outside school hours. He attracts an even smaller percentage of the Protestant pupils. The priest, who left the community in 1978 following a serious stroke in 1977, was perceived as a 'hardliner'. Though many admired his energy and his undoubted integrity, few applauded his tactics when he made a great fuss at Sunday High Mass in distributing religious trinkets to his best pupils and read aloud the attendance figures for each grade and the family names of the regular attenders.

Regular attendance at the Sunday service is no longer regarded as essential, and this now applies as much to the Catholic congregation as to the Protestant. There is a general preference for a quiet life on Sundays, and for maintaining a low profile in the Church. Many of those who regularly pay their dues do not attend more than once or twice annually. The sums collected at Sunday services are trifling, but the system of annual dues (about £2 Sterling (70 forints) per adult, with half-rates for pensioners) offers an ideal solution, since regular payment is now sufficient to guarantee a Christian burial. Undignified squabbles still frequently occur in cases when the priest wishes to apply the rules strictly and refuses burial. Weekday services are the most sparsely attended. At the Reformed Church chapel sometimes only the wife of the pastor is present. At the Catholic church the number varies seasonally but never exceeds a few dozen, mainly elderly women.

There is one major fete, the *búcsú*, when the Catholic church is always full. Each Hungarian village has a *búcsú* on a fixed date each year. In the village centre of Tázlár this is normally the first Sunday in June. In the

upper hamlet it is around the feast of the Assumption in the middle of
August. *Búcsús* were formerly events that one spent weeks preparing for
and participation in the *búcsú* of a neighbouring village was one of the few
occasions for travel outside the community. Nowadays, however much
the priest may stress its religious importance, for the majority it has come
to resemble the other major holidays and has a mainly social and secular
character. It is a time for families to reunite and for extended eating
and drinking. There was a time when joining the public procession after
High Mass around the village may have been construed as a political
act. But now, on account of the traffic on the road, the procession is
confined to the church grounds. (The only public march to take place
regularly now in Tázlár is the school-leaving parade, the *ballagás*, but
neighbouring Soltvadkert is sufficiently large to mount a May Day parade.)

It may be asked whether secularization *per se* is the dominant recent
trend in Tázlár, or whether what can be observed is the consequence of
a contraction in the sphere of activity of the Church itself, of its forced
withdrawal from secular life. It is of course hard to distinguish between
the two processes. Divesting the Church of its wide-ranging social control
functions has no doubt contributed to a weakening in the religious sphere
as well, although it should not be thought automatically to diminish the
capacity of the Church to influence and represent opinion. It is important
again to glance back over the peculiar history of the community. The
problems of social control affected the Church as much as the secular
authorities. The local records show that it was continually necessary to
make quite crude exhortations to improve church attendance. In the past
the Church regularly involved its ultimate sanction, the denial of a religious
burial, to those who shirked their financial obligations or those who did
not bother to sanctify common-law marriages. It was the poorer section
of the population that was always more liable to fall foul of God's ministers.
For some of them the Church hierarchy was as alien as the secular hierarchy of the State. The priest and the full-time cantor in the Catholic
Church enjoyed a high standard of living by comparison with most of their
congregation. The priest was entitled to receive tithe payments in addition
to the income he obtained from land in Church ownership. He employed
servants and was often the recipient of substantial gifts in kind from his
parishioners. Even today the meagre wages of the pastor are necessarily
supplemented in this way. Although the Tázlár clergy were poorly endowed
in comparison with the clergy in older communities (where there was
often considerable property and involvement in agriculture), in Tázlár
also individual priests were known on occasion to arouse the resentment of
their parishioners by their acquisitiveness.

The ministers still tend to be very conservative politically. The Catholic
priest is prone to dismiss the entire fourth zone as a 'proletarian zone'
and is occasionally criticised for neglecting certain scattered elements of
his flock. It is also true that the fine stained-glass windows of the new
church each bear the name of one or more of the traditional Catholic

families who were able to pay for them, a gesture corresponding to the pre-war custom whereby the leading families established public crosses at the community boundary. However, both religious denominations now have a more popular social base than formerly. At Sunday masses the collection plates are sometimes passed around by two former independent smallholders. One of them lost his land and his team as a result of the expansion of the State Farm. He moved into the village from his tanya and now works irregularly as a labourer, in addition to maintaining a small-farm. The other has of his own accord almost abandoned small-farming and works as a full-time labourer in the szakszövetkezet. It is difficult to imagine either man reaching any position of prominence in the pre-war Church. The two Church councils were perhaps of greater importance in the past, but as their importance has declined they have widened their social composition. The average age of the Catholic council members is high, and each one represents a small constituency in the community, just as a secular council member does. The selection of new representatives is in both cases under the effective control of the full-time minister, but as changes in the membership are rare the councils have institutional continuity and powers which may be brought to bear against the policies of a minister. This is particularly true in the case of the Reformed Church council, but because of the small size of the congregation this is not always the self-governing, democratic body it is meant to be.

A great deal still depends upon the character of the ministers. The relation between the Catholic priest and the council chairman is a formal one. In 1955, a new priest, accused by the secular authorities of being difficult to work with, had responded with a forthright public declaration of his political neutrality and intention not to intervene in secular affairs. Nowadays the priest and the chairman seldom meet, although they live next door to each other; but it is said that a priest in the early 1960s had rather warmer ties with the same chairman, frequently visiting him at his home. Despite the occasional diatribe from the pulpit, most commonly on declining moral standards and the moral price which the nation is paying for recent material prosperity, the ministers have generally maintained their neutrality, and they have earned general respect for their integrity as individuals. An observation in the Catholic priest's diary from 1957 shows the desire of the Church to avoid all secular taint. The priest declared as follows: 'The people of Tázlár say that the intellectuals who come here and work here all get rich – well, at no time will the priest come to live amongst you with these intentions.'

It may be that the increasing detachment of the Church from the secular society is making it 'marginal' to the community altogether. Membership of a Church council is no bar to membership of other councils and commitees, even Party membership. Several councillors figure prominently in the Church. It is true that teachers and the intelligentsia as a whole do not attend church, and that some of them follow with some reluctance what everyone sees as an unwritten rule. But it is only the ministers themselves and a few old people who see the secular authorities as constantly manoeuvring to destroy the Church. The age-structure of the population attending church, the lack of interest shown by the young and all non-peasant groups, indicate that the quietist stance of the Church is rendering it increasingly isolated in the new community and at the same time preventing it from expressing the conservative opinions of the old.

At this point it is important to correct in certain details the impression of a uniformity of religious practice in the major denominations. Currently, the most important difference is the lower profile and more strictly apolitical stance of the Protestant minority. In the past, the mere existence of a plurality of religions was of the greatest importance. Historically the Catholic Church has been dominant in the nation since the early Hapsburg days, and it has tended to maintain a strict attitude towards mixed marriages. Dispensations were regularly granted, but in families strongly identified with one denomination the problems could be acute. The ingenious solution sometimes adopted was to educate the children of different sexes, or each alternate child, according to different religions. Formal conversion of one partner, the partner of lower social standing if there was a substantial difference between the two, was a more common solution. Such problems have still not disappeared entirely, and a richer family may still be able to stipulate a religious wedding in the church of its traditional affiliation. Denominational conflict also surfaced in the election campaign for a szakszövetkezet chairman in 1975. Though in fact the religious identification of the candidates had virtually no effect on the result, candidate Rozinger belonged to the small Lutheran section of the minority, where sensitivity to discrimination from the Catholic majority is most acute.

There are major differences in style between the two ministers, which reflect to some extent the differences between their respective Churches in the national framework. The future of religious affiliation in Hungary, as in other socialist states, is a controversial subject, both as regards the overall speed of secularisation and the denominational variety within the process. There has been some consolidation of the institutional strength of the Catholic Church within the socialist state, and a more substantial weakening of all other denominations, partly because of poorly developed organisational hierarchies. The research of Miklós Tompa (1977) has shown that a larger proportion of Catholics than of those born into Protestant families describe themselves as 'actively religious', while for the latter the proportion is now below 50 per cent. Catholic congregations are younger (52.5 per cent of Protestants are over 60 years old), they contain more active earners (fewer pensioners and 'dependants'), and they are better educated (only two-thirds having failed to complete eight grades of 'general school', compared with three-quarters of the Protestants). On the basis of a highly dubious questionnaire and sampling techniques, Tompa reaches a conclusion which the evidence from Tázlár would tend to support, namely that in the near future secularisation will continue to wreak greater change upon the Protestant than upon the Catholic population. Active Christians in both denominations are demonstrably less well educated than the non-practising Christians, and further improvements in educational standards are likely to have a relatively smaller effect upon the Catholic Church.

From the Church's point of view the most depressing feature in the evidence from this one locality is the lack of interest shown by younger people and the failure of Christianity to attract any significant support amongst those white-collar workers who are not Party members. Admittedly, given the effective ban still enforced upon the teaching staff and the administration of the provisions for religious education, the Church has great problems in reaching the youth of the community. But in the rural community the Church is not limited by exactly the same constraints as the Church leaders concerned to perform a 'holding operation' in the nation as a whole. There are many who feel that the resources of the Catholic Church are not being optimally deployed, even though its strategies have been more successful hitherto than those of other denominations. Despite, and in part because of, its liberalism and conciliatory policies towards the State, it appears to fall short of giving a clear 'Reformist' lead which would attract the support of many young people and of intellectuals. At the same time it has given less of a lead in the nation than has been achieved by the Polish Catholic Church, and has forfeited any role as a conservative rallying force in the countryside, which is a role a man such as the priest in Tázlár might have eagerly cultivated in the secular sphere.

Instead we must conclude that the Church altogether does seem condemned to a 'marginal' role at all levels of the socialist state in Hungary. And with reference to our main theme, in the village of Tázlár the religious heterogeneity which dates back to the first decades of resettlement has also contributed to the failure of the Churches to become integrating political forces. In contrast with many Hungarian villages (e.g. Fél and Hofer, 1969, p. 380; Jávor, 1978, p. 336) religion could have no 'unifying functions' in the development of Tázlár.

V Cultural life – the example of the upper hamlet

Although there is a separate Catholic Church in the upper hamlet of Tázlár, the Churches, the secular administration, the Communist Party and almost all other bodies in the community today (such as the Hunting Society, or the Firemen's Association) are organised on a community-wide basis. In the case of the hunters, a single society covers the three communities of Tázlár, Soltvadkert and Pírtó. This is an exceptional society, the membership of which carries considerable prestige. It contains an unusual mixture nowadays of representatives of the old richer peasants and members of the new local elite including Party members.

Two of the new 'technocratic' leaders of the szakszövetkezet from 1975 were enthusiastic hunters. The local Firemen's Association has a long history and a more mixed membership, but meets infrequently and has no important social role. The same may be said of various other bodies and committees – a paramilitary organisation which organises rifle-shooting practice, especially for schoolchildren, the Consumers' Cooperative, which is now based entirely at Soltvadkert (although in the 1940s and again after 1956 there was an independent branch in Tázlár), the Patriotic People's Front, etc. For various reasons none of these community-wide bodies has developed any political functions in the community, either because they are identified with the monolithic State outside, or because they have chosen to withdraw from the social sphere, or because they are specialised groups meeting infrequently and are not socially exclusive.

Cultural policy in Tázlár has also been directed from the lower village centre and centred on the improvement of the cultural level of this centre. The cornerstone of these policies, for which there is one man in overall charge (a communist councillor and deputy head at the school), is the culture-house. However, for a number of reasons this is no longer well utilised. Besides the fact that only small numbers of young persons remain in the community beyond school age, there are many who consider the size and village-hall design of the building inappropriate for regular youth club meetings. Expensive structural alterations to the roof have become necessary. There have also been serious defects in organisation which have hindered the development of simple club and recreational facilities. The culture-house is not a complete white elephant, though. It is used occasionally by the school for concerts, and by the szakszövetkezet for its open meetings. It is sometimes used as the venue for a *lakodalom*, and for special dances and parties organised by a particular society such as the hunters or by the general committee at New Year, or to celebrate Women's Day, etc. Regular discos were held for a period in 1977 but these failed to attract much support, while the films screened on Sundays are of very bad quality and attract smaller numbers than in the past. There are also fewer visits to the village by outside artists and theatre groups than in the past, although a popular event such as a concert of zither music may still draw a large crowd. Theatre trips to Kecskemét are now arranged by the cooperative and a few, mostly white-collar workers, travel in their own private cars. Finally, the culture-house is used regularly by enthusiastic young table-tennis players, and its library serves a very small number of village-dwellers.

The disenchantment of many young persons is expressed by a few with conspicuous clothes and hairstyles, and in occasional rowdiness at the *bisztró*. They arouse some bewilderment and even resentment in the older generation. In the upper hamlet of Tázlár the problem is naturally muted. There is no *bisztró* there, and there are very few young people. But behind the placid appearance of this hamlet, which has been steadily deprived of its central functions over the last 70 years, and where even the schoolhouse

123

takes pupils for only the first four grades and faces possible closure in the
near future, there has in fact been a lively cultural organisation in recent
years. The older generation came together under the nominal umbrella
of the Women's Council, and began meeting regularly, arranging social
functions and mounting ambitious cultural events in a tiny hall, a former
Catholic group meeting-house. Within a few years their activities were
given national prominence and created a furious scandal in the lower
village centre.

It all began at the old schoolhouse with the initiative of the schoolmistress who has taught there during most of the socialist period. Mrs
Kádár's achievement was to exploit reserves of female energy which have
only become available since the formation of the szakszövetkezet. She
gave the women a group identification they had never before possessed
but needed greatly, as more and more men were absent through commuting and as both the size of the family and the scale of the farm continually shrank. Later the women began to involve the men as well. The
most successful field for their talents proved to be amateur dramatics.
Under Mrs Kádár's guidance a wide section of the hamlet, from farmers'
wives to skilled bricklayers, were persuaded to make costumes, learn lines,
paint each others' faces and finally carry polished performances to the
culture house in the lower centre, for the entertainment of the modern
community. This was all done with virtually no assistance from the council,
and contrasts with the stagnation of the Women's Council in the village
centre. Annual coach excursions organised by Mrs Kádár also became a
popular fixture, and one not duplicated in the main village.

There the story might have rested, but for the arrival of television
cameras and the screening of a documentary film about cultural life in
Tázlár in 1975. The television people were originally interested by a
novel feature in the structure of the school's teaching staff – the fact
that there were two deputy heads, one responsible for community-wide
cultural policy and the other more closely involved with the affairs of the
school who was, incidentally, the Party secretary at the time. Once in the
village the director found a more interesting theme in the contrast between
the cultural stagnation of the main village, where large sums of money
had been spent and still larger sums were being claimed by all the local
leaders, and the vitality of the upper hamlet arising out of traditional
self-help practices and the enthusiasm of one schoolmistress. The film
exaggerated the collective sociability of the upper hamlet and did not
point out a simple line of continuity with the traditions of the pre-war
néphaz. It also gave vent to the resentment born by a few residents of
the upper hamlet towards the council for its general neglect of the hamlet
and its failure to honour specific undertakings. Finally, it highlighted
plaintive cries of boredom and loneliness from certain village-dwellers,
expressed most colourfully by the first lady of the village, the wife of
the council chairman. The national press gave the documentary very

favourable reviews. The main point, that the allocation of material resources is not the key to a successful cultural policy in small communities, was generally accepted and it led most reviewers to reflect on the challenges socialist cultural policy now faces in the country as a whole. All this created much embarrassment and irritation in the leaders of the lower village.

Most inhabitants in all parts of the community felt that the film exaggerated. The complaints of the upper hamlet are not deeply felt by the majority of its residents. It is true that there is no piped-water system here, nor even a network of pavements in the side-streets, and that virtually nothing has been done by the council to improve the cramped hall which is the hamlet's only public building, apart from the church, the school and the shop. But this discrimination is consistent with national policy, which makes no attempt to raise such tiny centres to a higher level. It should also be stressed that the entire contrast between the hamlet and the village may rest upon the gifts of one individual, who was motivated, at least in part, by a strong personal antipathy towards the community leaders, whom she held responsible for her late husband's dismissal from the headship of the main school and his subsequent disgrace. Mrs Kádár was due to retire in 1979 and her departure from the community might well affect the activities of the Women's Council, which have already declined since the death of her husband in 1976. It may be entered as a further caveat that the dances held in the upper hamlet are based on exactly the same format as those in the main culture house and that young people have never been involved to any great degree. Finally, there should be no impression of general conviviality throughout the hamlet. Relations with neighbours are no more close and visiting houses no more important within the hamlet than in the main village. In fact there is a number of longstanding quarrels and Mrs Kádár herself has long been at loggerheads with her immediate neighbour, who, though a very resourceful woman herself, has therefore been excluded from much of the activity of the Women's Council.

With all these limitations the facts remain that something impressive was organised and that the motivations were not uniformly negative. The question which arises is whether consistent growth of the hamlet, material amelioration and the renovation of its culture centre would have improved the achievement or removed its fuelling-power. If the galvanising of the upper hamlet depended upon the gifts of one person it remains of importance that no one's imagination has yet been turned to such effect in the main village, or on a level which would embrace the entire community. Mrs Kádár found no panacea for the fundamental problems of the upper hamlet, which must continue to decline as a planned result of national and local policies; but she succeeded in bringing individuals together and firing them into action in the field of culture. Something similar is needed at the level of the community as a whole if tanya traditions are ever fully to be overcome.

VI *The democratic potential of the szakszövetkezet*

Nothing that we have looked at so far has brought much success in unifying the disparate elements of this community, let alone in representing them to forces in the outside world. Even the effect of cultural policies has proved divisive. It has been left to the szakszövetkezet itself to develop as a political forum, to promote the coalescence of fragmented tanyas into a real community of interest and vigorously to represent and defend that community against the administrative forces outside.

Ferenc Donáth has argued that some of the democratic spontaneity of the 1945 Land Reform could have been developed by the early cooperative movement, and that had the Land Reform been carried out in more favourable political and economic conditions there would have been more spontaneous support for the formation of cooperatives at that time (Donáth, 1969, p. 390). Even in the Rákosi period which followed, when other community institutions were completely divested of their representative functions and placed under outside control, the early cooperatives retained elements of the 'Direct Democracy' of 1945. This was why, as was noted in Chapter 3, in the implementation of the system of compulsory deliveries the cooperatives were treated in essentially the same manner as the independent peasants. The officials of these cooperatives, in what Kunszabó characterises as the earliest phase of spontaneous democratic organisation (1974, p. 78), were not distinguished from the main body of the cooperative, although a few were recommended to the members by outside forces and Party membership was recommended to all. They did manual work alongside the other members, in addition to their paperwork. The chairman had no security of tenure, and it was his job to represent all of the membership. In the antagonistic climate of the 1950s this made him not so much an intermediary with State or Party power as a collaborator with the rank and file against an over-weening bureaucracy. Former members tell of how animals were kept secretly, and driven off to the forest whenever outside inspectors appeared, in order to guarantee families a supply of winter meat. The general political climate may have strengthened certain features of internal democracy. Friction over the allocation of State aid was common, and squabbling over distribution between neighbours and within families tended to increase from year to year.

After the fluctuations of the 1950s these pioneer democratic associations were replaced by the mass-member production cooperative groups, which retained constitutions and an elected leadership very similar to those of the earlier cooperatives. In addition to their economic functions in developing the socialist sector and integrating private peasant farming, the new groups, in the tradition of their predecessors, saw themselves duty-bound to defend the interests of their members, if need be against forces outside. Hence the failure to pursue collectivisation during these years. In fact the socialist sector in the 1960s scarcely exceeded the size of the collectively farmed area in the early 1950s. Over the decentralized production of the members the leaders could exert only limited control. At the same time the records show that these groups were required by the Kiskőrös administration to influence production outside the socialist sector in each group. The members were exhorted, apparently by their own leaders, but also by visiting Party leaders, and we have seen already that there was considerable intervention from outside in the development of the socialist sector. As an example of the kind of attempt to influence the private sector one can find a district Party secretary in 1964, on hearing that the pig-fattening plan of the *Kossuth* group was only 50 per cent fulfilled, urging the group's leadership to 'make a list of those members who can afford to fatten pigs, and to ask them personally, and to convince them of the importance of the pig-fattening plan'. Later in the same year the executive brought the matter before an open meeting of the group and it is clear that the threat of sanctions was invoked: reference was made to 'those members who will be required to take up pig-fattening'.

The compromising of the local leadership and the regularity and variety of outside intervention in all the affairs of the group were new features in the cooperative movement in Tázlár after 1960. There was also a change in the all-important figure of the chairman. Rather than choosing a truly representative individual of average ability the mass-member groups tended to prefer more successful and respected peasant farmers from the former middle peasantry. In Kunszabó's terminology this was the phase of the *gazdálkodó* or 'farming' chairman (1974, p. 82). These men were popular choices and, unlike previous leaders, were capable of providing effective leadership. At the same time they were required by the administration outside to influence the membership in specific directions, and so we may see them as mediators, continual compromisers. Their fundamental loyalties were, however, firmly with the interests of their members, which coincided with their own private farming interests. The charactteristic reserve and modesty of most farmers was intensified by political hazards and caused most former middle peasants to be highly reluctant to accept any office in the new order. However, unanimous nominations could not be declined. In two of the three groups the same individual remained in the post of chairman for more than ten years. In the third, the *Rákóczi*, which not coincidentally we have seen already to be the weakest of the three, there was a series of leadership crises and incipient factional struggle within the five- or six-member executive. The longest-officiating chairman here, in the poorest of the zones covered by the groups, proved to be the veteran chairman of one of the earlier cooperatives, who found himself under continual pressure, partly because his individual record as a farmer was insufficient to warrant the respect of the full range of the new membership. The role of outside agents is seen most prominently in this group, whereas in the others external interference was generally limited to particular issues and to emergency situations.

The institution of *gazdálkodó* leadership, though removed from the small-group, direct democracy of the early cooperatives, offered important

127

guarantees to the mass of the members. In addition to the chairman there were places for numerous individuals on the various elected committees, and all of these leaders were more than the temporarily appointed spokesmen of an association of families. They were the products of a particular section of the peasantry but when they spoke to the administration outside they knew they had a local power base and they represented the peasantry as a whole. After the formation of szakszövetkezets and the introduction of the economic reform in 1968, which diminished the extent of detailed local planning, there was less interference from outside in the running of the members' farms and a chance for the associations to strengthen their democratic character.

The conditions for this democratic practice are fully specified in the constitutions of all cooperatives. Sovereignty is vested in open meetings of all the membership. The phrase *szövetkezeti demokrácia* (cooperative democracy) is a potent encapsulation of the democratic theory which has been grasped by most members. Leaders can only be nominated and elected at open meetings, and elections as well as other major decisions require a two-thirds majority of the total membership if they are to be effective. Open meetings must be held several times each year, including once in winter for the detailed reports of the leaders and the presentation of the accounts. The mass-member cooperatives thus became the first organisations to have regular mass-meetings in the community since the Catholic societies that had flourished before the Second World War. The membership of an agricultural cooperative was perhaps less voluntary, but the opportunity for the peasantry to organise as a socio-economic interest group was quite novel.

The typical production cooperative in Hungary has the same democratic theory, but despite its potential has never achieved the same novelty of local political expression. The shift to expert, 'managerial' leadership took place very early here, whereas at the end of the 1960s the Tázlár szakszövetkezets were still sharing the services of a single Soltvadkert agronomist and maintaining only a skeletal accounting staff in their offices. Beyond this, the production cooperative changed the family farm drastically, introduced large numbers of skilled workers and non-member workers alongside the peasant rank and file, and drove larger numbers to become wage-labourers, and a high proportion to leave agriculture altogether. In this context the open meeting can easily become an assembly of purely ceremonial importance, though valuable to the leaders and to the Party. It no longer exercises effective control over the choice of leaders and does not check their activity. This may be seen as a consequence of the success of policies designed to create a large-scale socialist sector in agriculture in the 1960s. The intended approximation to the conditions and working relations of industry, was largely achieved by the State Farms. Since 1967, when agricultural cooperatives were given full legal status as enterprises, and since 1968, when the general framework of enterprise behaviour was relaxed by the economic reform, the cooperatives have increasingly behaved as large commercial enterprises. They have grown rapidly and in most regions of the country cover an area now greater than that of the administrative territory of a single community. The szakszövetkezets have been the only major sector when an important part of production has been decentralised to full-time individual farmers and where the technical conditions have been conducive to releasing a democratic potential never realised in the production cooperatives proper.

Outside interference declined in the late 1960s, but then increased again as each of the szakszövetkezets experienced economic difficulties in the early 1970s. Pressure was applied to induce mergers, and in 1972 the *Kossuth* and *Rákóczi* szakszövetkezets amalgamated to form a single unit under the leadership of the recently elected chairman of the *Kossuth*, Imre Bugyi. Flouting the recommendation of the council chairman the new szakszövetkezet chose for itself the name *Egyetértés* (Harmony). Previous merger initiatives had failed because of wrangling within the executives, the reluctance of the rank and file, and the difficulty of excluding the *Hope* from the arguments for unity and securing the benefits of scale economies. Older members feared the loss of relative advantage and levelling downwards a single community-wide szakszövetkezet would bring.

Amalgamation with the *Hope* in fact followed two years later, precipitated by pressure from outside. An election was necessary in order to select a new chairman, for although the claims of the popular Bugyi may have seemed strong, the *Hope* also had a recently elected and younger chairman, who had a narrower group of strong supporters. The community-wide electoral contest which ensued was without precedent in local political history. By polling day, tension was at fever pitch. Controversial and slightly scurrilous slogans appeared everywhere, there was door-to-door canvassing and a spate of rumours alleging bribery and high spending by both candidates spread. There was no question of substantial differences of opinion between the candidates. The contest was essentially one of personalities. Voting required a judgement of the individual wanted as chairman, the man thought to be better equipped to represent and defend local interests. This did not prevent some supporters of Pál Rozinger, the chairman of *Hope*, from explaining his defeat as a conspiracy against the Lutheran minority by the Catholic majority. Following his defeat, to which most Tázlár people feel his religious and family background did not contribute, he made weighty charges of electoral malpractice and succeeded in having the whole election re-staged. On the second ballot he was heavily defeated. This election did not prevent his remaining on cordial terms with Bugyi, and from accepting office under him in charge of the new szakszövetkezet's crop production, a responsible and well-paid post which he still held in 1978, two chairmen later. The new cooperative was given the name *Béke* (Peace).

Consider now the position of Imre Bugyi at the end of 1974. His massive support in all corners of this scattered community made him the most powerful individual in the village and gave him incontestable bargaining authority in all dealings with higher organs. It goes without saying that had Bugyi been explicitly unacceptable to the outside administration then he would never have risen to prominence in the *Kossuth*. Members had no desire to make selections that were controversial, or provocative in this direction. In fact, his basic acceptability was proven by his election as a councillor in 1973. Thanks to his good relations with council chairman Trsztyinszki, he was still serving as a member of the controlling executive committee of the council in 1977, two years after he had ceased to reside permanently in the community. The election of 1974 is significant in retrospect as the last opportunity for democratic choice in the cooperatives. Bugyi's victory was probably the last victory of the archetypal successful *gazdálkodó*, of a man freely entrusted with the leadership of the szakszövetkezet on the basis of his private qualities as a farmer. The members saw no other valid criterion for the definition of a good leader. Hence they chose an individual whom ordinary farmers could recognise as one of their own kind, and with whom they could identify. The outside administration was less than satisfied, but it had found the task of engineering the mergers sufficiently daunting, and was not yet ready to impose its own leaders. I was told in 1977 by officials in Kiskőrös of how difficult it had been on occasion to deal with Bugyi, and in particular to win his backing for their many schemes to raise the efficiency of the szakszövetkezet, or rather of a rejuvenated socialist sector within the szakszövetkezet.

Thus it was no accident that Bugyi was displaced and effectively expelled after less than a year in office at the head of the *Béke* szakszövetkezet. Moreover, the manner of his departure and the election of his successors made it quite clear that the aberration of competitive elections was not to be repeated. The cause of his downfall was significant. It had been a frequent source of complaint, both within the szakszövetkezets and outside them in official reports and policy statements, that the *gazdálkodó* leader who retained his own land would resolve any conflict of interests by putting his private economic interests before the longer-term public good of the cooperative. A new treasurer arrived in 1975, a young man of local descent and the first trained expert of local origin to hold office in any Tázlár cooperative. A problem arose almost at once concerning the alleged abuse of szakszövetkezet supplies on the private farm of the chairman. There was no major scandal and no public campaign to discredit Bugyi. He remains convinced of his innocence, and is well liked and respectfully greeted by his former neighbours, who see him when he commutes out from Soltvadkert during the summer months to the land around his now empty tanya. But his resignation was immediate and his disgrace in the eyes of the outside administration was complete. It seems appropriate that the fall of the most popular and representative leader to have emerged in Tázlár in the socialist period was accomplished 'from above' on the evidence of charges which clearly emphasised the declared incompatibility between private peasant aims and the new socialist goals, the pursuit by the szakszövetkezet of some 'collective good' which was unconnected with the democratically expressed preferences of their rank and file members.

If the survival of the szakszövetkezet type itself was not yet called into question in the mid-1970s, the balance of socialist and private sectors was altered decisively by the downfall of Imre Bugyi. The seeds of change were sown under Bugyi, following the mergers, when a number of new young specialists with no commitment to the private sector arrived. Appointed to succeed as chairman was the agrarian engineer of the cooperative, not well known in the community, László Font. He was from a neighbouring village, of middle-peasant origin, young (born 1942), a dedicated professional and a longstanding member of the Party. He was unburdened by private farming interests. His nomination was accepted passively at the open meeting called shortly after Bugyi's resignation. Rozinger was undoubtedly still ambitious, but the memory of his defeat was too recent, and he was in any case a friend of Font. Thus there was only one name on the ballot paper and the choice of the outside administration was accepted without significant protest.

This election is now seen by many Tázlár farmers as a watershed in the history of the community. Given the previous career background of Font, the years he had spent in another village in a production cooperative, it was inevitable that the direction would now change. Even had he possessed any of Bugyi's strength in the community, he was not interested in using such locally-vested power to counter the proposals of the outside administration. Instead there was now an identity of views on the need to modernise the szakszövetkezet and to compensate for the years of neglect of the socialist sector. The new 'managerial' group took over the szakszövetkezet. The treasurer (born 1943) possessed a degree in agricultural economics from the Karl Marx University, Budapest. A new qualified engineer was recruited (born 1947), as well as two agronomists, the elder of whom was only in his early thirties. The last three were all strangers to the village, and the agronomists did not even establish residence but commuted daily from nearby towns.

While it would be an exaggeration to claim that everything was transformed in the next two years, the economic profile did change considerably, as was described in Chapter 4. The collective sector initiated a great expansion of extensive sheep-farming on the vast empty pastures that had fallen into cooperative ownership. The quality of the services provided to members improved, as did the level of investment and the readiness to use State credit when available. Much more important for the rank and file was the move against the land area of the private sector, which antagonised the membership at large and certain important elements in particular. The identification for the first time of the policies of their own leadership with the anti-peasant policies attributed hitherto to the outside administration caused the profound estrangement of the rank and file. This led firstly to a successful assault on the new managerial group, partly spontaneous, partly provoked by the executive committee, which emerged as the new custodian of unchanged *gazdálkodó* interests. In the longer run, however, the reassertion of local power within the cooperative served only to strengthen the resolve of the outside administration to carry out major reform and to disarm the szakszövetkezet as a vehicle for the mass organisation and defence of peasant interests.

The crisis of 1977 developed in the following way. A foretaste was given in autumn 1976, when a meeting of the executive committee heard a report from the internal control committee, which had investigated the large losses recorded of *közös* sheep, and the semi-starved condition of most of the remainder. Responsibility was laid at the door of the chief agronomist. He listened passively that afternoon to the criticism from the executive committee, and was not seen in Tázlár again. A year later the szakszövetkezet was still unable to find a successor. In the meantime Font himself was criticised by certain members of the 12-man executive. They found a measure of support in the treasurer, who was believed to cherish personal ambitions of his own and, proudly responsible for the sacking of one chairman, was keen to claim another. He accordingly precipitated a crisis by asking to be relieved of his treasurer's responsibilities at the executive meeting on the eve of an open meeting in February 1977. This request was not granted and quietly pushed into the background in the following weeks.

It was, however, impossible to shelve the issues and the bitter taste left by the February open meeting. The discreet criticisms of the executive were now voiced loudly by the rank and file in the presence of the outside administration. There were angry personal attacks on the chairman, which cited, for example, the house he occupied at a low rent and the car he had ordered on behalf of the szakszövetkezet without due consultation with the executive committee. Other speakers attacked the new aggressive collectivising policies, particularly the confiscation of the important reed areas and the sale of the reeds to mechanised outside contractors. Similar strictly commercial criteria had led to the transfer of fishing rights to outside institutions, to the fury of the handful of local fishermen. All the criticisms were roundly answered by the visiting Party spokesman in the most general ideological terms. He finished his speech with great difficulty because of loud interruptions. Praise and full backing for Font came from Trsztyinszki the council chairman. However, when Font himself arose towards the end of the meeting to answer the attacks, he sounded a broken man. He apologised for his temperament, his nervousness and other character defects which had impeded his contact and harmony with the rank and file. Behind these euphemisms there was no retraction on any matter of principle or of current policy. Yet it seemed to many of the 400 present that Font had lost the will to continue as chairman.

In fact, despite strenuous efforts in the following weeks by outside officials to restore equilibrium and heal the dispute with the treasurer, his resignation was submitted to the outside administration and accepted in the following month. This followed the departure of the engineer, a long-expected move made largely for personal reasons, but which also added to the crisis in the leadership group. No replacement was found for him either, and after a two-month hiatus it was a local artisan and member of the executive committee who stepped in at the machine centre and did an admirable job in preparing the combine harvesters for the summer season. The final assessment of Font's reasons for resigning is difficult. He was a very complex, intelligent character.[1] Some were of the opinion that it was the long squabble with the treasurer that precipitated his departure. Others referred to his wife's desire to return to her native village some 30 miles away, which was where the family moved shortly afterwards. This became the version put about by the outside administration. It was true that the marriage had been under strain in Tázlár, that neither partner had found friends in the divided ranks of the local intelligentsia. Both regarded the community as unusually cold towards outsiders. These 'personal' factors are thus important, but it is the conjuncture of events which resulted from deliberate policies and the mass opposition of the peasantry that are of greater interest and must be included in any complete account of why he resigned when he did. The following is based on his own account.

Font believed himself by virtue of his background in a production co-operative to be unsuited to managing the szakszövetkezet as a non-socialist, non-collectivising amalgam of private interests. After the February open meeting he also felt he lacked the essential power resources to continue the attempt to reform. He drew this conclusion because of the attitude of those members of the executive committee who had acted as the self-interested representatives of wider private-peasant interests. The executive was composed of precisely those respected private farmers who had been dislodged from the very top in 1975. It is extraordinary to observe just how well the executive represented the cream of richer farmers today. For example, the average sum of produce sold through the cooperative between 1975 and 1977 by members of this committee was more than double that of the average for all the active members. This group, which had never before articulated policy opposition and even now was far from displaying a coherent united front, saw itself nevertheless as the representative of the private interests of the membership at large. The individual most persistent in his complaints was perhaps the man best placed to do so – the former chairman of one of the earlier cooperatives and a veteran Party member, but also a fisherman, whose family had lost substantially through the confiscation of the reeds. His dedication to the future of his own family farm and the private future of the membership at large proved to be his most fundamental loyalties. It could certainly not be local Party policy to criticise the reforms of Font. He was too widely admired in the outside Party on account of the sweeping changes that had taken place since he had taken office. However, despite the support given at the open meeting, it was suggested by other well-placed informants, and suspected by Font himself, that the solidarity of the council chairman was withdrawn in the weeks following that meeting.

It is worth considering the implications of this possibility. Could this be seen as a judicious concession to the strength of local opinion, as demonstrated at the open meeting? Although that was indeed the effect of his action, a more plausible explanation is one of self-interest. Font, a radical 'new broom' unwilling to make compromises in the old ways, was a power threat. The chairman, hitherto the dominant representative in the community of the outside Party, had reason himself to fear the commitment of an over-zealous communist at the head of the szakszövetkezet. He had preferred to deal with several leaders whose activity on the land prevented their threatening his monopoly in full-time administration. It had been his practice to dispose quickly of any threat, whether it emerged within the council bureaucracy, where the turnover of executive committee secretaries had been very high for exactly this reason, or in ancillary institutions, such as the school, where he had played an active role in the dismissal of Mr Kádár and his replacement by a more amenable headmistress, who is aware that her job depends in some measure on his support. It is possible that the chairman was actually approached by individuals or groups to further the conspiracy against Font. He was, for example, seen in frequent consultation with the treasurer, not himself a Party member. In any case many suspect that the chairman has a strong personal interest in preserving a vigorous private sector in agriculture, which would be always liable to need favours from the council and able to pay for them.

Whether or not the council chairman was directly involved, the resignation of Font became effective early in April, and from that time until the end of July the szakszövetkezet had no full-time chairman. A senior communist executive committee member took over on an interim basis, but effective control passed to the treasurer, who governed in the style of a garrison chief with a very small staff. A new agronomist arrived in May to take responsibility exclusively for the sheep, and, in addition to the artisan who took over the machine centre, another member of the executive was hired to assist the remaining household agronomist in the marketing of small-farm produce. Meanwhile, during the next few months the curious in the village would occasionally catch a glimpse of well-dressed strangers who arrived in State cars and paid visits to the cooperative offices and the chairman's empty house. At last in mid-July the members, who still knew nothing officially of the departure of Font, were summoned to an open meeting in the Culture House for the business of electing a new chairman. The candidate was József Pénzes, qualified agronomist, Party member, only seven years away from retirement and previously employed in a small enterprise in the district centre, Kiskőrös, and with large private farming interests in that area. Only members of the executive committee had met him before the open meeting. They had elected him a member of the szakszövetkezet the previous week, to establish his eligibility for the chairman's job. It was widely expected that there would be only one name on the ballot paper at the Sunday afternoon election. However, Pénzes was not accepted as readily as was hoped, and it is worth considering some of the questions asked at that meeting and the issues raised for the future of the szakszövetkezet by the flagrant abuse of its normal procedures through the will of the outside administration.

The fundamental problem was the reality of an election with only one name on the ballot paper. The frustration of the rank and file was intensified by the strict adherence to the formalities of democratic procedure. These included the ratification by the open meeting of a nomination committee, chaired by a member of the executive committee, which ceremonially withdrew and then returned with a carefully prepared speech recommending Pénzes. Several speakers then re-stated the opinions expressed in February and in addition criticised the electoral procedure. The most interesting moment came when an individual, searching for potential candidates in order to permit a choice to be made by the members, hit upon the names of the treasurer and the household agronomist. No local *gazdálkodó* candidate could establish eligibility because none possessed the new qualification of a formal higher education in agriculture. The treasurer and the agronomist were obliged publicly to decline nomination. Each asserted the need to preserve unity and a strong collective leadership. The agronomist stressed the essential point when he stated that if elected he would be powerless to further the interests of the cooperative outside the community, since only Pénzes had the full confidence of the outside administration. In other words, both managers and executive committee men were constrained to urge acceptance of the man presented to them by the outside administration. Members were told that it was now in their own interests to approve the decisions taken elsewhere because this was the way to elect the individual best able to represent their interests outside the community. The spokesmen for the Party and the council chairman restricted their contributions to a justification of the recruitment process, the careful sifting which they said had preceded their selection.

The next telling contribution was made by Pénzes himself. In a short speech he emphasised his peasant origins, his own private farming interests, his financial standing and current job security irrespective of whether he came to Tázlár. In the ballot which followed there were significant abstentions and a very few votes of opposition, but members were inhibited from scratching out the candidate's name by the presence of a district official next to the urn, who simply stared hard at anyone who moved away with his paper instead of dropping it straight into the urn. Moreover the 'polling booth' was not opened for much of the time, nor was any writing instrument supplied. In any case with only just over a third of the membership present, there was no way in which the required two-thirds percentage of votes could be obtained. However, the cars of the Kiskőrös officials appeared in the village several times during the week that followed. Membership lists were revised and large parts of the official minutes of the meeting were dictated by the same official who had supervised Sunday's polling.

That meeting broke up in good humour with the distribution of free beer. Pénzes took up his job in August in a generally neutral climate. In the treasurer's quarter, however, he was already seen as another Imre Bugyi, but lacking the latter's popularity. It is too soon to give any verdict on the Pénzes szakszövetkezet. The danger from the treasurer passed with his resignation after only a few months when he was replaced by an elderly lady from Soltvadkert who expressed her astonishment at the young expert's pecuniary management and general irresponsibility. The chairman continued to commute in the szakszövetkezet's car from Kiskőrös, which at least saved the expenses of a chauffeur, even though there were those who complained and suggested that the chairman could quite well use his private car for travelling to work each day. The former chairman's house has been occupied by a new young agronomist who was making valiant efforts to raise production in 1978, especially on the large areas of abandoned land which, as a result of government policy, he is now attempting to bring back into cultivation. Pénzes is going ahead with the same policies for full collectivisation as his predecessor, but he has also tried to reassure the members, and to muster support for a collaborative vineyard in which the members will invest and retain limited ownership rights while the szakszövetkezet will ensure that varieties of grape are optimally chosen, that the distance between the rows permits mechanised spraying etc.

It is clear that Pénzes has certain bargaining reserves *vis-à-vis* the outside administration, or at least some room in which to manoeuvre, as a direct consequence of the local hostility which was expressed in 1977. There was a general feeling that he was a 'last chance', that another failure could not be contemplated because the outside administration would never be able to find another man to take on the job. The executive and the szakszövetkezet officials had to work with Pénzes, given the preclusion of an internal *gazálkodó* solution. The mass of the members probably felt they had the next best thing to one of their own kind – physically, Pénzes somewhat resembled Bugyi and he was in most respects the opposite of Font. This was the balance of forces as it crystallised in 1977, and it is now up to Pénzes to negotiate a path between them, helped by the fact that no one wishes to provoke his early downfall.

A chronological exposition has been given as the best method of bringing out the great changes which have taken place since the formation of the first cooperatives 30 years ago. Three phases of the movement have been identified in Tázlár. The first, from 1949 until the establishment of the mass-member szakszövetkezet in 1960, includes the period of greatest authoritarian abuse in the national sphere. The cooperatives were small, almost familial in character, and in Tázlár at any rate the leaders were responsive to the needs of the members. These cooperatives received small subsidies and much ideological support from the State, but played no major part in enforcing external controls and did not unduly disturb local peasant opinion. Some of their land had formerly belonged to richer farmers, but they did not actively seek to expand and were indeed much too weak economically to undertake any embryonic collectivising role.

In the second phase, following mass collectivisation, the cooperative group, or szakszövetkezet as it was later called, became a doubly representative political institution. To an extent it represented the will of the State in the locality, but it also transmitted local peasant opinion to the outside administration through able, popular, freely chosen leaders. The szakszövetkezet remained too weak to fulfil the socio-economic role which the State intended for it, but not only the economic strength was lacking. The representation outwards and the self-managing attributes of the szakszövetkezet at first increased after the economic reform and reached a peak with the amalgamation of the early 1970s and the community-wide election of Imre Bugyi as chairman in 1974.

The third phase has been characterised by 'managerial' leadership and the active implementation for the first time of the commitment to collectivisation. The political function of the szakszövetkezet has now become one of negative protest, but it has survived in substance as well as in form. Control over policy has now been removed entirely from the rank and file and vested in an alien leadership largely drafted in by the outside administration. Yet in 1977 the strength of the protests became too much for the first wave of the new managers. There was no sign in the resolution of that crisis of any fundamental concessions being made by the outside administration. Given national policies and the extent to which Tázlár already lags behind other communities in the region, this is hardly possible. It seemed to the farmers that the szakszövetkezet had at last confirmed its anti-peasant intentions. And it might have seemed to an observer that not only had Tázlár been obliged to conform on the issue of collectivisation but that the emergent political role of the szakszövetkezet in the community was being transmuted to conform to general local government practice. Yet so long as the open meeting persists as a forum the new leaders and the outside administration cannot help but take note of mass opinion – and if they should attempt to ignore it, there is the szakszövetkezet executive with which they must maintain working relations. Even if mass opinion is no longer able to influence any actual decision field, it may still exercise a delaying effect upon all fields, and the possibility of further crises such as that of 1977 cannot be excluded.

If we try once again to see Tázlár in the national context we must first note that collectivisation did not in general disturb the established relations of power within the rural community or its relation to higher levels of administration. In contrast to the szakszövetkezet communities, the higher rate of migration out of agriculture, the earlier substitution of managerial leadership (even if not always in the position of chairman), and the organisation of Party groups within the cooperative were just three factors which facilitated the incorporation of the production cooperative into the local polity. Mass-membership was not a danger if members never regarded the cooperative as a potential arena for the expression of interests which might be antagonistic to those of Party and State. Personal interests could be taken up in other quarters, such as the council, as in szakszövetkezet communities. In practice, *group* interests are not articulated. 'The public, theoretically plugged into the control and information channel, . . . realises its subordinate status and uses this vehicle for the promotion of individual interest. It does not criticise nor check the bureaucracy, but it begs for personal favours' (Piekalkiewicz, 1975, p. 210).

Tázlár followed a different path. The peasant landholdings which were not collectivised in 1960 survived to become both the material and symbolic basis of private interests. In 15 years during which there was no attempt to implant an alien leadership or an active policy of collectivisation the szakszövetkezets emerged as the unifying mass-based representative organs of the traditional independent peasantry. They were not a substitute for political parties, which had at no time organised successfully amongst the scattered tanya peasantry. In the last resort membership was obligatory and self-management an illusion. Behind the local leaders the Tázlár farmers generally perceived the encroaching agents of an anti-peasant State. Nevertheless, over a sufficiently long period the szakszövetkezet proved compatible with the pursuit of private farming interests. In 1974 it generated massive participation in a non-sectarian, non-ideological electoral contest. A few years later it seemed that this unusually 'open' experiment in gradualist transition to full collectivisation had been abandoned. Despite the protests of the members against the aggressive new tactics of the first leaders they had not freely elected (1975), and later against the abuse of the democratic character of the szakszövetkezet in the appointment of new leaders (1977), the traditional pattern of State-community relations in Hungary was reaffirmed. Democratic-centralism proved unable to assimilate the democratic szakszövetkezet. Some have tended to argue (e.g. Pusic (1975) for the case of Yugoslavia) that socialist states may be able to cope better with interest-group confrontations at grass-roots level and afford more local independence when they reach a higher stage of socio-economic development, or, in other words, when the crucial issue of collectivisation has been settled and the distinctive interests of the landholding peasantry have vanished from the scene. In Tázlár it is possible (and will be considered again in the next chapter) that within the landholding peasantry the benefits of the szakszövetkezet were far from equally distributed, and on these grounds alone one may wish to approve of its suppression. However, the evidence of the more 'developed' communities in Hungary today is not encouraging. In the end the full costs of the events of 1977 in Tázlár must include a certain moral damage caused by the July open meeting which ratified the choice of Pénzes, and this may never be understood by the outside administration.

The szakszövetkezet community – society

The sociology of the szakszövetkezet community is decisively influenced by two aspects already covered – on the one hand by the limited integration of small-farms into the szakszövetkezet, and on the other by the inability of the szakszövetkezet to develop its representative functions and of any other group or organisation to assume the tasks of political and social integration. In spite of great changes in family size and household structure, in the differentiation of groups and in the system of values and norms, there is still much continuity with the tanya past. In particular, no new social structure has yet been generated by the changes we have seen in the occupational structure, and the continued vigour of small-farming has preserved certain features of the old social hierarchy. Recently, in the period of 'market socialism', individualist attitudes and values seem to have maintained pre-eminence. At the same time, specific social problems, such as the integration of the new intelligentsia, the improvement of the conditions of minority groups, of the deviant and aged, remain unsolved.

In their own analyses of culture, family life and 'normative structure', some Hungarian sociographers and ethnographers have been unable to refrain from stating strong personal opinions about the phenomena observed. In the case of the sociographers a commitment to certain values and a didactic approach to writing are easy to defend and have brought impressive literary and political achievements in the twentieth century. It is less clear why an ethnographer such as Zsigmond (1978, p. 169), at the end of a discussion of family types in the village of Varsány, judges it necessary to denigrate village architecture and to criticise village families from a privileged urban standpoint. If the reader thinks that subjectivism has been pushed far enough in earlier chapters of this book, he may be reassured that no blanket 'objectivist' models will be imposed here, least of all in the discussion of stratification. At the same time it is hoped that the pervasive influence of the szakszövetkezet will be clear, especially in the final section on values and norms.

I Family and household

It is common to begin the analysis of household structure with more or less adequately documented reference to a large traditional household which contained more than two generations and often enough more than one family. In the case of Hungary it has been shown that there was considerable regional variation in the incidence of complex households at the end of the eighteenth and beginning of the nineteenth centuries (Andorka and Faragó, n.d.). The conditions which prevailed on the sparsely populated 'frontier' regions of the Great Plain, the only large region where land was not scarce even at the end of the nineteenth century, give credence to the common ideal-type in the case of Tázlár. Andorka and Faragó argue that the complex family was not necessarily an ancient phenomenon but became common amongst serf-peasants, especially the better-off peasants with substantial land resources, because in communities remote from markets and biased towards subsistence production complex households permitted a more efficient division of labour. In Tázlár in the period of mass resettlement, given the virtual absence of any housing stock, household size was large; it was, however, usual in the late nineteenth century for sons to leave their parents within a few years of marriage and build new dwellings on land made available by the parents (but not always inherited until after the death of the father). In 1892 a total population of 2,021 persons inhabited only 246 dwellings.

Average family size began to decline in most groups, except the poorest and the landless, before the war, under the influence of adverse economic conditions and the diminishing availability of land. However, the most substantial contraction occurred in the 1950s and 1960s, in association with high rates of outmigration, the appropriation of the substantial land resources of many traditional farms, and very low, almost negative, rates of natural increase in the national context. The rate of natural increase has remained low nationally in the 1970s, and there has been a steady decline in the proportion of economically productive age-groups. The marriage rate has remained stable but the average age of marriage has fallen for both males and females in the socialist period (to 21 for females and 24 for males in 1972). Fertility is considerably higher in villages than in provincial towns or Budapest.

The average household in Tázlár today contains 2.99 persons and the average age of its head is about 55 years. The total numbers of males and females are almost equal, but at any time a larger number of males are resident outside the community in workers' hostels, or in further education, or in the army. Following Laslett's typology of households (1972, p. 31), in 1976–7 almost two-thirds of Tázlár households could be classified as 'simple family households', i.e. as households which contained a married couple alone, parents with their children, or a widowed parent plus children. The next-largest group is that of solitaries – over 100 households altogether including 59 widows or widowers. The most common type of extended family household is the 'upwards' extension, i.e. where the family is supplemented by one or more elder relatives. The number of households which contained more than one family ('multiple family households') was 32. Of these, 23 had a 'secondary unit downwards': in most cases these secondary units would in due course build new houses and become 'simple family households'.

There are some striking differences between the village and the tanyas. The tanya population is older: in the case of the head of the household by an average of three years. The simple family household dominates everywhere, but while the majority of 'married couples with children' are found in the main village the majority of 'married couples alone' reside on tanyas. In the village the average age of household heads is boosted by the large number of widows and widowers who live alone (36, compared to 23 on tanyas). Yet the total number of solitaries is much greater on tanyas (65, compared to 39 in the village) owing to the larger number of single persons and a few cases of nominal tanya residence where the individual now has his principal residence elsewhere. Only 8 multiple family households are found on tanyas, compared to 15 in the village. Because of a small number of very large households, including a few which occupy State Farm-owned accommodation, mean tanya household population is only slightly below the village and community mean.

The general pattern shows that a high proportion of families in Tázlár realise what seems to be the 'ideal family-type' in the national context (cf. Zsigmond, 1978, pp. 155–6). This is commonly said to be based on the urban family. The family is small, attaches high value to the occupancy of independent accommodation (and its material amelioration) and to the achievement of full independence from the authority and influence of the older generation at or as soon as possible after marriage.

Marriage choice has long been effectively 'individualised', i.e. determined by the couple involved and not substantially influenced by their families. There were, nevertheless, many cases in the pre-war period when differences in religious belief led to serious friction within families and even disinheritance. There were also many examples of marriages where property interests were carefully calculated by both generations, e.g. when a stepson married his cousin and a large property was saved from division. The marriage of genetic first cousins was discouraged, and though there were cases when romantic attractions led to the breaking of this rule such 'individualism' was sternly rebuked.

In recent years the proportion of intra-community marriages has remained high in Tázlár even amongst those who have not resided in the community full-time after the completion of the general school. The young couple have the final say in most matters, in contrast to the village examined by Zsigmond where important issues, such as the timing and location of house-building, are still said to be subject to parental interference. In Tázlár the price of building plots in the village still encourages young men to accept the parents' offer to divide their own plot and to share a common yard and outbuildings. Where there is significant status difference between the marrying partners the richer family may lay down conditions in return for their larger endowment. There is little respect for the son-in-law who is obliged to reside with or beside his wife's parents and does not make strenuous efforts to begin independent house-building.

The older generation may be puzzled and hurt at the refusal of the new couple to build in the immediate vicinity of the old home (on either the male or the female side). Some couples prefer to move to the new streets being built on the northern side of the main road. Yet at the time of marriage and throughout the years of house-building (which frequently dominates the early years of the marriage), the new couple are dependent upon substantial material support from their families. The inheritance of land has lost its overriding importance, but the transfer of other goods, and above all of cash, is essential to the establishment of the new family. If neither family is willing to cooperate to fund a substantial *lakodalom* on the occasion of the wedding the financial penalty to the new couple is immense. In this way certain powers and moral rights are established by the older generation.

The modern *lakodalom* exceeds the bounds not only of the modern family but of the traditional kin group as well. It is commonplace nowadays for 400 or 500 persons to be invited. In addition to neighbours and kin on both sides there is an indeterminate number of friends and acquaintances who will be flattered by an invitation, overwhelmed by the hospitality on the day, and obliged to contribute heavily to the fund for the new couple. The preparations, by the family with the assistance of many friends and neighbours, take several days. The festivities themselves invariably continue until the following morning. But the central moment comes late in the evening, following a large supper, when the dancing and the good humour is at its zenith. The 'bride's dance' is an opportunity for all guests to dance a few steps with the bride. The steps completed, a donation is made, on behalf of the guest's family, to the couple's future prosperity. (In the case of kin and close friends substantial presents may be given instead of, or as well as, money: such presents are generally major household durables.) Then silence is demanded and it is usually the bride herself who announces the sum that has been raised and thanks the revellers. Later the women will discuss whether the outcome was better or worse than expected, and the whole wedding will be remembered by the quantity of cash grossed. In Tázlár a *lakodalom* with 400 guests might raise over 50,000 forints in cash and bring in the furniture for one or two rooms in the new house, kitchen equipment and, inevitably, a television set. Depending on their means the parents may also make separate gifts: in rich communities such as Soltvadkert it is common to give a car or a very substantial sum towards the house.

The couple's dependence upon their immediate families and upon a range of close friends continues during the period of their house-building. None of the problems of the developmental process of the family, the sociology of work and leisure, status differentiation and the system of norms and values can be understood without a knowledge of the working of the private housing market.

The housing stock in Tázlár is being continually improved, yet despite the growth of the village centre in the socialist period and the abandonment of many tanyas, at the last detailed survey in 1970 more than three-quarters of all houses had been built before 1944. In the district as a whole 21 per cent of housing was nineteenth-century and 44.5 per cent had been erected between 1900 and 1944. The comparable figures for Tázlár were 8.7 per cent and 67.1 per cent. Only 35 per cent of houses had been connected to the electricity supply in 1970, 9 per cent had bathrooms and fewer than 3 per cent had modern flush toilets. The statistics also show that each house contained only 1.38 rooms, but that each room was occupied by almost two persons.

The great majority of housing in the village is privately owned (although in recent years the council has bought certain buildings when an individual's death occasioned a sale, and the szakszövetkezet too has a number of houses which it puts at the disposal of leaders recruited outside the community). There is a basic difference between the countryside and the larger towns in the general means of obtaining housing. The major builders in towns are councils and cooperative associations, and the main problem is how to qualify for such housing, which is in very short supply but not distributed at 'market prices'. In some rural communities local councils have taken similar initiatives and younger couples in certain categories of employment have been able to benefit from cheap housing, but this has never taken place in Tázlár. There has therefore been an obligation to build privately. The national savings bank offers substantial long-term loans to all first-time builders, at very low interest rates, but these loans

11. House-building

are not sufficient today to cover even half of the cost of the materials required for a small family house. Only a few exceptional loans to individuals in special categories of employment, such as teachers or civil servants, come anywhere near to covering the costs of materials alone.

Because of the considerable sums involved it may take several years before the new couple can tackle the job. The plot might be bought in the first year, the bricks ordered in the second, the foundations put down in the third, etc. Then, in one concentrated summer season, the family will try to build the entire main dwelling. Moving-in may be further postponed while outhouses and extensions are added, and new houses usually must wait years before finances permit the luxury of a final exterior plastering. During the summer of the most concentrated work there are numerous occasions when, in addition to the small band of the hired builder, the future owner must raise large workbands from amongst his own kin and friends. From the laying of the foundations to the packing of mud for the insulation of the roof he is grateful for all the help he can get. Such informal cooperation has become extremely widespread with the recent growth of the main village. Some older people allege that it is quite without precedent in the tanya community where building was the task of the simple family household plus any number of hired specialists. It is said that the village doctor was the first to call together such a large band of 'volunteers' for collective labour at weekends. In fact, given the size of the building bands, the nature of certain tasks is such that they could scarcely be performed in any other way, except at extraordinary expense through hiring day-labourers. The kin group is unlikely to be large enough or susceptible to regular and intensive mobilisation.

Private house-building relies therefore upon a collective labour system, and is the only such occasion for significant cooperation in 'private sector' activity. In return for ample food and drink the house-builder is given command temporarily over large resources of labour. He is then, of course, bound to reciprocate this service when invited by other house-builders, and for some years after his house is completed he can be obliged to sacrifice many of his summer weekends in assisting those who once extended their assistance to him. These are very demanding years for most couples. Children are not usually postponed more than a few years and indeed are commonly born while the couple is still living in rented accommodation or with one set of parents. Whatever the occupations of the couple, there is very likely to be some small-farming, to help cover the escalating costs of building and to furnish the new house. It is rare for the people of Tázlár to take honeymoons or any substantial trips away from the community at this time: in the summer any holiday entitlement is fully used up by the demands of the house or of work on the land.

The importance of the family as a production unit was emphasised in Chapter 4, particularly in the section on the integration of small-farming. After the initial years of marriage, when heavy burdens are shouldered by both partners, it is common, especially in worker-peasant households, for an increasing proportion of the labour burden to be shifted on to the wife. It is she who is responsible not only for the house and the animal-breeding, but also frequently for the landholdings still associated with the farm. Even if she too had a full-time job at the time of the marriage, more work devolves on her in the agricultural sphere in the years when she is at home receiving the child-care allowances. If she returns to work, the agricultural jobs remain hers in the first instance. The consequences are more severe if her husband is a long-distance commuter. He, meanwhile, commonly reaches a stage where the pressures to reciprocate labour services are reduced (more men of his age having completed their houses), and where he is not necessarily sympathetic to his wife's demands to improve the interior decoration and comfort of the home.[1]

It has been argued that the main consequences of the division of labour within the family are more deleterious for women than for men in other Hungarian communities, where the men have almost all been drawn into public, wage-labour employment and where, as a result, small-farming has been most thoroughly feminised. The strains upon women in the traditional farm enterprise were not negligible but they have certainly increased in recent years. In Tázlár too, as in Varsány (cf. E. Kovács, 1978, pp. 188–9), many women complain about the short-time available for their housework. Families do not eat together regularly and parents do not go out together socially in the village except on rare occasions when special parties are held in the *bisztró* or culture-house. There is a high incidence of nervous disease amongst women, and of other illnesses which can be brought on by overwork, including alcoholism. The rate of divorce or of irretrievable breakdown of marriages does not appear to be much higher than in the past, but this may be partly attributable to the extent of the joint investment in property and the daunting task of repeating this accomplishment in a second marriage.

It should be pointed out that some of these problems are experienced on a lesser scale in the szakszövetkezet community where the 'full-time farms' still outnumber the 'worker-peasant farms', although the latter are gaining in strength all the time and dominate amongst the young. The alternative to the 'worker-peasant' strategy of 'mixed' households, which is that most typical of the young couples who have built in the community in the 1970s, is less attractive in the longer term. The increase in mixed households proves that there is no absolute commitment to private farming and ensures that the szakszövetkezet community does not become an isolated pocket in the nation, a prosperous pocket today admittedly, but a potential rural backwater tomorrow.

Within the present framework the role and the situation of women are in any case, eased by a number of factors which have not yet been considered. Firstly, there is the assistance frequently provided by the family on either side which enables the young mother to leave her children with elder family members while she herself performs some productive task. Such child-minding is an important consideration which often influences the newly-married couple to build in the vicinity of elderly kin (not necessarily parents).

Secondly, the labour contribution of older children themselves still deserves to be taken into account, particularly in full-time farm families resident on tanyas. Children may be seen as a significant 'economic cost' by parents today. In 1977 only seven households in the entire community had more than three children under 16 (29 had three, 99 had two, and 119 had only one). It is also true that, as most children are absent from the community after the age of 16, in further education or in some urban employment, children may contribute less to the farm than in the past, and that parents, or the mother alone, are thereby forced to allocate more of their time to tasks formerly performed by the entire family. Yet all children, including those studying outside the community or those already with urban jobs, form part of the family labour unit at peak periods, while the children living at home are brought up to help out regularly in the yard, to run errands, etc.

Women have also benefited from new opportunities and national legislation in the socialist period. The introduction of the child-care allowances had its desired effect in raising the birthrate from the low levels to which it had fallen in the 1960s. In association with improved pre- and post-natal care at the village surgery, it also induced important changes in the attitudes of families towards bringing up children, including the attitudes of older 'full-time farm' families who did not benefit directly from the allowances. A certain solidarity and tempered competitiveness has developed amongst young mothers, who dress themselves and their babies in best holiday attire for summer walks around the village pushing modern prams. The general acceptability of shopping at the self-service shop, the purchase of canned and conserved foods and of fresh meat at the butchers, has simplified the woman's work in the kitchen, though it remains true that even younger households strive to make the maximum use of private gardens and set aside large quantities of home-made fruit and vegetable preserves every summer. Women benefit also from the existence of the nursery school, which may take children as young as three. Those who return to work later are helped in so doing by the provision of a school-meals service at the general school. Some schoolchildren have virtually no breakfast at home but go out to the shop for bread rolls during the school break, eat lunch at school, and then go directly to the shop again for sweets or ice-cream in the afternoon when school has finished.

Sociologists have naturally associated the demise of peasant economy in socialist nations with an increase in the importance of the consumption functions of the family, at the expense of its former role in production. The effect of incorporation into a production cooperative removes the need for economic cooperation between households and the social security system of the modern state means that: 'Contemporary rural families are nowhere near as totally dependent on their neighbours as they were in the past' (Hegedűs, 1977, p. 168). It may be doubted whether this dependence was in fact very great in the past in the case of the tanya community. The szakszövetkezet community of recent decades has continued to rely upon the productive effort of the family but, as we have seen, the links between households are but feebly developed in agricultural production and informal cooperation is limited in modern 'mixed' households to the process of house-building. The simple family household is both the ideal and the dominant reality of household structure in Tázlár today, but the reduced size of the family, the weakening of kin ties by migration, the importance of individual family housing, and the intensity of labour commitment required to finance it, all combine to make the isolation of the modern family comparable to the isolation of the tanya family of old. As András Hegedűs notes at the end of his chapter discussing the family, there are as many suicides and psychiatric cases in Hungarian villages today as there are in towns (1977, p. 178).

II Differentiation and stratification

One general problem in the analysis of group differentiation and stratification in peasant communities has been that no matter how variegated and heterogeneous the community, it may still seem to display a certain unity and homogeneity in any larger context. It was shown in Chapter 2 that Tázlár was a 'community' in only a loose, administrative sense before the Second World War and one that was subject to wide class divisions consequent upon the penetration of capitalism. Great improvements in communications since the war and the changes in the occupational structure associated with the rise of the worker-peasantry have brought Tázlár into ever closer contact with the national society. At the same time, Land Reform, the anti-*kulák* levelling of the 1950s and eventual loose integration of virtually all farmers into the szakszövetkezet have destroyed the foundations of the traditional system of stratification, which even in the ecological conditions of Tázlár had been based primarily upon the quantity of land owned by the family. Yet even now essential differences between town and countryside (e.g. in housing conditions) make some sociological concepts that are valid at the national level quite inapplicable to rural communities. The concern of this section is only with Tázlár, where co-operative integration has been of a 'vertical' type, and this in itself creates a quite different situation from the 'horizontal' consolidation of small farms achieved by the production cooperative, and more typical of villages in the national context.

It has been shown by Yoon in a study of Provençal wine cooperatives that in the context of capitalist markets vertical cooperation accentuates class distinctions in the rural community (Yoon, 1975, p. 76). The relaxation of political pressure on small-farmers in Tázlár after 1956 and the ever greater incentives offered to small-farmers in the szakszövetkezet period have resulted in comparable phenomena in a context of socialist markets. In spite of the rise in the number of worker-peasant households and greater uniformity in living styles amongst younger households in the community today, small-farming has remained the major economic activity and full-time farm households still constitute the 'backbone' of the community. The wide variation in the incomes derived from small-farming was documented in Chapter 4 and attempts to account for this in terms of demographic variables and in terms of key differences between full-time farms and worker-peasant farms were only partially successful. The higher incomes of many regular commodity-producing worker-peasant households depend upon one or more members remaining full-time in agriculture and are partly attributable to the larger mean population of these households compared with those of full-time farms. The latter are able to generate very high incomes not only through drawing upon the supplies and services of the szakszövetkezet and perhaps through cooperating with fellow full-time farmers, but also through a revived use of traditional labour-hiring (see Chapter 4, pp. 88–9).

There is a continuity here with the pre-war pattern of stratification. Most of the larger hirers of labour today are farmers in their fifties and sixties who belong to the traditional middle and well-to-do families of the community. A few of them were once branded as *kulaks* in the 1950s. Some have seen their sons and daughters through advanced schooling and have encouraged them to settle in remote towns. Many have accepted the fact that their farms will have no successor, but strive in the mean-time to accumulate the largest possible nest-egg for their families and for themselves before retirement. Some have built new houses in the village in late middle-age, others have returned to the family home in Soltvadkert from where the family migrated two or three generations previously. Some of them retain great pride in their family's pioneering exploits and high status in the pre-war community. One or two families (including that of Lajos Égető, the most dynamic small-farm producer in the community today) are able to claim descent from the lower nobility in the regions from which they originated.

Even in villages characterised by production cooperatives, this stratum of 'middle peasants' retained its identity over a long period (cf. Juhász, 1975). They did not perform the same jobs in the cooperative as other members, and they were always more likely to see their children through further education; a few underwent a 'sea change' and became Party members and leaders of the new community in the council or the co-operative. In Tázlár the persistence of this differentiation is stronger, and it is still associated with the ownership of property and of the means of production. Because this differentiation has persisted without a break (even in the 1950s when some of this stratum were obstinate and refused to flinch under political pressure), and because the mass of farmers have never worked alongside each other in any form of collective labour system, there remains a stratum of 'prosperous' (*jómódú*) families whose higher status is beyond question within the farming population.

This is not to deny that great socio-economic mobility has characterised the entire post-war period. A few 'middle-peasant' families abandoned agriculture in the 1950s. Some have only reached the ranks of the 'prosperous' in recent years, starting from lowly positions on the pre-war hierarchy. Yet such upward mobility has not been easy: the mere achievement of high farm incomes through heavy purchasing of the szakszövetkezet is insufficient to establish a family at a higher place on the social scale. On the other hand, differentiation with respect to the ownership and control of the means of production remains important in a number of ways. Firstly, there is land itself. Although the traditional prosperous families have all ceded or otherwise abandoned a large acreage, the small areas they still control tend to be of a very high quality. More especially, the ownership of vineyards and orchards is a durable source of wealth with which the government has yet to interfere, and it may be stressed again that it is in this branch that labour-hiring and 'class differentiation' is most conspicuous. We have already seen in Chapter 4 that the ownership of machines enables some small-farmers not only to save labour on their own farms but to extract rents from their neighbours. There are considerable economies of scale within small-farming, and though the capital requirements to establish a farm are very small and the assistance of the szakszövetkezet is extended to all, it is those who have some capital in building, land and vineyards that are best placed to profit from szakszövetkezet services. Indeed, the rich can become richer through looking beyond the local szakszövetkezet. For example, some have sold their wine elsewhere, or purchased root crops for use in pig-fattening in black-soil villages to the south. These are opportunities which only a few rich 'maximisers' are able to exploit.

The perceptions and judgements of the farming population still dominate in the community. Even the basic yardstick of class and social status in the old system, the ownership of land, has not been as effectively eroded as in villages which formed production cooperatives. This has to some extent held back the emergence of differentiated groups within the 'worker-peasant' households. The latter are by no means regarded as a homogeneous group. Yet the differences between families where the adults are skilled workers who commute to local towns, and those where all family members are labourers with the State Farm, are not so great as might be supposed. Younger persons may perceive a status difference more clearly here, and they may have a greater valuation of comfort and satisfaction during work. The differences in incomes in the public sector are small. In the eyes of many older farmers it is a tragedy that so many smallholders have freely exchanged farming for unskilled wage-labour, and there is bitter sympathy for the small number of traditionally prosperous farmers who have been forced to abandon farming (e.g. through the expansion of the State Farm). However, most farmers now encourage their sons to obtain skilled-worker qualifications. The blanket stigma against wage-labour will continue to weaken and finally it will disappear. Given the current wage-structure, however, and the relatively small spread of income differentials, it may be a very long time before the new occupational structure can be associated with a well-defined status hierarchy. Until then the most important general determinant of social rank will continue to be related to small-farming, not only to the resources and the production of the enterprise today but also to what the family represented in previous decades.

This implies that the impact of new elements in the socialist period has been small. It was suggested in Chapter 5 that the liquidation of the genuine collective farms and their replacement by mass-member szakszövetkezets at the time of mass collectivisation may have influenced the failure of a class of careerist officials to emerge within Tázlár through the Communist Party and to exert its influence through the leadership of the council and the cooperative. Instead the upper levels of the 'intelligentsia' (*értelmiség*) in Tázlár have had to be recruited from outside. The council chairman and the chief secretary at the council offices have long been appointed from Kiskőrös. Since the fall of Imre Bugyi after the unification of the szakszövetkezets the same has been true at the cooperative. A high proportion of the teaching staff are also strangers not just to the community but to the region, and many stay only a few years in Tázlár. The priests may stay for a longer period but eventually they too move on. The provision of housing at a low rent for most of these representatives of the intelligentsia means that there is no incentive for them to build and settle in the village. Building is in any case no easy task for those on fixed incomes with little opportunity or experience in small-farming, although the doctor and several long-serving teachers with no links with the land did built private houses in the 1970s. Teachers' salaries were exceptionally low before 1976, and even afterwards their average level in Tázlár is boosted to respectability only by heavy overtime working.

The incomes of the intelligentsia are low primarily in comparison with those commanded by the most entrepreneurial small-farmers. They are not low in an urban context, and when bonuses and holidays are taken into account their lot is not a hard one. Nevertheless, a few intellectuals resent the material rewards available elsewhere. There is no idealisation of the life-style of the few 'fully intellectual' households which are not active in farming, and sometimes a rueful cynicism is expressed when such households seek means to supplement their fixed incomes, as when the council chairman proposes a price for administrative services which will benefit an individual, or the teachers sponsor dancing parties at the culture-house, or the 'landlord' of the *bisztró* organises all-ticket social evenings. The leaders of the community today do not command the respect that previous leaders commanded. The single young policeman is not respected as was the large local gendarmerie in the past, but he is preferred to his immediate predecessors who were dismissed for various misdemeanours. Corruption is suspected wherever money is handled and sadly at the szakszövetkezet and elsewhere in recent years suspicions have been amply confirmed.

It is possibly the knowledge that they do not command the respect which they feel they merit that contributes to the ill-will and quarrelling that

have persisted within the intelligentsia, and even within the staff-room
at the school. With the exception of the priests and a few of the teachers
they are not admired for their intellectual qualities, and few of the brighter
young people of the community would aspire to occupy their jobs. Officials
are granted a certain deference primarily in official places, especially by
older tanya farmers whose gratitude shown for any petty favour is sometimes grossly exaggerated. Outside these places they are subject to the
same kind of gossip as everyone else. The status of the director of the
spinning factory does not protect him against criticism of alleged romantic
involvement with younger employees (though his status as the boss may well
help in launching an affair). The only place where the 'intelligentsia' hangs
together well is when the doctor and his cronies organise informal football
matches during the summer and adjourn to the *bisztró* afterwards: yet
even on the football field the intellectuals sometimes appear as a 'foreign
body' in the village. They commonly play challenge matches against a
similar scratch team from Soltvadkert but are not always so keen to compete against other teams formed within Tázlár.

There is thus a general problem in integrating the new intelligentsia,
and part of the problem has been caused by the szakszövetkezet and by
the relatively small number of white-collar workers resident in the community. Of the 43 households containing such workers in 1977, 32 contained only one white-collar worker and many of these maintained some
commodity production in agriculture. So did several of the 11 households
which contained two white-collar workers. The locally resident intelligentsia is therefore still in close contact with the land. Although those
who come from outside may be uneasily accepted, and although white-
collar work does have a higher status in the eyes of some younger persons,
the intelligentsia is not therefore a distinct group or class in the community.[2] On the contrary, the growing number of 'mixed' marriages,
where one partner is a skilled manual worker and the other a teacher or
administrator, should be accounted a healthy development in the breakdown of the hegemony of occupations associated with small-farming.

A comparable problem of integration is posed by elements in the
modern community which in the terminology of Kunszabó (1970, p. 1302)
can be classified 'distressed'. Not much more than half of the total number
of households could be classified as regular small-commodity producers
between 1975 and 1977. Even after we have added the small number of
all-white-collar households, those pensioner households to which, in
addition to State benefits, family and neighbours extend regular assistance,
and the small numbers of homogeneous worker households, there remains
a substantial proportion who live at or very near the poverty line in certain
seasons, and where even basic subsistence needs are frequently not met.

Many of the households in this group consist of old persons unable to
take care of themselves adequately and sometimes, following migration,
without family in the community. There are also a number of cases of
subnormality, where able-bodied individuals live alone in the most squalid

tanya conditions. In the winter, when there is no *napszám* work available, they lead a beggar-like existence and obtain occasional food and warmth at the houses of their kin. The tanya of József Szőke is pictured in Plate 12: the outer door was removed and burnt as firewood in 1977. He walks barefoot throughout the year. The *napszám* population is of course recruited not only from amongst the subnormal. Alcoholism is also very common in outlying tanya areas. Addiction usually renders a man (and, less frequently, a woman) incapable of paying regular attention to his own farm, condemns him to seasonal labour on the farms of his neighbours and often to winters of frozen misery.

The major role in public assistance is performed by the council through one clerical employee at the council offices. Apart from the small numbers who obtain regular assistance, mainly aged widows, fourteen persons benefited from a special hardship allowance in 1977, awarded specifically to alleviate winter fuel shortage. Various other benefits and allowances may be awarded if eligibility can be proven. About a dozen persons received a special allowance for the blind. Aid may be given to ease the expenses of a funeral. Special assistance is available for the mothers of large families, but this has not been claimed in recent years in Tázlár. There were, however, in 1978 an estimated 21 children (under the age of 18) living in conditions classified as prejudicial to their well-being, either because of the quality of the housing or, in the majority of cases, 'because of the parents' alcoholism and improper conduct'. A further 14 Tázlár children had been removed from their families and placed in State care, normally with foster-parents in other communities. Such action is taken only as a last resort after parents have received several warnings. It is not council policy to offer regular aid to such families, because there is no guaranteeing the purposes to which the money would be put. Instead children are likely to have winter clothing bought for them directly.

The council administrators have done their best to deal with the causes of the problems, but there is little they can do apart from keeping households where women and children are in danger under some surveillance. They rely for information upon the goodwill, or possibly the malice, of neighbours. They can recommend the prolonged treatment of chronic alcoholism in detoxification centres, but very few persons have received such treatment and the administrators say that the 'cure' never survives the return to the community.

The administrators also have the power to recommend the admission of certain old persons to special homes, and of the subnormal to various institutions. The lack of places is a constraint upon the numbers accepted, and in any case even those utterly incapable of looking after themselves generally prefer to continue in Tázlár with a little help from the council rather than enter a home.

Not surprisingly, because of the age structure of the population and the migration of the young, it is the care of old persons which poses the greatest problems for public welfare administrators in Tázlár today. It

12. The tanya of József Szőke, in the fourth zone

was estimated that 28 individuals over the age of 60 needed public assistance in 1978. Nineteen of them lived on tanyas. The total number of persons over the age of 60 was 550 (out of a total community population not far in excess of 2,000). More than 300 of them live on tanyas, where the men slightly outnumber the women, while in the village there are 141 females to only 98 males. The administrators made a special investigation into their conditions in 1978 but took no specific action apart from criticising negligence within certain families. The names of those suffering the greatest hardship, in a typically fatuous gesture, were passed to the local branch of the Red Cross: fatuous, because this organisation has a formal existence only. In the past, though it cannot be said with certainty that families accepted much responsibility for their neighbours, all strata did offer greater security to old persons than they do today. Landholdings were commonly transferred only at the death of the household head. Today old persons are often forced to fend for themselves long after the age where their own parents would have abandoned manual work, and individuals in late middle-age expand their farmwork instead of contracting it, in order to guarantee with cash the security that the modern family and State combined do not provide.

The earlier cooperatives had a genuine 'welfare' role and even the szakszövetkezets in the 1960s made a range of special payments to members unable to sustain themselves, and organised communal parties and even summer picnics by the lakes. The new szakszövetkezet is too large and, committees notwithstanding, has played no active welfare role: for old persons in 1977 it sponsored one sparsely attended tea-party at the culture house, costing rather less than the leaders' entertainments allowances. It is difficult to blame the council administrators, who do their job conscientiously. Special praise should be given to certain members of the school staff, who liaise with the council in monitoring the conditions of certain children, and in general make brave attempts to compensate for adverse conditions in the home that no public agency has come forward to improve.

There is one 'marginal' group which even the teachers have failed to help, the only group to be denied support by the council administrators after specially applying for it in 1977. These are the three gypsy households in the main village. In fact there are two families and both of them are recent arrivals to Tázlár. The exact size of the households is difficult to estimate because in one there are a great many children and, at certain times of the year, a fairly constant stream of relatives and in-laws from outside. The two families are not treated in exactly the same way, for one, it is admitted, works much more steadily than the other, 'almost as if they were Hungarians'. In the other, the house and personal appearance and hygiene are neglected, the younger members work irregularly as casual labourers, and there is occasional involvement outside the community in traditional low-status gypsy activities, including horse-dealing. Hungarians constantly assert that this family steals, and that gypsies in general steal. Many refuse to employ them as *napszámos* (day-labourers) no matter how severe the labour shortage. In the school, talents that would be carefully nurtured in a Hungarian child are wasted. Teachers claim that they can do nothing because of the home background, but, perhaps understandably, they do not always take the proper action when gypsy children fail to report for school. At the council offices, assistance has been extended on occasion in the past but was refused in 1977 on the grounds that the family concerned had some land in its name (and actually fattened one pig that year). They were told to work their land decently for a living, and lost a further appeal against the administrators' decision.

In the past there were other small groups which stood out conspicuously in this predominantly Hungarian community. Comments of a racialist kind could be (and occasionally still are) directed against small clusters of settlers of *Sváb* German descent (they are said to be more *Skót* (Scottish, or miserly) than other nationalities). The council chairman today is occasionally mocked for his large Slovak nose. Religious affiliation was also in the past a cause for some social ostracism, in the case of a few small sects and possibly the Baptists. However, no other group is so irrevocably isolated as are the gypsies. The prejudice is deep inside many Hungarians in the national context, despite consistent policies of the government to improve the status and living conditions of gypsies. Tázlár itself has no major problem, with only two families, who serve to bring in a little more casual labour for beleaguered maximisers unable to recruit elsewhere. But it is the very failure of the gypsies nationally to benefit from what are seen as generous policies favouring them at the expense of Hungarians (e.g. in public housing in towns such as Kiskunhalas) that confirms their 'otherness' in the eyes of the people of Tázlár. In contrast to the Hungarians of the szakszövetkezet community they appear to reject every new possibility the State proposes for their self-improvement. It is said that they are not prepared to work, because one of the two families does not work but makes a living in the same way as do numerous Hungarian families. Although the gypsies of Tázlár all live in the centre of the community, like the gypsies of Atány they are regarded as 'being created different' (Fél and Hofer, 1969, p. 227). The death of a young gypsy boy under a bus near the Solt-vadkert boundary was not received with anything like the depth of concern which would have been the response had the victim been Hungarian.

There is relatively little overt expression of status ranking and differentiation in face-to-face encounters in everyday life, but in the case of the gypsies this rule is easily broken. Their lower status is commonly expressed by a refusal to use the polite, third-person form of address in conversation with them or in the customary exchange of greetings in the street. The Hungarian language and kinship terminology is in fact a rich field in which to look for signs of differentiation and stratification. Though the comparison is not one that space permits to be pursued here, there would appear to be significant differences between Tázlár and the Hungarian-speaking community in Rumania examined by Vincze (1978). In Vincze's case solidarity is argued to be strong and the asymmetrical exchanges in kinship relationships function to inject ' . . . a measure of hierarchical order into a society with minimal social differentiation' (1978, p. 114). In Tázlár there is little need for the injection of further hierarchical elements. Relative age is a most important factor in status differentiation here also, but the diffuse concept of *tisztelet* (respect) is more closely associated with the wealth a family controls, or controlled in the previous generation. Exaggerated attention is paid to address usage. The drinking of a special toast, the *pertu*, marks the transfer of two men to the personal mode of address, but even after such a toast the younger man must speak carefully and follow the friendly '*Szervusz*' (French '*salut!*') with the name of the older individual and some general kin term (*bátyám*: my elder brother). Children are taught to greet all adults they pass in the street, usually with the polite '*csókolom*' ('I kiss you'). Men usually use this address to women whom they are acquainted with; a more flowery '*kezicsókolom*' ('I kiss your hand') is used in formal situations in offices, while strangers in the street commonly receive a cursory 'good-day!'

In fact nowadays there are relatively few well-known and well-respected citizens (*köztiszteletben állók*) who can count on being greeted by most people they recognise in the village, and it is at least equally common to walk with one's head down while passing others in the street. In trans-actions with strangers it is virtually obligatory to use the third-person, but it is also common to enter any transaction with reserve, to utter the customary phrases in a most perfunctory manner and only after the 'fare-well' turn aside to a family member and express what one really feels about the personality and the status of the other individual. In such contexts a well-specified address system does, as in Vincze's Rumanian community, minimise the conflict which can arise out of social differences. It is possible to go along with his conclusion, that address usage '. . . may be regarded as a cultural device which counterbalances the divisive conse-quences of atomisation' (1978, p. 115), but with the proviso that 'atomis-ation' and differentiation are more pronounced in Tázlár than in his community of Gyarak.

There are certain uses of language and forms of address which are not used outside the farming population (such as the common farewell: 'God bless you!'), and other forms which have been recently introduced and are confined to an official sphere. As Fél and Hofer (1969) stress, the peasants of Atány conceived themselves as a very distinct group. Officials, teachers and pastors could never properly become part of that community. The same is true in Tázlár today. The old term of address which expressed the higher status of the teacher or official was *úr* (gentleman) commonly added after the stating of the profession, e.g. *a tanár úr* (the respected teacher). The term is still used occasionally today, especially by older persons, in referring to teachers, priests, or even the director of the factory. It is used most widely in addressing the doctor, which is an accurate indi-cation of the greater freedom this professional retains within the new intelligentsia (for example he is perhaps the only individual amongst them who can send his children to church with impunity). It is, however, quite inappropriate to refer to a chairman, be it of the council or the szakszövetkezet, as a 'gentleman'. The correct term here and in all modern bureaucratic etiquette, and in the Party, is *Elvtárs* (comrade). The szakszövetkezet chairman under criticism at an open meeting in 1977 (see p. 132) was addressed as an *úr* instead of as an *Elvtárs* by a peasant speaker from the floor, with calculated cynicism designed to convey disaffection with his policies.[3] As in Gyarak it is also an insulting sarcasm to use such a title to a fellow-farmer (Vincze, 1978, p. 111). A peasant told also of the insult he experienced when once the council chairman called to him from the council offices while he was walking in the street, in the third-person but shouting his surname only — an impoliteness which would never be committed within the farming population.

The analysis turns again and again upon the standards and behaviour of 'the farming population'. Although the number of full-time farms is in decline, and although the great vigour of small-farming in the conditions of the szakszövetkezet has led to wide income disparities in both full-time and worker-peasant enterprises, there is still a fundamental unity in the community's social structure, from which only the intelligentsia and certain small numbers of 'deviant' households are excluded. This is not to be confused with 'communal solidarity', yet as in the more integrated community of Átány it is not thought to be anti-social if a household keeps very much to itself, in its religious convictions, its economic activity and its social profile (Fél and Hofer, 1969, p. 305). The goals are decentralised and the society is 'atomistic'. Excluded from the unity of the community are those elements which challenge these traditional values: on the one hand, the socialist intelligentsia with its mission, on the other, the 'deviants' and the marginals who create a real need for effective intervention from outside, in the absence of internal community solutions.

There is little hope of an improvement here in the near future. What is possible, depending upon the future of the szakszövetkezet and the government's policies towards small-farming, is that a class of rich farmers will emerge from amongst the maximising elements analysed in Chapter 4. The most hopeful sign preventing this is the attitude of the young, and it is an appropriate point on which to end a discussion of stratification. Older families still take great pride in family names and genetic parentage: it is of great importance to know that X is not really a member of prosperous family Y but only an adopted member, the son of one of Y's farm-servants. For young people these values do not count. They are equally indifferent to rank in socialist officialdom. They respect individuals on the basis of individual traits and achievements: performance on the football field, dancing in the culture house, driving ability, generosity in the *bisztró*, etc. For many of their parents their style of dress and objection to authority in the home are signs of unruly 'hooliganism', a rejection of all values. A more optimistic interpretation would see in the egalitarian but individualist spirit of youth continuity with the openness and atomisation of the past

157

and the means not only to overcome the stratification system of the past but to avert the tyranny of any new hierarchy.

III Values and norms

The preceding sections have implied a good deal about the values and norms accepted and observed in the community today. This final section will concentrate on what has survived from the past, on what is most characteristic of the present situation and on the association of many of these factors with the szakszövetkezet. The 'unity' of the community as described at the end of the last section is the justification for proceeding as if the values and norms outlined were recognised and observed by all sections of the population. At the end of this section one should have a better understanding of the nature of this 'unity'.

Fundamental values have been retained from the pre-socialist period. The attack upon property-based status ranking, the transformation of community government, and the conflict with the Church (e.g. over the secularisation of the school) could not prevent individuals from clinging to the old order. In many cases personal religious convictions were strengthened as the Church lost its former institutional importance. We have noted that it was following the years of intense political pressure that local energies in both major denominations were harnessed in the building of new places of worship. Since then religion has retained overriding importance in many older households, where the only books in the house and all the pictures on the walls are religious in nature. Catholic women organise regular trips to traditional national shrines and in 1977 there was pious support amongst the women for a diocesan pilgrimage to the Holy City, the first time that many of the participants had travelled outside Hungary.

Organised party politics was never well-developed in Tázlár. In the years following the war there was general support for the populist peasant parties and amongst a few intellectuals for the social-democrats.[4] The gendarmerie was identified with right-wing groups and opinion in the pre-war period. For a majority of farmers over 50 the political grievance they have born all their adult lives has been the 'mutilation' of their country by the territorial provisions of the Treaty of Trianon in 1920. The movement for a 'great Hungary' was one of the antidotes to the depression years. Although realistic hopes of enlarging the territory of the country are no longer entertained, there is still concern, especially amongst the post-First-World-War immigrants from Transylvania, about the treatment of the Hungarian minority there by the current regime in Bucharest. Some people of Tázlár also keep up ties with relations in Slovakia and in Yugoslavia. In the latter case there is frequently some envy of contemporary conditions e.g. greater religious tolerance and the availability of consumer goods. People of Tázlár with their own cars frequently go for one-day shopping trips across the border, taking with them whatever latest gossip

holds to be in demand from Hungary. The image of everyday life in the
Soviet Union (which very few Tázlár families have visited, except in the
course of the war) is biased in the opposite direction from the idealised
image of Yugoslavia and the West. 'Talking politics' is not a common
pastime of any group in Tázlár, but anti-Soviet jokes are the stock-in-trade
of humorists. The undisciplined behaviour of elements of the Red Army
in 1944 after the Liberation of the territory is still recalled with horror
by some persons. A few individuals were convicted on trumped-up charges
of defying soldiers and held in the Soviet Union until the 1950s.

Patriotic values are powerfully held by all age-groups, though expressed
in different ways. Older men justify the compulsory military service in
patriotic language. For the young the call-up is something which is awaited
with the utmost apprehension. But for them too the national flag, the
anthem of the Hungarian nation, the poems of the hero of the 1848
Revolution, Sándor Petőfi, are all most powerful, evocative symbols.
Perhaps because of her long history of domination by foreign powers
and her linguistic and cultural isolation in the Carpathian Basin, there
is a great concern in Hungary with the image projected abroad. In scientific
achievement just as in sport the successes of Hungarians and of foreigners
of Hungarian descent occasion deep pride. There was universal joy when
Hungary's football team defeated the Soviet Union to qualify for the
1978 World Cup Finals in Argentina, but dismay and almost shame at the
performance of her team in the final stages of the competition.[5]

Other powerful values are those which anthropologists have found
characteristic of peasant communities in many parts of the world. Some
of these remain strong in seemingly incongruous situations. For example,
consistency is greatly respected in an individual, especially if strength of
principle conflicts with material interest. Most people would admit that
a *nagy kommunista* (raving communist) and sincere atheist could be a
good and honourable man by his own standards, though they might
recognise few such honourable men in the Tázlár cell. Similarly, respect
can be earned by the mere fact of the stability and duration of an institution or a relationship over time. This applies to many common-law
marriages, especially in cases where old people come together for com-
panionship or where considerations relating to State welfare benefits
mitigate against legislation of the marriage. The same factor underlies a
widespread resignation of the farming population to socialism itself – for
over two decades now it has not assailed them directly and in recent years
it has brought them a prosperity they never previously knew.

The council chairman merits respect for the duration of time through
which he has fulfilled his duties. His status falls, however, on another
score: the traditional expectation of higher intellectual qualities as well
as certain professional qualifications in the white-collar leaders. The
former 'middle peasants' led the way even in the pre-war period in seeking
for their children the best educational facilities they could afford. Nowadays
it is a great deal easier for all families to keep their children in some form

of further education after the elementary school. Yet the status differences between traditional *gimnáziums* (grammar schools) and newer technical schools for training skilled workers are still considerable. A higher degree from a teachers' training college, various forms of polytechnics or in a very few cases, universities, still carries very great prestige. It was shown in Chapter 5 that educational qualifications above elementary level are now essential for szakszövetkezet leaders. In the case of the council chairman there should be similar high standards, but it is widely alleged that the present chairman was appointed at a time when political rectitude was considered much more important and that he failed even to complete the full eight grades of the elementary school.

Those with any ambitions in the local public employment sector can improve their qualifications through occasional adult classes in the village and also, through the Party, by application for part-time courses right up to degree level. This is the so-called 'Marxist University'. It is not especially difficult to gain acceptance at lower levels. Many of the courses taught are highly theoretical and ideological in character, and much of the study can be done in lieu of normal office working-time. It is also possible to study for other higher specialist qualifications on a part-time basis, and at the council offices new young clerical recruits are encouraged to attend the *gimnázium* at Kiskőrös part-time. While those who succeed in this way in completing the *gimnázium* in the standard four years are deservedly admired for their application, there is considerably less respect for the explicitly political courses and qualifications. Some of those who attend them, or who intend to keep applying each year until they are at last admitted, are frankly cynical, but welcome the break from routine office work and the possible advantage the qualifications might bring in their careers.

If the modern intelligentsia does not receive the same deference as that generally awarded the community officials in the past, and is indeed prevented by its own precepts from taking active steps to recreate such deference, nevertheless in all dealing with the administration, at the szakszövetkezet as well as at the council offices, a traditional code of behaviour has survived. The overt payment of bribes has probably increased in recent years as a result of relatively low official salaries. The scale varies from simple gifts of chocolates to junior clerks for performing routine tasks with exceptional speed, to large payments to a policeman for his acquiescence in a spirit-distribution network, or to a council chairman when the council purchases a private house at an inflated price. It is assumed that the officials have their prices, and the blank refusal of Font when he was szakszövetkezet chairman even to listen to such offers astonished and angered some small-farmers. This is part of a complex mentality which extends well beyond the sphere of the administration. When an individual is convinced of the importance of a goal to him, he mentally allocates a certain sum for the purpose. Even if the matter could be easily handled through the normal channels, he will seek to ensure their efficacy by

'greasing palms'. If the concern is over a health matter the sum will be
effectively offered up to the doctor, in the belief that seeing him outside
regular surgery hours for a fee will guarantee higher-quality medical
advice. If the concern is for a relative's soul the Catholic Church too has
limitless ways and means of absorbing the restless cash. On All Souls'
Day in the cemetery the priest and cantor move from tomb to tomb singing
a special hymn until the bidders desist and everybody can go home and add
up the accounts.[6]

For those with sincere socialist convictions there are other domains
where the policies of the government and of the government's representatives
in the locality must have caused much soul-searching in recent decades.
This is most acutely so where government policies (acting, for example,
through price incentives) have undermined traditional moral controls and
protective devices, inadequate as these generally were in the tanya community. The effective acquiescence of the government in the illegal production of spirit, and of local officials in its unrestrained distribution on
the market, is the extreme case of a *carte blanche* from the government
to produce for private profit without regard to wider social consequences.
In such a case it is the government which has acknowledged the 'atomised',
'individualist' values of the community in a context where the community
itself finds such values inadequate (see the discussion on the alcohol
market in Chapter 4).

There is general recognition of the impulses which the government has
sought to activate. They are 'materialist' in character, they are bound up
with a desire for higher standards of living and material comfort. They are
not always realised, because of the tenacity of old habits and the life-
styles of the past. For some families little changes as wealth accrues. Some
have built large new houses which are seldom entered, the entire family
continuing to reside in an old dwelling adjacent, or in a 'summer kitchen'.
In other cases, amongst younger households, and in the families of former
prosperous peasants, the new house is genuinely to be lived in, and there is
less preoccupation with the perfection of the exterior after building.
There is no way of knowing the size of a family's savings at the bank,
but interest rates are not much incentive to investment. Astute individuals
put down deposits for new cars with great regularity and make large
profits from their re-sale. Competition in material goods is most conspicuous and least susceptible to rebuke in the cemeteries, where large
and ornate tombs and headstones have become fashionable in recent years.

Only a few worker-peasant and all-worker households have avoided the
excesses of this 'materialism'. Instead of devoting all their efforts to the
construction of expensive houses and to the purchase of motor vehicles
they are prepared to spend larger sums on entertainment within and occasionally outside the community, and even to take proper holidays. In
many older households there is a comparable distaste for the new norms
and for all materialist status competition. This distaste is associated with
a puritanical, almost ascetic impulse and the denigration of all contemporary

values. It is commonly echoed by the local clergy. Such individuals extrapolate from the *jólét* (prosperity) of Tázlár to the nation at large, which, as some of them are well aware, possesses large foreign debts. Nation and people are said to be living off borrowed assets and one day, it is held, the day of reckoning will come. Some of these characters, unfortunately, not only conform to the norms and work harder than many of those they criticise, they fail to extract the smallest tangible benefit from their labours and, instead of using the savings bank, store large wads of banknotes under beds and in lofts. The greatest public display of 'materialist excess' is at the *lakodalom*, but here too a certain sourness has appeared in recent years. It is now more common to refuse an invitation than was ever the case in the past. The musicians at the *lakodalom* come by a part of their payment in a curious, symbolic way, being required to scratch up money from the earth where it has been buried by the host while the entire assembled company stand around and chant 'Dig it out!'

Behind the accumulation of material goods there lies a value system based on the respect for and the integrity of human labour, primarily of manual labour. First impressions of the melon-growers after their arrival in the community were highly unfavourable: these people did not even occupy proper houses. When it was seen that, in addition to being masters of their speciality and astute hirers of labour, they were also, each and every one of them, hard workers individually on their fields, opinions changed quickly. The virtues most commonly praised are those of hard work. Those held in least esteem are the *igénytelenek* (those without wants), while the man who is *szorgalmas* (diligent) exceeds the man with *ész* (a fine brain) in public estimation (cf. Jávor, 1978, p. 365). The continued unity of the enterprise and the family home makes it easy to judge individuals on the quality of their labour in the szakszövetkezet community. The criterion can, however, be applied outside the farming population: it is not much use having a doctor who is brilliant but erratic and prone to negligence (*hanyagság*).

In recent years the estimation of industry and manual work has remained high, but it has been tempered by new elements. It is considered foolish to invest large quantities of labour in some tasks which szakszövetkezet machinery could perform more efficiently: better to free the labour for deployment elsewhere on the farm than obey the instinct to oppose all outlays of cash in the production process. There remains suspicion of those who attain very high levels of production through purchasing large quantities of supplies at the szakszövetkezet and without personal graft on the land. There is now an ambivalence towards the *ügyesség* (ingenuity) of those producers, especially in the alcohol market, who live comfortably without appearing to exert themselves. In small sections of the well-to-do there is a lingering willingness to defend the man who is able to *dolgoztatni* (have others work for him) as opposed to *dolgozni* (to work – but implying here manual work on the land). Outside these ranks it is the quality of performance of the traditional tasks on the land that is the primary basis for status and reputations for all those active in small-farming.

The place of such values at the centre of the value system of the szak-szövetkezet community, given the atypical character of this community in the national context, leads to specific views about various factors which appear nowadays to be undermining the integrity of 'honest work on the land' and to distorted opinions of 'socialism' and 'capitalism' as economic systems. There is widespread respect for a system (capitalism) in which it is felt individual farmers have more scope for self-improvement and therefore must work harder than farmers lacking the security of private property and the explicit approval of society for efforts to expand their enterprise. There is a widespread belief that individuals work harder in the West than is general in the socialised sector in Hungary. At the same time, they are equally firmly convinced of the special 'enclave' status of the szakszövetkezet within Hungary. They have a *kis kapitalizmus* (little capitalism) as the local structure, which is why so many individuals work as hard as they do. But in the absence of guarantees which could only be given in the national context, theirs is a hand-to-mouth capitalism. There will be no substantial investment in the farm's capital because ever since the foundation of the szakszövetkezet the future of the family-farm has been in jeopardy. Hence, over this entire period and in spite of the ever greater incentives from the government to the small-farm sector as a whole, there has been primarily intensified exploitation of the labour factor, and hence the continued dominant role of labour as the basis of the value system.

It is doubtful whether this respect for individual work should be identified with an absolute commitment to 'private', 'individualist' values, with an 'atomised' ideal of how society should be organised. We have seen that this is not the case with regard to spirit production and distribution. More significantly, the general readiness of szakszövetkezet farmers to seek work in the 'public' sector of the labour market when not obliged to do so shows that there is no sentimental loyalty to the patrimony on these sandy soils (though it can still be maintained that given greater security on the land they would not have been so quickly attracted by the guaranteed pay-packets of industry and the socialised sector in general). Some credit must be given here to the success of a generation of the dissemination of socialist norms and the expectations that people hold for the future of socialist society. The people of Tázlár articulate praise most readily for material prosperity, for visibly higher standards of living and of public utilities in the main village. The circulation of newspapers shows that in addition to about 40 copies of the major Party daily which are distributed almost entirely in the village there are also 146 subscribers to the county daily which is published at Kecskemét, and about once or twice each year contains an article which reviews some event or the general socialist progress of Tázlár. A still larger number subscribe only to the agricultural weekly newspaper *Szabad Föld* (*Free Land*). The circulation of other national papers with greater news coverage and of cultural and scientific magazines, etc. is minimal. However, with radio and television in Hungary both devoting high proportions of peak viewing and listening time to news analysis and political programmes there are many channels for the constant exposition of socialist goals and for the inculcation of socialist values (cf. Völgyes, 1975, pp. 107–15).

It is therefore paradoxical but unexceptional in the community today to hear the government's current policies and general programme called into question from the standpoint of socialist ideals themselves. If the government itself has abandoned doctrinal purity, can individuals them-selves be blamed for selfishness, for greed, for responding to an economic juncture in exactly the way in which the government wishes them to respond? The limitations on individual economic initiative, e.g. through the continued squeeze on land, are obviously contradictory. They are still attacked from a moral conviction of the righteousness of private ownership, but, 20 years after this moral issue was settled in the nation as a whole, the people of Tázlár are often content merely to point out the manifest inconsistency with the goals of increasing small-farm sector production.

There are elements which still attach the highest value to the continued possession of family landholdings. Of greater importance in fact is the opportunity to work freely and independently without supervision. These are 'private sector' values which conflict with the proclaimed values of the government, but they by no means entail the 'exclusion' of moral judge-ments from the sphere of economic activity. There is a distinction between an activity that it is 'private' (*maszek*: the word which is formed from *magán* (private) and *szektor* (sector)), and one which is explicitly con-demned by public and private sectors alike as *zug* (black market). It is true that the labelling of a privately-owned boar used for insemination by *maszek* farmers in preference to the breeds of the szakszövetkezet as a *zugkan* (black market boar) might not be accepted as a correct use of *zug* by the farming population. Similarly a *zugkocsma* is, in the eyes of the State, any private retail outlet for illicit spirit, but local opinion would distinguish between the small-scale provision of a neighbourhood service and large-scale commercial distribution. The derogatory conno-tations of the word '*maszek*' refer to contravention of an abstract socialist standard which no one nowadays relates to the real world: those of the word '*zug*' imply the legal infringement of a specific rule, the desirability of which few in the private sector would wish to challenge. The necessity for a wide range of *maszek* activity in the interstices of the socialised sector of the economy has long been admitted (cf. J. Kovács, 1978), but it is only in exceptional spheres in recent years that great efforts have been made to stimulate such activity and that explicitly *zug* activity has been more or less openly condoned.

The major value which underlies the unity of the szakszövetkezet community is the value of *maszek* independence, yet there is resentment against the way in which this value has been exploited and cheapened in recent decades. The unity is something to which the population is inhibited from owning up both collectively and privately, and as a result the homogeneity of the norms and values of the szakszövetkezet community becomes deeply paradoxical. As in other communities the greatest stress has fallen upon family values and the approximation to urban life-styles through the exaggerated imitation of material elements. This has come to mean, in Tázlár, a norm virtually to dispense with norms; those families which diverge from the statistical pattern (e.g. the few families who value their leisure time as do city families and make heavy purchases at the shop) are subject to no social rebuke or sanction. There is no 'control' of any kind. In general 'unity' may have been better preserved in Tázlár because there was no nuclear centre before the Second World War and because there was no large group of landless whose behaviour could be contrasted with that of the former smallholders in the socialist period. Although there is general perception of polarity, it is based on purely personal factors since there is little basis for the formation of differentiated groups (cf. Jávor, 1978, p. 368). There has been, if anything, an increased passive homogeneity of values and norms in recent decades, and as in the case of the village studied by Jávor, the 'levelling' has been downwards. The richer farmers of the past may have been expected to follow stricter moral standards, but the same is not expected from Party members today. An offence is mitigated, or even entirely legitimised, when large numbers are party to it, but the problem of the szakszövetkezet community is that where there is no collective labour there is no concrete knowledge of the deceit being practised by one's neighbour. Unity here lies in this *absence* of any collective, community-wide framework.[7]

This unity cannot be described as 'peasant' because this word (in Hungarian *paraszt*) as in other languages, has a strong pejorative flavour today, certainly when applied to anyone below the age of 30 who has no full-time occupation and no specialisation (cf. Gyenes, 1973, p. 48). Within the older generation there is still immense respect for traditional peasant virtues. The new szakszövetkezet chairman, Pénzes, like other leaders in the socialist sector today, was proud to boast of his *'paraszt'* origins at his first open meeting. Nor is the term *maszek* ever likely to become a rallying cry, for its derogatory force is perceived by many of those to whom it is sweepingly applied. They admit jocularly that the szakszövetkezet community is a *maszek világ* (private world) within contemporary Hungary, but when describing themselves they prefer the traditional *földmüves* (cultivator) or the more impressive sounding *magán gazdálkodó* (private farmer). Similarly, artisans describe themselves as private craftsmen or by the specific name of the craft. Despite the eagerness for security and guaranteed incomes, even in the worker-peasant households the freedom to work on the side is greatly prized, and the extent and the skill with which 'free time' is exploited is often the basis for social ranking in this group just as the quality of labour on the land or in craft specialisation remains the primary basis of social ranking in the fully private sector.

The conflict today is with an ideal socialist theory and not with socialist practice, although there are instances when it is felt that current practice diverges excessively from proclaimed standards, as in the alcohol market. When steps are taken or even mooted to bring the theory and the practice of the szakszövetkezet community into greater alignment, there is danger. Collectivisation is more than just a powerful symbol since, as Chapter 4 demonstrated, larger landholdings make an important contribution to small-farm production in Tázlár. It also became apparent in that chapter how limited the extent of 'integration' really was, in that in addition to technical integration through the szakszövetkezet, traditional features of peasant economy and features such as labour-hiring to which the government is explicitly opposed, have maintained their importance. At the same time, there is great difficulty for the population of the former tanya community in coming to terms with the extent of their present integration. They like to feel still that they are independent producers with respect to the szakszövetkezet and are isolated exceptions in the national context. There is some truth behind these sentiments, but their willingness to produce today may still be dependent in part on a certain false consciousness in failing to recognise a large measure of socialist control over their production process and the socialist definition of the framework of all their economic activity. Perhaps this 'false consciousness' could now survive even the final stage of collectivisation to establish formal conformity with the national pattern, while all the inconsistency with the abstract socialist principles would remain.[8] As long as large numbers of Tázlár farmers are not obliged to seek their livelihood in the public sector they will retain their illusion of independence: they do not consider themselves substantially integrated today and for the pragmatic reasons we have discussed it is unlikely that the government is prepared to pay the price of changing this consciousness overnight.

7 Conclusion

'Now you must explain to me what sort of thing your village community is,' Bazarov would interrupt [the peasant]. 'Is it the same world which we are told sits on three fishes?'

'It's the earth, master, that is stood on three fishes,' the peasant would explain soothingly in a good-natured, patriarchal sing-song, 'An' over an' above our world, our village community, I mean, we all know there's the master's will; on account of you bein' like our fathers. An' the more strict the master rules, the better it be for us peasants.'

Turgenev, *Fathers and Sons*, Penguin ed. (1965), p. 217.

The conclusion does not set out to summarise the material and the analysis of previous chapters. Rather, it attempts to relate them to other theoretical and empirical approaches to peasant communities and peasant societies, beginning at an abstract level with Marx and looking briefly at the results of studies of other European peasantries before returning to Hungary.

The quotation above is not intended to imply that patriarchal relations were ever of great importance in Tázlár outside the family, nor that the problematic of Tázlár's status as a 'village community' has been resolved. Nor is the mutual contempt which it turns out Bazarov and the peasant have for each other necessarily an appropriate characterisation today of the relation between peasant communities and their elites. That relation, however, is the final problem which must not be evaded. If special features of 'peasant economy' have persisted, if the development of the agricultural sector has been distorted under socialism, in what respects, if any, is it correct to speak of the continued 'exploitation' of the countryside and its inhabitants?

The writings of Marx on the peasantry are not central to his work but they do deserve attention. Some recent writers have been concerned quite correctly to show that Marx's praise of the English yeomanry and the sympathy which he occasionally expressed for 'the free property of independent peasants' do not add up to support for a theory of a peasant mode of production 'in the full sense' (Ennew *et al.*, 1977; Littlejohn, 1977). Because the family-labour farm is always subsumed by a larger system of social relations, it cannot itself be used to define an autonomous mode of production. However, this need not necessarily preclude the use of the term 'mode of production' (or preferably something less confusing) as Marx

167

himself certainly appears to use it on several occasions to characterise the special features of the organisation of peasant farms.[1]

Later socialists, in their theoretical analyses if not in their empirical works, ignored the special characteristics of peasant farms as enterprises and analysed peasant economy as a problem specific to the general system of capitalism. The best example of such an approach, where the theory is in a continual tension with the observed facts about the peasantry, is that of Lenin in *The Development of Capitalism in Russia*. The neo-populists were the faction which continued to uphold the 'autonomy' of peasant economy, while not necessarily denying the penetration of capitalist social relations in the countryside. It is necessary to preserve a distinction between the 'autonomy' of peasant farm organisation and the compatibility of this form of enterprise with a diversity of social formations and class structures in order to explain the persistence of peasant economy after the abolition of capitalism.

Modern analysts of peasant economy in socialist states in Europe have confirmed its character as a special domain that is potentially compatible with various social systems (cf. Tepicht, 1973, pp. 17, 45–6). However, there is relatively little scope for comparative empirical studies of this domain. Immense difficulties beset all attempts to generalise about peasants, even if we begin by basing the comparisons on other European peasantries. (cf. Dalton, 1972). Many of the phenomena described in this book appear in similar forms in Western Europe. Amongst these can be included the general decline in the size of the family, the emigration of younger members and their early withdrawal from the family labour force through the demands of the education system, the emergence of the 'mixed' households of the worker-peasantry and the feminisation of agricultural work which commonly occurs when the head of the household becomes a breadwinner in industry. On these points and many others it will be useful to relate the experience of the Tázlár inhabitants to rural trends elsewhere in Europe. Yet although Tázlár has been unaffected directly by the two basic transformations through which most socialist states have passed in the twentieth century, those achieved by Land Reform and by mass collectivisation, it would be a mistake to neglect the indirect effect of these changes working through the national context.

If we return to the model of Tepicht (1973), an outline of which was given in Chapter 4, we find that it is intended to have general relevance for the socialist states of Eastern Europe. Tepicht's analysis of sectoral interdependence in modern socialist agriculture leads to a reformulation of peasant economy as a special domain. His claim that peasant farms are merely 'agglomerated' and not 'transformed' by their incorporation into a production cooperative (*kolkhoz*) needs some additional explanation, for it would seem that the production of the individual farm is necessarily modified through its contraction and redirection into the 'irreducibly labour-intensive' branches, and integration into the cooperative. Never-theless, Tepicht's concept of the continued 'marginality' of peasant labour inputs in those branches where small-farm production is most vital establishes his model in direct line of descent from theories of the specificity of peasant economy implicit in Marx and most highly developed by Chayanov and the neo-populist school.

The possibility of a single model having a general relevance for Eastern Europe is nevertheless questionable. Most of the empirical examples of Tepicht (1973) are drawn from Poland, where mass collectivisation was abandoned after setbacks in the 1950s. In Hungary, in spite of similar set-backs, the political decision was taken to press ahead with collectivisation in 1958. While the szakszövetkezet community of Tázlár has many points of resemblance to the general structure of Polish agriculture, it is now an isolated exception in the Hungarian context. In Hungary the socialised sector, and hence the government, has developed greater control over agricultural production as a whole, including small-farm production, than has been achieved in Poland. This pattern may be more typical of the countries which have undergone mass collectivisation. Control over the 'small-farm sector' (substantial production from which is still required in all socialist countries) is not prejudiced by reliance on 'indirect' incentives, i.e. on material incentives through the price mechanism.

The issue of control is important. Critics of a 'compromise' with the small-farm sector have nowhere been more vociferous than in the case of Hungary, where its persistence has been unusually strong, as typified by the szakszövetkezet, and where economic decentralisation and reliance on material incentives have been taken to greatest lengths. Cynics in the West have found in such phenomena an abandonment of socialist principle. Within Hungary concern was expressed at the excessive differentials which developed after the introduction of the economic reform in 1968 and at the continued scale of private-sector activity in agriculture and elsewhere in the economy. The evidence of this study of a szakszövetkezet community (which is an enclave in the national economy where 'individualism' and the forces of the market are given greater scope than almost anywhere else) shows such fears to be groundless. There are some weak signs of capitalist tendencies, notably in one branch of production, that of wine, which has the greatest need of labour hiring if production is to be expanded. The government's concern to raise small-farm production in this branch is encouraging these tendencies, and the general reliance on material incentives has certainly widened income differentials. But there has been no substantial private investment in agriculture because the small-farm sector remains fundamentally suspicious of the government's intentions. Small-farming as an exclusive occupation has not become any more attractive to the young, and even in the szakszövetkezet community there has been a general rise in the proportion of mixed households and of outside commuting to industry. At the same time, at farm level the application of capitalist concepts such as 'rate of return on labour' remains as inappropriate as in the past in all branches, including that of fruit and wine production.

Equally mistaken is the criticism from the right which is still frequently heard within Tázlár. Collectivisation has not proved to be, in the Hungarian case, part of a protracted political campaign waged by the government against the peasantry. Inevitably the appropriation of landholdings, the symbol of peasant independence but not necessarily crucial to the persistence of peasant economy, gave collectivisation this colouring. In Tázlár now there is still a widespread fear of the eventual realisation there of mass collectivisation. Yet if collectivisation is judged on the basis of its general social and economic results the conclusions may be highly favourable from the point of view of the peasantry. Tepicht is aware that the virtual abandonment of collectivisation in Poland makes that country atypical, but he is correct to stress the resources and the power now commanded by the peasantry even in those countries which experienced the shock of collectivisation. In view of the high prices now paid for smallfarm output he is quite correct in observing that '. . . at present Hungary offers a particularly instructive example of the concessions imposed upon the national economy by the agricultural sector, and which are reflected in the price levels' (1975, p. 261).

The issues raised here are great indeed. Recently it has been suggested that collectivisation did not succeed in extracting a 'net economic surplus' from the agricultural sector for the development of other sectors during Soviet collectivisation, but was a politically inspired campaign against peasants which forced millions into starvation and at the same time enfeebled agriculture's capacity to contribute to national growth (cf. Millar, 1970; Ellman, 1975). According to Tepicht's view of more recent collectivisation in Eastern Europe (1975), its non-utility as an instrument of general surplus-extraction is confirmed, but its social and political effects can be seen as highly beneficial to the peasantry. It is *their* revolution because it has helped their capacity to bargain with the government over small-farm produce and in the absence of coercion to force even reluctant governments to raise the prices of peasant produce. The fundamental point is that modern governments are not likely to be reluctant since they represent peasant-class interests, recruit their elites in the main from those of first-generation peasant descent, draw much solid support from the peasantry and especially from mixed households, which are content to maintain well-rewarded small-commodity production in agriculture and are proud that one day their children will have the opportunity to succeed in the town. Hence the fact that in Hungary today there are some urban and white-collar workers with fixed incomes who feel resentment of the high earnings generated by worker-peasants, and both these groups may envy the few who, in addition to wage-labour earners, have household members active as full-time small-commodity producers in the framework of the szakszövetkezet.

Neither Millar nor Tepicht would judge it correct in an economic sense to speak of the 'exploitation' of peasant economy by the national economy in socialist states, for the agricultural sector has not made a positive contribution to economic development as a result of any process of surplus extraction. In the case of Soviet collectivisation it is reasonable to argue that an attempt was made to develop in this way, but coercion does not necessarily imply exploitation (cf. Dalton, 1974). In the case of East European collectivisation, in retrospect the policies put into practice may be seen as paradoxically 'Bukharinite' and consistent with the policies pursued under the New Economic Policy in the Soviet Union and with remarks made by Lenin in that period about the need to 'satisfy the middle peasantry'.[2] The general performance of agriculture, the recent steep rises which have been necessary to stimulate small-farm production together with the vast costs of the investments which have saved so much peasant drudgery in crop production and established an 'industrial labour sector' within agriculture since collectivisation make it unreasonable to speak of the continued exploitation of the agricultural sector in Hungary.

The rejection of a theory of exploitation in the version in which it is commonly expressed by conservative opponents of collectivisation within the peasantry and by ideological opponents in the West does not prevent us from recognising and criticising the persistence of the special domain of peasant economy and the national economy's continued reliance on inputs of 'marginal' peasant labour. The szakszövetkezet community in Tázlár is an instructive setting for a final assessment.

Tázlár and the loose form of cooperative known as the szakszövetkezet can be conceived as the realisation of Chayanov's call for the vertical integration of the 'elemental peasant farm' through cooperatives (Chayanov, 1966, p. 267). This he envisaged as the basis for a new social structure under State capitalism and ultimately for a 'social cooperative economy'. Vertical integration was the only alternative in the short term to capitalism and the further proletarianisation of the mass of the peasantry. In most socialist countries horizontal consolidation to form production cooperatives was what eventually took place. In Tázlár too, where there has been little significant integration of a horizontal type, the family base and the production sphere of the 'elemental peasant farm' have been transformed by the szakszövetkezet but not yet replaced by the anticipated 'industrialisation of the countryside'. In fact, neither vertical nor horizontal integration has abolished the dependence upon the marginal labour of peasants, although the peasantry as a whole has been well integrated into the national economy and indeed, far from being proletarianised, has forced numerous political and material 'concessions' from the national economy. Some socialist critics have condemned Chayanov's interim approval of vertical integration as '. . . an idealisation of petty commodity production' (Littlejohn, 1977, p. 132). But if, after at least several decades of experience with all forms of integration, certain elements in the peasant farm enterprise have *not* changed, then one is faced with admitting that the enterprise has proved its compatibility with a variety of systems, capitalist, State capitalist, or socialist, or alternatively proving that the existence of peasant farm enterprises entails elements of capitalism wherever it is found.

This study has shown that distinctive features of peasant economy have persisted up to now in the small-farm sector in socialist Hungary. High prices have been an exceptionally but unevenly effective incentive to marginal peasant labour in the szakszövetkezet community. High incomes have resulted but successful groups have continued to work exceptionally demanding hours to obtain these rewards. There has as yet been relatively little change in rural life-styles, but some notable rise in conspicuous consumption and in status competition through house-building. The different working of the housing market in town and countryside is an example of the mechanisms which have developed to redistribute wealth away from the active small-farmers; but in many cases it is their own traditional attitudes and 'consciousness' which prevent many benefits from actually reaching the direct producers. The exploitation which persists, then, is clearly of the sort that is correctly called into question by Dalton (1974).[3] Despite their relative prosperity within the national context, few in Tázlár have the positive support for their government which Tepicht ascribes to the contemporary peasantry in Poland (1975, p. 261). Perhaps there is a need for a further and stronger dose of cruelty-to-be-kind, at least with regard to the remaining pockets of vertical integration. It might now be desirable that the national economy should face the massive investments necessary to enable agriculture to dispense altogether with small-farm production and thus with the remaining features of peasant economy and the exploitation of marginal labour which have so characterised the szakszövetkezet community.

Notes

1 Introduction

1 This is, of course, a very unsatisfactory account of the breadth of writing on the 'tanya problem' or 'tanya question'. For background in English on the historical origins of tanya settlement see den Hollander (1960–1); for information on more contemporary issues see Lettrich (1969) and Petri (1969) and (in Hungarian) Romány (1973). Theory and policy have been greatly influenced over the last three decades by the writings of Erdei (1957, 1970, 1976, etc.). However, because Erdei is concerned above all to stress the 'dual settlement' characteristics of the tanya system (specifically, the links with large 'agrarian towns' which replaced the former village network in many areas of the Great Plain during the Turkish occupation), he consistently neglects the problems of the truly isolated tanya areas such as Tázlár. Instead he has on occasion put forward confusing recommendations that the 'tanya problem' be resolved not by any more attempts to build 'socialist model villages', but by the eventual incorporation of all tanyas into agricultural towns (cf. Erdei, 1962).

2 The case was brought to trial before the Kiskőrös barber in 1809, according to the County archives (Bács-Kiskun Megyei Levéltár, Kiskőrös, Protocollum Sessionale 1799–1811). The incidence of such violence is one point advanced by den Hollander in his elaboration of similarities between the Great Plain and the American 'wild west' frontier (see den Hollander, 1960–1, 1975).

3 I have avoided alternative usages such as 'local ecological community' or 'rural collectivity' and preferred the simple 'community' throughout, even when there was no possibility of any cultural unity or identity between settlers. In Hungarian there is a distinction between the term denoting an administrative unit, *község*, and that which denotes the unity or 'commonwealth' of a group, *közösség*. Tázlár became an independent *község* by decree in 1872, but the evolution there of a *közösség* is the longer process which forms the subject of this entire book. I am not assuming that all nuclear villages with long histories of continuous settlement are necessarily cohesive communities, but it is clear that the conditions which prevailed in Tázlár were fundamental obstacles over a very long period to the emergence of *közösség*.

2 The tanya problem

1 Lenin's formulation of the problem is of some interest as, despite his

173

strong opposition to the romantic narodnik view of the capacity of the peasant community to resist capitalism, he too finds that many factors associated with that community are able to slow down the penetration of capitalism and hence of social development as a whole (cf. 1956, p. 347). Factors such as 'the absence of full freedom in the purchase and sale of peasant lands and in the movement and settlement of the peasantry' establish major differences between Tázlár and the traditional community, despite the correct insistence of Lenin that the latter was itself inevitably disintegrating under capitalism.

It is remarkable to note how narodnik conceptions of the peasantry have continued to influence the analysis of peasant economy since Lenin wrote. Besides Georgescu-Roegen (1970), Shanin has often emphasised the village as an economic unit (e.g. 1974, pp. 72–3), while Scott (1976) has constructed an elaborate theory of the 'moral solidarity' of the peasant community on the basis of the functioning of 'the village as an institution'. Hungarian studies have generally adopted a similar standpoint. To Erdei's impressions of Kiskőrös society, cited in the text, could be added the detailed analysis of Atány by Fél and Hofer (1969). Indeed the authors of the latter work freely admit that they set out to describe homogeneity where it had no statistical basis at all: 'Numerically, the proper peasants were in the minority, but their way of life was the more or less generally adopted *model* for the whole village, and, more importantly, it was the way of life we wished to describe' (1972, p. 481). In Varsány, despite abundant evidence of stratification in the pre-war period, Jávor does not see the village as significantly affected by capitalism (1978, p. 297). Extreme patterns of stratification are perfectly consistent with the model developed by Scott (1976) who should not therefore be criticised for paying little attention to such factors in his empirical material. It is necessary to distinguish Tázlár from even the practice of 'conservative village egalitarianism' in which no one can be exploited because everyone is assured subsistence (cf. Scott's views on 'the peasant's view of relative equity'): nothing whatsoever was guaranteed to the pioneer tanya settlers in Tázlár.

Curiously, it is Chayanov (1966) who comes closest to a theory which will help us to understand the tanya community. This is because he openly avows a 'private economic viewpoint', and though unable to account for the great changes taking place in the national economy which define the framework for the farm, he does not mystify, nor move dishonestly in his analysis from the level of the household to that of the community. For detail relevant to the early conditions of resettlement in Tázlár, see his analysis of 'an isolated economic machine', 'the almost natural economy' in Tot'ma (1966, pp. 121–5).

2   See Erdei (1976, p. 11) for an opinion on the ineffectiveness of feudal controls when economic factors began to favour prolonged residence on tanyas. The socialist ban on farmstead construction was proclaimed in 1949, but it is now generally admitted that the attempts to deal with the 'tanya problem' by administrative measures (such as the creation of 150 new 'tanya centres' from 1949) were relative failures.

By the 1970s the Minister of Agriculture confessed that the regulations
which governed tanya residence and production were contradictory
and in need of revision. He noted that in practice many were simply
disregarded and that in the 1960s some 3,000 new tanyas were built
in Bács-Kiskun County alone (Romány, 1973, p. 54).

3 The concept of the 'farm-tanya' is also used by Erdei (1976, pp.
148–9), but in a sense quite different from the way in which some
people in Tázlár use the term today. For Erdei the peasants of the
farm-tanya are resident on an isolated farm but still closely bound to
a town, and the endowment of the farm may be insufficient to maintain the family except through specialisations such as market gardening.
For the people of Tázlár today the word denotes the large, prosperous
family farm of capitalist agricultures in the West.

There have been relatively few attempts to relate the development
of Hungarian agriculture and of the tanya system in particular to
developments in other countries, but steps have been taken in this
direction by Hofer (1974).

4 Controversy continues to surround economic reform in Eastern Europe
generally, and the pedigree of the Hungarian reform in particular. Karcz
(1973) is one who views Hungary as the 'market extreme' amongst the
COMECON countries and has seen an explicit debt to the tradition
of Bukharin. However, some critics of the reform argue that it is has
never been substantially implemented at all levels of the economy.
For example Szelényi, in a stimulating paper (1977), has argued that
market forces remain subordinate to a 'redistributive sphere'. Much
of the liberty given to specific groups was modified and withdrawn
in the 1970s, and as will be shown, policies towards the small-farm
sector also oscillated. Nevertheless, some measure of decentralisation to enterprises and a greater reliance upon market-price signals
were fundamental changes. The controversies which took place in
the media centred upon the impact of the reforms upon distribution
and crystallised their 'spirit' in the popular mind as associated with a
greater reliance upon a profit indicator and upon material incentives.
For an early account of the political and social effects of the reforms
see Nyers (1969); for a brief but slightly more realistic appraisal
after ten years, see Csikós-Nagy (1978).

3 The transition to a socialist agriculture

1 The little material that has apparently survived from these years is
not systematically filed and I came across this information almost by
accident in the Kiskőrös district offices. It is, of course, difficult to
obtain access to certain recent archival material.

Lists of peasants branded as *'kulák s'* were drawn up in most Hungarian communities. The word has entered Hungarian from the Russian,
where it meant originally 'fist'. For a good discussion of the *kulák*
stratum and other strata of the Russian peasantry prior to collectivisation see Lewin (1968).

2 This account of the events of 1956 in one community may not satisfy
those aware of the rising's popularity and active support in other

areas of the countryside; but if Orbán (1972) deliberately understates
the political importance of the disturbances, it is grossly exaggerated
in the account given by Coulter (1959), who writes of peasants 'able
spontaneously to create a governmental apparatus' (p. 539). It is fair
to point out that several young men in Tázlár received prison sentences
for their part in pulling down communist flags and in damaging
property; but this was seen in the community more as youthful
bravado than as a calculated political protest. In the longer term,
1956 certainly marked a decisive turning point in rural conditions,
for there was to be no return to the system of compulsory deliveries
under the new Kádár government. For interesting detail on the
activity of peasants during what is still officially described as the
'counter-revolution' see Lomax (1976) and Fryer (1956, pp. 58–63).

3   Widening differentials were general except where the government was
able to intervene directly, e.g. in controls over the wage-rate in production cooperatives. See Donáth (1977) for an interesting discussion
of the problems faced by the government in ensuring that the more
efficient cooperatives obtain a fair reward, while at the same time differentials do not widen too rapidly. Of course in the szakszövetkezets
the greater part of individual incomes is not subject to any direct
government control.

4   Blanc (1977, pp. 32, 36) accounts for declining performance on the
household plot in terms of the increased leisure preferences of their
holders; he finds that decline is most serious in highly labour-intensive
branches of production (such as dairy farming), where the full-time
farmers of the szakszövetkezet are well placed to expand, given
adequate incentives and a minimum of security.

4   The szakszövetkezet community – economy

1   All bodies in the State apparatus have, in the system adapted from that
of the Soviet Union, their own control committees. In addition to
the performance of an internal control function the committees may
also investigate problems at lower levels, as in the case here, both
inside and outside the apparatus of government; an initial report
might or might not have come from the internal control committee
of the szakszövetkezet.

2   The term 'managerial leadership' is chosen because the newcomers
were trained experts in their professions who could be expected to
exploit the new scope given to 'management' in general by the economic
reforms. In fact it can be doubted whether the leaders of agricultural
enterprises, even of large State Farms and production cooperatives,
benefited to the same extent as industrial management from the reforms.
As socialised agriculture enjoys considerable subsidies from the
government it is perhaps to be expected that greater controls be maintained, particularly by the apparatus at district level. However there
was undoubtedly a great increase in the autonomy of richer cooperatives
less dependent upon the government for investment funds (cf. Csendes
and László, 1970).

3   The private plots have long been integrated into the crop rotation plans

of production cooperatives (cf. Varga, 1965, p. 33). But full 'collectivisation' of the plot has become widespread only in the 1970s. The members right to the plot is commuted into either a specified quantity of produce (e.g. 2,000 kilograms of maize, to encourage him to remain in small-farming) or into a cash payment.

The flexibility of sharecropping schemes is one of the main reasons for the success of Hungarian collectivisation policy in many areas of the country; for the proliferation of the so-called 'Nádudvar system' see Lázár (1976, p. 66).

4 There are special problems in arriving at the population of 'active earners' in a szakszövetkezet community. According to statistics collected during fieldwork in 1977 (see note 5 below), there were 142 manual workers employed 'full-time' in the socialised sector of agriculture (i.e. in the szakszövetkezet, the State Farm and the Forest Farm). There were also 256 individuals employed in wage-labour outside agriculture, including daily commuters, 70 long-distance commuters, 50 white-collar employees, and 31 'artisans' (individuals who practised a non-farming specialisation on a 'full-time' basis). If we add all of these together, and then add the numbers of children, of those in further education or in the army, of those in receipt of pensions and of all those over the age of 70, and then subtract this total from the total population of the community, this leaves a figure of 932 who might be considered as full-time earners in small-farming. Some of these will correctly be classified as 'housewives' by the national statistics; others will rely on day-labouring or other casual work for their livelihood and do not maintain independent farms. Nevertheless the production figures for 1977 show that the units which marketed produce through the szakszövetkezet in that year included 674 adults to whom no wage-labour occupation or full-time specialisation could be assigned; if we add to these the large numbers of workers, artisans and 'intellectuals' (white-collar employees) who are active part-time commodity producers in agriculture, plus the 142 agricultural wage-workers, we have an idea of the continuing importance of agriculture in the community economy.

5 The figures relating to production marketed through the szakszövetkezet were painstakingly collected from the system of cards used by the szakszövetkezet accountants. The cards describe the production of each member in each year, as well as taxes and levies paid, social security contributions (if any), and services obtained from the szakszövetkezet ('transactions'). Since considerable use will be made of these and other figures in the course of this chapter it is as well to make clear certain reservations.

Figures can give only an approximate guide to the actual production of each enterprise, because the szakszövetkezet has no monopoly over the farm sales of its members. In the case of dairy production the approximation is very good, since there are few other channels for the marketing of milk. Yet, there are village households which sell milk to neighbouring families without cows at the same price as that paid by the szakszövetkezet. Such production will not show up in the statistics. Nor will that of a household which uses its milk to produce curd cheese for sale on the local market. In the case of wine production, those with means of transportation have plenty of marketing opportunities in neighbouring communities. In 1976 a number of large producers benefited from the higher prices which prevailed elsewhere, but were then heavily penalised by the szakszövetkezet, whose regulations (seldom invoked nowadays) guarantee it the right to claim a certain proportion of the member's produce. In the case of pig-production, there are many opportunities on local markets where animals can be sold at prices roughly comparable to those paid by the State through the szakszövetkezet. Tázlár farmers do not resort to this market because of a price differential (except with specific classes of animal, such as high-quality piglets, where a higher price could be expected on the open market), but when there is a long waiting period at the szakszövetkezet, or when the animal has not been properly castrated as the State enterprise requires, etc. A further channel, through the Soltvadkert-based Consumers' Cooperative, is consistently preferred by a minority of farmers, including some who see this as a 'half-way house' between the State and the private market: they argue that animals slaughtered and processed locally will return to the village butchers for local consumption.

The statistics obviously do not comprise the component of production which is retained for domestic consumption. Some households with relatively large landholdings do not market large quantities of produce, but they seldom purchase food at the self-service shop. Some slaughter as many as five pigs annually. Almost all households keep some poultry and a small garden for subsistence needs. The systematic marketing of small commodities produced in the farmyard and garden takes place outside the framework of the szakszövetkezet. The Consumers' Cooperative is the major buyer of eggs, rabbits, and fruits such as apricots and cherries. Vegetables, fruits, and special commodities such as paprika can be sold on the Thursday market in the community or in Soltvadkert, or informally from the house, or to licensed traders who will dispose of them on large urban markets. Other products have their own specific channels. Some wine is retailed privately, or on the black market (for the distinction see the account of the 'alcohol market' which begins on p. 99). One household is a large producer of honey and contracts with a remote cooperative for its sale; another draws substantial income from a private flock of sheep; a third has contracted with another outside cooperative to raise large numbers of geese.

All of these factors create small distortions in the statistical analysis of small-farming, and if a family specialises in one of the activities listed above (at the expense of production in one of the major branches) the distortions are serious. Further problems are posed by the 19 recognised cases of 'multiple families' where more than one 'enterprise' can be identified within the household. In a few cases the decision to recognise a separate unit had to be taken on the basis of separate accounting records only (without evidence as to separate cultivation of the land, division of buildings etc.). In other cases the nominal production of a dependant (e.g. one who still owns a large vineyard)

has been included with that of the family members who actually
performed the labour. It was also difficult to ensure that all and only
the production of current Tázlár-based enterprises be included in the
statistics: small numbers of migrants, and current residents of Soltvadkert in particular, have retained landholdings and vineyards in
Tázlár and may continue to market produce through the Tázlár
szakszövetkezet.

Nevertheless the production figures accurately describe the main
branches of production in the community and they do comprise a
very high proportion of all produce marketed by the small-farm
sector. Units for which there was no three-year run of production
figures (except where it is known that one or more years saw no
production) have been disregarded. Thus for example, a family active
until 1976 which then migrated has not been included at all. New
arrivals in 1977 are similarly disregarded in the analysis of production,
but details on the composition of their households and the employment of their members are included in the general sample. It should
be stressed that the information on the employment of household
members, as well as on the numbers of children, of dependent adults,
etc., refers to the first half of 1977; the records of land ownership
(including vineyards) were obtained from the tax officials at the
council offices and refer to 1976 (except in a few cases where a
revised 1977 figure was known to give a more accurate estimate of
land actually used in preceding years). In general, no account could
be taken of all the changes which occurred over the three years in
the size and composition of the household, in its permanent place of
residence, in the employment of its members and in the resources at
their disposal.

A closer analysis might well show that 'demographic' variables
were of considerable importance in the explanation of changes in household production, and errors must inevitably result from the crude
assumption that family size, pattern of employment, etc. did not
change between 1975 and 1977. Small errors may also have resulted
in the processing of data from a failure to subsume the 19 'secondary
units' under their respective households. Despite these and other
potential sources of error, I have preferred to present statistical results
with these imperfections, because of the advantages of having a three-
year run of production data for a large sample. Certain enterprises
have a tendency to dispose of their wine in alternate years only;
production in any one year can be highly sensitive to climatic factors
and to the prevailing configuration of prices: this was particularly
true in 1976, when the grape harvest was bad and small-farming had
declined as a response to State moves against the sector which were
speedily reversed when their economic consequences became apparent.
The run chosen gives a sound basis for a statistical analysis and enables
one to pick out significant trends in the small-farm sector as a whole
and in each of its major branches.

Additional material based on these figures, together with a fuller
account of the reservations concerning their use, will be found in the
author's doctoral thesis (in preparation).

6   Cf. Franklin (1969, pp. 223–6), who finds the concept of a 'modernised peasantry' ambiguous in itself, and, noting that such a peasantry has nevertheless become the aim of governments in Poland and Yugoslavia, doubts that anywhere 'the paysans évolués will attain parity with comparable industrial earnings'.

7   Nor has there been any unemployment in the last quarter of a century in Hungary. This is more than an impressive propaganda claim: it is a legitimate indication of the 'socialist' character of the economic system. Hungarian experiences in recent years has reversed that of capitalist countries (e.g. that of Britain, a country similarly dependent upon foreign trade and hard hit by developments in the international terms of trade in the 1970s). Whereas the capitalist nation has responded to crisis by increasing unemployment, the socialist nation has attemped to increase production through the proliferation of opportunities for second jobs outside the 'socialised sector' (cf. Kovács, 1978) and has maintained constant excess demand in the labour market.

The very existence of a labour market in State socialist society has been questioned by Szelényi, who argues that direct producers have no power to bargain with the State and that the 'core institution of the State socialist redistributive economy is the non-market trade of labour' (1977, p. 12). He perhaps underestimates the extent to which the 'rational redistributive' socialist society now compromises with market forces, especially in agriculture. Szelényi claims that a party of the working class in Hungary might need to fight for the right to be 'unemployed', but in the szakszövetkezet community the direct producers already have this right, and as the fluctuations in the production reveal they do not hesitate to withhold their labour from society when prices are considered low.

8   Policies to maintain over-full employment have inevitably resulted in high labour turnover, and attacks in the media upon 'wander-birds' have had little effect. It has been argued that increased mobility in the labour market was the major advantage (curtailed by law since) obtained by the working classes and especially by unskilled labour, from the economic reforms (cf. Kemény, 1978).

9   The worker-peasantry is not, of course, unique to Hungary, but because of the relative neglect of urban housing conditions and the small size of the country, which facilitates long-distance commuting, it is exceptionally large here. Franklin (1969, p. 220) makes a distinction between worker-peasants, who tend 'to assimilate to a form of industrial labour, the proletariat' (cf. Gyenes (1973) on the rise of a 'worker type' within Hungarian cooperatives), and part-time farmers, who tend to acquire 'the characteristics of the petit-bourgeoisie'. A third group of 'labourer-peasants' who never work outside the agricultural sector would also find members in Tázlár, but for simplification in this chapter, households are classified as 'worker-peasant' if they have any member who enjoys regular income from outside small-farming (in socialised sector agriculture, in industry, as a long-distance commuter, a white-collar employee, or as an artisan), while all remaining households are 'full-time farms'.

10   Sociologists anxious to demonstrate the trend towards an equalisation

of rural and urban incomes have not always pointed out that in many areas this depends upon the organisation of a 'dual economy'. Sociologists have emphasised the transitional character of the worker-peasantry, but have realised at the same time that some families are tempted to prolong commuting patterns and working highly unsocial hours because of the undoubted material benefits of such a life-style (cf. Márkus, 1972, 1976).

Szelényi too (1977) offers a justification of the 'dual economy'. Worker-peasants according to him can be seen as typical products of the class struggle, who are anxious to keep their farms because it increases their independence from 'the bureaucratic labour organisation'. But his earlier research on the housing market in Hungary (Szelényi, 1972, pp. 269–97) may be thought to offer more cogent reasons for the persistence of a large worker-peasantry.

11 The analysis of demographic differentiation between peasant farms is primarily associated with Chayanov, though he did not argue that all social differentiation could be attributed to demographic factors. On the contrary, he stated explicitly that 'purely economic causes' can also intervene, while remaining in no doubt that 'demographic causes play the leading part . . .' (1966, p. 249).

For a summary of more recent work done with 'standard labour units' and the dominance of the two-unit enterprise in western agriculture in recent decades, see Franklin (1969, pp. 17–20, 36–7).

12 This is confirmation of the ineffectiveness of State bureaucratic control in the labour market. It would be useful to have more information on the extent of private labour-hiring in other socialist societies (cf. Halpern and Halpern (1972, p. 132) on the scope for the use of 'the supplementary labour of others' in Yugoslavia).

13 For the modern theory of 'satisficing' see Simon (1957). It should be stressed that unlike the satisficing of, for example, the modern business corporation, that of the peasant farm enterprise cannot be construed as 'maximising in conditions of uncertainty', or as optimising behaviour of any 'economic' variety. The peasant satisficer is not responsive to market-price signals, has no awareness of return on labour, etc. and for these reasons he may be closer to the traditional models of the peasant farm than is the modern maximiser.

14 For background to the accomplishment of collectivisation and forced industrialisation in the Soviet Union, which is relevant to the Hungarian experience, see Erlich (1967), Gerschenkron (1966), Lewin (1968). Tepicht (1975) has claimed that there was substantial support for Stalinist agricultural policies even in the countryside, while Ellman (1975) has shown that the urban proletariat may have suffered relatively more than the peasantry as a result of the use of coercion, for the actual terms of trade remained on the whole favourable to agriculture.

15 Maximisers may resemble the *paysans évolués*, or they may be striving only to attain higher levels of production in the short term without any change of techniques. In Tázlár the latter are more numerous. They are more interested in the short-term maximisation of income than in the long-run improvement of their farms, because many feel

that the szakszövetkezet does not offer them a long-term future in farming. Kunszabó identifies a similar category in a production co-operative community, and he classifies such individuals as *'feszitők'* (1970, p. 1303).

16 Poland and Yugoslavia offer the best possibilities for comparison with the small-farm sector in Hungary, although both countries have stepped back from full collectivisation and the evolution towards higher forms of socialist property is less advanced than in Hungary. The future of family farming as an occupation seems uncertain in both countries. For Poland see Galeski (1972, 1977); for Yugoslavia see Halpern on 'the negative attitude toward working the land' (1967, p. 319).

5 The szakszövetkezet community – politics

1 In addition to obtaining excellent qualifications at the Agricultural University, he was also a gymnast of outstanding ability. However his exceptionally small height was the subject of some pointed jokes: unlike his predecessor, who could be considered a 'big man' not only in physical stature but also as regards social standing in the community, Font was doubly condemned to be a *kis ember* (small man).

6 The szakszövetkezet community – society

1 See Jávor (1978) for an analysis of the 'womens' society' that has evolved in a village where a very high proportion of males are com-muters, and on the crude 'materialism' which is stronger in the women than in the men. See also Brody (1973) for a description of how most of the recurrent tasks in agriculture have devolved upon women in the west of Ireland. Many comparisons may be sought on this point with other European peasantries; see Cernea (1978), Morkeberg (1978), First-Dilić (1978).

2 The higher status of white-collar work was made plain in 1977 by the fate of one of the szakszövetkezet wage-clerks. It was considered a heavy punishment for rather minor misdemeanours to dismiss him from the offices and employ him instead in the technical centre as a lathe operator, though he would receive more pay as a manual worker. He was not, of course, obliged to quit his low rent, council-owned accommodation as a result of this move. Within a year he returned to the offices with a new post under new chairman Pénzes.

It is perhaps unreasonable to expect recent theories of class conflict in State-socialist societies to be confirmed by much visible evidence in the rural community although the fundamental lack of integration of the intelligentsia might be taken as such an indication. For a recent theoretical approach see Szelényi (1978).

3 Fryer (1956) notes that the State Farm workers in Bábolna during the 'counter-revolution' rejected the term *'elvtárs'* for the slightly old-fashioned *polgártárs* (citizen).

4 For a useful account of populist politics in Hungary in the period before 1948 and interesting comparisons with other East European countries, see Jackson (1974); but see also Tepicht (1975) for a

somewhat different view of the extent of peasant support commanded
by the new, communist governments.

5 In a perceptive note on nationalism and in particular on the impact of
1956 on national consciousness Vali considers such sentiment to be
'the most persuasive motivating force which engenders antagonism
towards the main facets of Soviet-communist rule' (1966, p. 152).

6 Jávor (1978, p. 364) emphasises the prevalence of such behaviour in
Varsány and argues, quite correctly, that individuals mistrust other
methods, including a reliance upon the objective impartiality and
efficiency of official channels. The ecclesiastical archives in Kalocsa
contain numerous examples of favours sought through Church patronage, in the period when the Church was still a great secular force. It
is more appropriate to emphasise the continuity with past modes of
behaviour than to criticise current phenomena by reference to utopian
socialist morality or to some other standard of an 'upright society' (cf.
Völgyes' exaggeration, 1975, p. 126).

7 See note 1 to Chapter 2 for an emphasis on past divergences between
Tázlár and the 'traditional village community'. It would seem that,
while the old communities are all in the process of losing their enigmatic
unity of the past (cf. Jávor, 1978, pp. 367–8) Tázlár has now found
in the szakszövetkezet an institution which corresponds very well
to their most basic values, and one which they would like to defend.
This is not to deny that many of the phenomena excellently described
and analysed by Jávor are not to be found in Tázlár as well. Her village
is perhaps more typical of general tendencies than is Tázlár, but many
aspirations, beliefs and aspects of social behaviour are identical.
For example, even though the proportions of the socialist and the
small-farm sectors differ so greatly there is a similar general attitude
towards work in the *közös* and towards so-called 'social work', while
real effort and resources are conserved for *personal* activities, be this
the management of a large full-time farm or merely the maintenance
of a smart-looking house and garden. Ultimately, it seems that an
emphasis upon the values of the atomised family is everywhere
dominant, but only in the szakszövetkezet community with its history
of tanya settlement could such values become a positive basis for
unity. 'Isolation' is still a major feature of Tázlár society, but the
problems it creates are not 'chronic' for the majority, as Brody describes
them in Inishkillane (1973), nor has depopulation been accompanied
by so many negative features. See also Tepicht's concept of 'family
individualism' (1975, p. 261).

8 For a perspective on the future evolution towards higher forms of
socialist property in Hungary (where the ideological categories still
resemble closely those of the Soviet Union), see Donáth (1977).

7 Conclusion

1 Both Tepicht (1973) and Littlejohn (1977) draw on the same passages
from Marx (1970–2, Vol. 3, pp. 804–7), recognise the same implications
in them, but then come up with different conclusions. In these pages
Marx describes the 'free self-managing peasant proprietorship of land

parcels' as the basis for a 'mode of production' which is potentially compatible with a wide variety of social formations, including those of classical antiquity, feudalism and capitalism (socialism is not mentioned). Tepicht and Littlejohn both recognise that there is an ambiguity in the use of the phrase 'mode of production', which Marx elsewhere in *Capital* tends to use when characterising social formations in their entirety. Obviously it is desirable to find some other phrase to describe what Marx perceived to be the remarkable durability and flexibility of peasant economy. But it is only Tepicht who accepts the substance of this perception and builds on it his own model of how elements of peasant economy have persisted in socialist societies. It would seem from passages elsewhere in Marx that he did not anticipate that this would happen. Instead he believed that other countries would copy the English model (where the very existence of a peasant yeomanry, which Marx took for granted in preindustrial England, has recently been questioned by Macfarlane (1978)) and also that the peasant, who was above all a 'man of reckoning', would soon see for himself the advantages of cooperation to form larger units (cf. Marx, 1933, p. 46).

Littlejohn (1977) denies that the brief remarks of Marx in Volume 3 of *Capital*, where there are obvious similarities with the later views of Chayanov on peasant-farm organisation, are consistent with the main body of Marxian analysis.

2 It is instructive to follow the development of Lenin's thinking on the agrarian question, particularly in confronting practical problems in the years after the Revolution. See for example his remarks on 'protracted transition' (Lenin, 1965, Vol. 30, p. 112) and his political approach in the *Report* on the substitution of a tax in kind for the system of surplus appropriation, where he argued unequivocally that the 'needs of the middle peasantry must be satisfied' (Lenin, 1965, Vol. 32, p. 216). Although there were great differences between the vague 'Cooperative Plan' championed by Lenin during the years of the New Economic Policy and the cooperatives which Chayanov envisaged creating, it is nevertheless worth reflecting what course the Soviet industrialisation debate might have taken, had Lenin lived to shape events over another decade (perhaps creating at least a small sector to compare with that of the szakszövetkezet in Hungary, in the framework of which in recent years large numbers of the former middle-peasantry have been materially 'satisfied'). See the references on the industrialisation debate note 14 to Chapter 4.

3 Szelényi (1977) sees the new class war as being fought between, on the one hand, the intellectuals, and on the other, direct producers in both industry and agriculture. In my opinion his model of the 'rational redistributive' economy cannot be a sufficient basis for explaining how the small-farm sector is exploited in Hungary today. As a result of *transactions* on the market, small-farmers are able to secure considerable advantages, which *may* nevertheless be outweighed by patterns in the 'redistributive sphere'. The economic power of the small-farm sector, and of strategic groups such as full-time szakszövetkezet

farmers in particular, certainly sets limits to their exploitation and has won for individuals the apparent freedom to decide for themselves to a large extent the labour they wish to expend in small-farming. Small-farmers may then be exploited 'to a lesser degree' than industrial workers who, as Szelényi convincingly shows, have not (except briefly in certain respects after the introduction of the economic reforms) possessed the resources to transact and bargain with the government through the market.

Some residents of Tázlár

Mrs István Lázár, born in 1895. Her husband committed suicide in 1951, the day before he was due to go before a committee in Kiskőrös to defend himself against the charge of being a *kulák*. She now lives alone in the main village and recalls her husband's suicide with mournful clarity. She receives a monthly allowance from the szakszövetkezet and some infrequent attention from two *jómódú* sons resident on nearby tanyas.

Ferenc Hadfi, born in 1949 into a well-to-do family. He qualified as a mechanic, and later graduated from a *gimnázium* as a part-time student. He is a szakszövetkezet member. He works primarily with his own tractors on the small-plots of other independent farmers; the pigs which he markets and the wine he produces from the vineyards he inherited are the responsibility of his wife, with some assistance from hired labourers.

Tamás Kazi, born in 1942. He is the leader of the largest group of builders in the community (the most profitable specialisation in recent decades) and a very hard worker during the building season. He is active also as a Party member, with 'white-collar' friends in occasional football matches, and as a small-game hunter.

András Farkas, born in 1930. He is a resident of the Szank corner, about
6 kilometres (4 miles) from the village centre. He procures a livelihood
through day-labouring when strong enough to work. He was deserted by
his wife in 1977 and his five children are now scattered: one living with
his mother, two in State care, and two still with their father, but frequently missing school to work for richer small-farmers (not for full
wages, but for a pittance plus a little food).

Mrs József Krizsán, born in 1940. She is an 'employee' of the szakszövet-kezet, and works in the dairy collection-point several mornings a week throughout the year. She lives in a council-owned house in the centre of the village, by virtue of her second marriage to a former policeman who now commutes to Kiskunhalas. A son by her first husband has qualified as a tractor driver, and a daughter is being trained by the Kiskunhalas hand-industries cooperative. She maintains substantial farm activity with only occasional help from other family members.

Ferenc Papp, born in 1913. He was chairman of the relatively successful *Remény* (Hope) szakszövetkezet in the 1960s and is very well-liked in the community today. Still a council member, but no longer involved with the szakszövetkezet, Ferenc Papp also runs an active and innovating small-farm. His children have all obtained considerable help in settling in the main village; he and his wife have recently electrified their tanya and continue to produce high-quality cheeses for the local market and to experiment with highly profitable lines in greenhouse production.

Mrs Sámuel Kőrös, born in 1929. She lost her husband in 1978, but
continues to reside alone on his tanya, about 3 kilometres (2 miles) from
the centre, where she maintains breeding-hogs owned by the szakszövetkezet. Farm production was fully diversified between 1975 and 1977,
but she is unlikely to maintain production in all branches. Her son is
employed in the machinery centre of the szakszövetkezet and has recently
built a large house in the village.

192

Pál Trsztyinszki (second from right), born in 1925, of poor Kiskőrös origin. He came to Tázlár in the mid-1950s as a tax official and has served as council chairman for the last 20 years. He lives in a large council-owned house in the village centre and, apart from tending the vines in the garden, neither he nor his wife performs any agricultural work. They have three sons: one works as a waiter in Kiskőrös, another is an excise inspector, also in Kiskőrös, and the third, having finished at the *gimnázium*, will possibly follow his father in local government by graduating from the 'Councils' Academy'. Trsztyinszki is here pictured in consultation with district and county officials during the open meeting to elect chairman Pénzes in July 1977 (see pp. 134–6).

János Fenyvesi, born in 1921. He is a skilled wheelwright who still finds opportunities to be active in his workshop (e.g. making barrels and agricultural tools) although his traditional craft has disappeared. A resident of the village, with ancestors who were lesser nobles on the Great Plain beyond the Tisza, he is a lay leader of the Reformed Church council, and an important public figure on several bodies and committees. His wife is also active in the community, one of his daughters is a nurse and the other a teacher.

Imre Bugyi, born in 1921. He was excluded from membership of the szakszövetkezet of which he was chairman in 1974–5, for alleged abuse of
supplies on his own farm. He is now resident in Soltvadkert, maintains traditional family links with a town beyond the Tisza, and commutes out to
his tanya on the Tázlár/Soltvadkert border during the agricultural season,
although he has reduced the scale of his farming and abandoned a large
vineyard area. He is still widely respected in the community, where he is
now seldom seen.

Glossary

bisztró: the new form of the *kocsma*: bar, cafe
cseléd: a farm servant (in pre-1950s agriculture)
elvtárs: comrade
felső telep: upper hamlet
Futóhomok: *Running Sands* (title of Erdei's ethnography/sociography of
    the Danube-Tisza Interfluve, 1936)
gazdálkodó: farmer
hold: measure of area, = 0.58 hectare (5,755 square metres)
jólét: prosperity
kocsma: inn, bar
közös: joint, collective (as a noun: the socialised sector of agriculture)
kulák: rich peasant (pejorative)
lakodalom: wedding reception
magán: private
maszek: the private sector; (person: one who is self-employed, on the land,
    as a craftsman, or otherwise)
napszám: the rate for a day's hired labour
napszámos: day-labourer
népház: the village hall (pre-socialist equivalent of the 'culture-house')
pálinka: fruit brandy
paraszt: peasant
puszta: lowland plain, steppe, waste
szakszövetkezet: specialist cooperative
tanya: isolated farm
zug: 'black market'

Bibliography

Andorka, R. and Faragó, T. (n.d.) Pre-Industrial Family and Household
Structure in Hungary. Manuscript

Asztalos, I. and Sárfalvi, B. 1960. *A Duna-Tisza köze mezőgazdasági
földrajza* (Földrajzi Monográfiák IV). Budapest, Akadémiai Kiadó

Balogh, I. 1965. Az alföldi tanyás gazdálkodás *in* I. Szabó (ed.), *A
parasztság Magyarországon a kapitalizmus korában 1848–1914*,
Vol. 2, pp. 565–615. Budapest, Akadémiai Kiadó

Beeson, T. 1974. *Discretion and Valour: Religious Conditions in Russia
and Eastern Europe*. London, Collins, Fontana Books

Beluszky, P. 1976. Functional Types of Rural Settlement in Hungary *in*
Gy. Enyedi (ed.), *Rural Transformation in Hungary* (Studies in
Geography in Hungary 13), pp. 41–58. Budapest, Akadémiai
Kiadó

Berend, I. 1976. *A szocialista gazdaság története Magyarországon 1945–
1968* (1st edn 1974). Budapest, Kossuth, Közgazdasági and Jogi
Könyvkiadó

Berend, I. and Ránki, Gy. 1974a. *Economic Development in East-Central
Europe in the 19th and 20th Centuries*. New York, Columbia
University Press

1974b. *Hungary: A Century of Economic Development*. Newton Abbot,
David and Charles

Berényi, I. 1971. Development of the Agricultural Structure around
Kiskőrös *in* B. Sárfalvi (ed.), *The Changing Face of the Great Hun-
garian Plain* (Studies in Geography in Hungary, 9), pp. 123–32.
Budapest, Akadémiai Kiadó

Blanc, M. 1977. Les Paysans en Hongrie. *Structures Sociales en Europe de
L'Est* (Notes et Etudes Documentaires 4 mars 1977), pp. 29–39.
Paris, La Documentation française

Borovsky, S. (ed.) (1910) *Pest-Pilis-Solt-Kiskun Vármegye*, Vol. 2.
Budapest, Országos Monográfia Társaság

Brody, H. 1973. *Inishkillane: Change and Decline in the West of Ireland*.
Harmondsworth, Penguin Books

Cernea, M. 1978. Macrosocial Change, Feminisation of Agriculture and
Peasant Women's Threefold Economic Role. *Sociologia Ruralis*,
Vol. xviii, no. 2/3, pp. 107–25

Chayanov, A. 1966. *The Theory of Peasant Economy* (ed. D. Thorner,
B. Kerblay, R. Smith). Homewood, Illinois, Richard D. Irwin for
the American Economic Association

Coulter, H. 1959. The Hungarian Peasantry: 1948–1956. *American and
East European Review*, Vol. xviii, pp 539–58

Bibliography

Csendes, B. and László, J. 1970. Développement et Gestion de l'Agriculture en Hongrie. *Economie Rurale*, No. 83

Csikós-Nagy, B. 1969. The New Hungarian Price System *in* I. Friss (ed.), *Reform of the Economic Mechanism in Hungary*, pp. 133–62, Budapest, Akadémiai Kiadó

1978. Ten Years of Hungarian Economic Reform. *New Hungarian Quarterly*, Vol. xix, No. 70, pp. 31–7

Dalton, G. 1972, Peasantries in Anthropology and History. *Current Anthropology*, Vol. xiii, Nos. 3–4, pp. 385–407

1974. How Exactly are Peasantries 'Exploited'? *American Anthropologist*, No. 76, pp. 553–61

Dányi, P. 1976. A községi tanácsok működése, szervezete, feladataik *in* V. Kulcsár (ed.), *A valtozó falu*, pp. 287–319. Budapest, Gondolat

Donáth, F. 1969. *Demokratikus földreform Magyarországon*. Budapest, Akadémiai Kiadó

1977. Economic Growth and Socialist Agriculture. *New Hungarian Quarterly*, Vol. xviii, Nos. 65, 66, pp. 33–43, 107–23

Ellman, M. 1975. Did the Agricultural Surplus provide the resources for the increase in investment in the USSR during the first five year plan? *Economic Journal*, Vol. 85, pp. 844–63

Ennew, J., Hirst, P. and Tribe, K. 1977. The Peasant as an Economic Category. *Journal of Peasant Studies*, Vol. IV, No. 4

Erdei, F. 1957. *Futóhomok* (originally published 1936). Budapest, Gondolat

1962. The Tanya, the Hungarian 'Homestead'. *New Hungarian Quarterly*, Vol. iii, No. 8, pp. 61–82

1968. (ed.) *Information Hungary*. Oxford, Pergamon Press

1970. The Changing Hungarian Village. *New Hungarian Quarterly*, Vol. xi, No. 38, pp. 61–82

1976. *Magyar tanyák* (originally published 1942). Budapest, Akadémiai Kiadó

Erlich, A. 1967. *The Soviet Industrialisation Debate, 1924–1928* (second printing). Cambridge, Mass., Harvard University Press

Faber, B. (ed.) 1976. *The Social Structure of Eastern Europe*. New York, Praeger

Fekete, F. 1973. The Major Social and Economic Features of Cooperative Farming in Hungary. *Acta Oeconomica*, Vol. xi, No. 1, pp. 19–32

Fél, E. and Hofer, T. 1969. *Proper Peasants* (Viking Fund Publications in Anthropology, No. 46). Chicago, Aldine

1972. Authors' Précis of *Proper Peasants* in *Current Anthropology*, Vol. xiii, No. 3/4, pp. 479–81

First-Dilić, R. 1978. The Productive Roles of Farm Women in Yugoslavia. *Sociologia Ruralis*, Vol. xviii, No. 2/3, pp. 125–39

Franklin, S. 1969. *The European Peasantry; the final phase*. London, Methuen

Friss, I. 1969. *Economic Laws, Policy, Planning*. Budapest, Akadémiai Kiadó

Fryer, P. 1956. *Hungarian Tragedy*. London, Denis Dobson

Gadó, O. 1976. *Közgazdasági szabályozó rendszerünk 1976–ban*. Budapest, Kossuth

Bibliography

Galeski, B. 1972. *Basic Concepts of Rural Sociology*. Manchester University Press
1977. Quelques Réflexions sur la question agraire dans les democraties populaires (1945–1975). *Structures Sociales en Europe de l'Est* (Notes et Etudes Documentaires 4 mars 1977). Paris, La Documentation française
Galgóczy, K. 1877. *Pest-Pilis-Solt-Kiskun megye monográfiája*. Budapest, Pest Megye Közönsége
Georgescu-Roegen, N. 1970. The Institutional Aspects of Peasant Communities: An Analytical View *in* C. Wharton (ed.), *Subsistence Agriculture and Economic Development*, pp. 61–94. London, Frank Cass
Gerschenkron, A. 1966. *Economic Backwardness in Historical Perspective* (second printing). Cambridge, Mass., Harvard University Press
Glied, K. (ed.) 1970. *Bács-Kiskun megye élelmiszergazdaságának 25 éve*. Kecskemét, Bács-Kiskun Megyei Tanács
Gyenes, A. 1973. Restratification of the Agricultural Population in Hungary. *Acta Oeconomica*, Vol. xi, No. I, pp. 33–49.
Gyenis, J. (ed.) 1971. *Az egyszerűbb mezőgazdasági szövetkezetek*. Budapest, Mezőgazdasági Kiadó, Kossuth
Halász, Z. 1975. *A Short History of Hungary*. Budapest, Corvina Press
Halmos, P. (ed.) 1972. *Hungarian Sociological Studies* (Sociological Review Monograph 17). University of Keele
Halpern, J. 1967. *A Serbian Village* (revised edition). New York, Harper Colophon Book
Halpern, J. and Halpern, B. 1972. *A Serbian Village in Historical Perspective* (Case Studies in Cultural Anthropology). New York, Holt Rinehart and Winston
Hegedűs, A. 1977. *The Structure of Socialist Society*. London, Constable
Hofer, T. 1974. Kisérlet a magyar tanyarendszer összehasonlító vizsgálatra. *In Tanyák* (vol. 3 of Proceedings of Magyar Néprajzi Társaság conference). Szolnok, Damjanich Museum
Hollander, A. den 1960–61. The Great Hungarian Plain: A European Frontier Area. *Comparative Studies in History and Society*, Vol. iii, pp. 74–88, 155–69
1975. A Magyar Alföld és Turner 'frontier' hipotézise. *Ethnographia*, Vol. xxxvi, Nos. 2–3, pp. 313–23
Horváth, Z. 1965. A községi önkormányzat és a parasztság *in* I. Szabó (ed.), *A parasztság Magyarországon a kapitalizmus korában 1848–1914*, Vol. 2, pp. 565–615
Hough, J. 1969. *The Soviet Prefects*. Cambridge, Mass., Harvard University Press
Ignotus, P. 1972. *Hungary* (Nations of the World series). London, Ernest Benn
Jackson, G. 1974. Peasant Political Movements in Eastern Europe *in* H. Landsberger (ed.), *Rural Protest: Peasant Movements and Social Change*. London, Macmillan
Jávor, K. 1978. Kontinuitás és változás a társadalmi és tudati viszonyokban

in T. Bodrogi (ed.), *Varsány: tanulmányok egy észak-Magyarországi falu társadalomnéprajzához*, pp. 295–373. Budapest, Akadémiai Kiadó

Juhász, P. 1975. A mezőgazdasági szövetkezet dolgozóinak rétegződése munkajelleg csoportok, származás és életut szerint. *Szövetkezeti Kutató Intézet Evkönyv 1975*, pp. 241–71.

Károlyi, J. 1904. *Fejér vármegye története*. Székesfehérvár, Fejér Vármegye Közönsége

Karcz, J. 1973. Agricultural Reform in Eastern Europe *in* M. Bornstein (ed.), *Plan and Market: Economic Reforms in Eastern Europe*, pp. 207–43. New Haven, Yale University Press

Keefe, E. *et al.* 1973. *Area Handbook for Hungary* (Foreign Area Studies Handbook). Washington, U.S. Government Printing Office

Kemény, I. 1978. Hol tart a társadalmi kompromisszum Magyarországon? *Magyar Füzetek*, No. I (ed. P. Kende), pp. 21–46. Budapest-Paris

Kovács, E. 1978. A családi háztartásszervezés atalakulása *in* T. Bodrogi (ed.), *Varsány*, pp. 173–200. Budapest, Akadémiai Kiadó

Kovács, J. (pseudonym) 1978. A szabadság egy rejtett dimenziója. *Magyar Füzetek*, No. I (ed. P. Kende), pp. 5–20. Budapest-Paris

Kozlowski, Z. 1975. Agriculture in the East European Socialist Countries *in* L. Reynolds (ed.), *Agriculture in Development Theory*. New Haven, Yale University Economic Growth Centre Publications

Kulcsár, K. 1976. A magyar tanya ma és holnap *in* F. Erdei, *Magyar tanyák*, pp. 261–71. Budapest, Akadémiai Kiadó

Kunszabó, F. 1970. Szine és vissája. *Kortárs*, Vol. xiv, pp. 1294–304
1974. *Elnök tipusok a szövetkezetekben*. Budapest, Akadémiai Kiadó

Lane, D. 1970. *Politics and Society in the USSR*. London, Weidenfeld and Nicolson

Lane, D. and Kolankiewicz, G. (eds.) 1973. *Social Groups in Polish Society*. London, Macmillan

Laslett, P. (ed.) 1972. *Household and Family in Past Time*. Cambridge University Press

Lázár, I. 1976. The Collective Farm and the Private Plot. *New Hungarian Quarterly*, Vol. xviii, No. 63, pp. 61–7

Lenin, V. 1956. *The Development of Capitalism in Russia*. Moscow, Foreign Languages Publishing House
1963. *What is to be Done?* (ed. S. Utechin). Oxford, Clarendon Press
1965. *Collected Works*, Vols. 30, 32. Moscow, Progress Publishers

Lettrich, E. 1969. The Hungarian *Tanya* System: History and Present-day Problems *in* B. Sárfalvi (ed.), *Research Problems in Hungarian Applied Geography* (Studies in Geography in Hungary, 5), pp. 151–68. Budapest, Akadémiai Kiadó

Lewin, M. 1968. *Russian Peasants and Soviet Power: A Study of Collectivisation*. London, George Allen and Unwin

Littlejohn, G. 1977. Peasant Economy and Society *in* B. Hindess (ed.), *Sociological Theories of the Economy*, pp. 118–56. London, Macmillan

Lomax, B. 1976. *Hungary 1956*. London, Allison and Busby

Macfarlane, A. 1978. *The Origins of English Individualism*. Oxford, Basil
  Blackwell
Mályusz, E. 1924. A helytörténeti kutatás feladatai. *Századok*, Vol.
  lviii, No. 1–6
Márkus, I. 1972. Post-Peasants and Pre-Citizens. *New Hungarian Quarterly*,
  Vol. xiii, Nos. 46, 47, pp. 79–90, 185–95
  1976. Tanyaiak. *Forrás*, Vol. xiii, No. 7/8, pp. 28–37
Marx, K. 1933. *The Civil War in France* (first published 1871). London,
  Martin Lawrence
  1970–2. *Capital: A Critique of Political Economy* (3 Vols; first published
  1867–1895). London, Lawrence and Wishart
Millar, J. 1970. Soviet Rapid Development and the Agricultural Surplus
  Hypothesis. *Soviet Studies*, Vol. xxiii, pp. 77–93
Morkeberg, H. 1978. Working Conditions of Women Married to Self-
  employed Farmers. *Sociologia Ruralis*, Vol. xviii, No. 2/3, pp.
  95–106
Nagy-Pál, I. 1975. *Soltvadkert 1376–1976*. Soltvadkert
Nagy-Pál, I. and Apró., J. 1972. *Adalékok Soltvadkert történetéhez*.
  Soltvadkert
Nagy Szeder, I. 1926. *Kiskun-Halas város története*. Kiskun-Halas, The
  Author
Nyers, R. 1969. Social and Political Effects of the New Economic Mechanism.
  New Hungarian Quarterly, Vol. x, No. 34, pp. 3–24
Orbán, S. 1972. *Két agrárforradalom Magyarországon*. Budapest, Akadémiai
  Kiadó
Orosz, G. 1969. Mezőgazdasági szakszövetkezetek Bács-Kiskun megyében.
  Pártélet, No. 11, pp. 77–81
Petri, E. 1969. The Collectivisation of Agriculture and the Tanya System
  in B. Sárfalvi (ed.), *Research Problems in Hungarian Applied Geography*
  (Studies in Geography in Hungary, 5), pp. 169–83. Budapest,
  Akadémiai Kiadó
Piekalkiewicz, J. 1975. *Communist Local Government: A Study of Poland*.
  Ohio, Athens
Pusic, E. 1975. Institutions and Realities: Local Government in Yugoslavia
  Public Administration, Vol. liii, pp. 133–52
Rásonyi, L. 1958. Les Noms Toponymiques Comans du Kiskunság. *Acta
  Linguistica*, Vol. vii, No. 1/2
Romány, P. 1973. *A Tanyarendszer Ma*. Budapest, Kossuth
  1977. Hungarian Agriculture in the Seventies: the Period of Intensive
  Progress. *New Hungarian Quarterly*, Vol. xix, No. 71, pp. 74–81
Sárkány, M. 1978. A gazdaság átalakulasa *in* T. Bodrogi (ed.) *Varsány*,
  pp. 63–150. Budapest, Akadémiai Kiadó
Sarlay, S. 1934. A Wattay-csalad birtokszerzeményei. *Turul*, Vol. 48,
  No. 3/4
Scott, J. 1976. *The Moral Economy of the Peasant*. New Haven, Yale
  University Press
Shanin, T. 1974. The Nature and Logic of the Peasant Economy. *Journal of
  Peasant Studies*, Vol. I, Nos. 1, 2, pp. 63–80, 186–207
Simó, T. 1971. *The Career of an Experiment: Experiment of independent*

enterprise-like rational farming in specialised vine and fruit growing cooperative societies in Hungary. Budapest, Hungarian Cooperative Research Institute (in Hungarian English)

Simon, H. 1957. *Models of Man, Social and Rational: Mathematical Essays on Rational Human Behaviour in a Social Setting.* New York, John Wiley and Sons

Sinor, D. (ed.) 1977. *Modern Hungary* (readings from the *New Hungarian Quarterly*). Bloomington, Indiana UP

Stiller, O. (ed.) 1976. *A háztáji és kisegitő gazdaságok termelésfejlesztésének feladatai és módszerei az V. ötéves tervidőszakban.* Budapest, Mező-gazdasági Könyvkiadó

Szelényi, I. 1972. Housing System and Social Structure *in* P. Halmos (ed.), *Hungarian Sociological Studies* (Sociological Review Monograph 17), pp. 269–97. University of Keele

1977. Social Inequalities in State Socialist Redistributive Economies – Dilemmas for Social Policy in Contemporary Socialist Societies of Eastern Europe (draft of a paper written at the Flinders University of South Australia School of Social Studies, for publication in *International Journal of Comparative Sociology* in 1978)

1978. The Position of the Intelligentsia in the Class Structure of State Socialist Societies. *Critique*, No. 9

Szigetvári, F. 1968. *A kiskőrösi járás szőlőtermesztés helyzete.* Kecskemét, Központi Statisztikai Hivatal

Takács, J. 1975. A tanyai népesség helyzete. *Szociológia*, Vol. iv, No. I (with English summary)

Tálasi, I. 1977. *Kiskunság.* Budapest, Gondolat

Taras, R. 1975. Democratic Centralism and Polish Local Government Reforms. *Public Administration*, Vol. 53, pp. 403–26

Tepicht, J. 1973. *Marxisme et Agriculture: le Paysan Polonais.* Paris, Armand Colin

1975. A Project for Research on the Peasant Revolution of our Time. *Journal of Peasant Studies*, Vol. ii, No. 3

Tepliczky, J. 1880. *Kis-Kőrös mezőváros leirása.* Budapest (printed by Bagó Márton és fia)

Tompa, M. 1977. A felekezeti arányok és a szekularizáció Magyaror-szágon. *Világosság*, Vol. xviii, No. 4, pp. 235–9

Triska, J. 1977. Citizen Participation in Community Decisions in Yugo-slavia, Romania, Hungary, and Poland *in* J. Triska and P. Cocks (eds.), *Political Development in Eastern Europe.* New York, Prager

Vali, F. 1966. The Regime and the Nation *in* T. Aczél (ed.) *Ten Years After.* Letchworth, Macgibbon and Kee

Varga, Gy. 1965. A Cooperative Village. *New Hungarian Quarterly*, Vol. vi, No. 19, pp. 16–34

1978. Hungarian Agriculture in the Seventies: Rural Development and Food Production. *New Hungarian Quarterly*, Vol. xix, No. 71, pp. 82–8

Vincze, L. 1978. Kinship Terms and Address in a Hungarian Speaking Peasant Community in Rumania. *Ethnology*, Vol. xviii, No. 1, pp. 101–17

Völgyes, I. 1975. Hungary: from Mobilisation to Depoliticisation *in* I.

Bibliography

Völgyes (ed.), *Political Socialisation in Eastern Europe*. New York, Praeger
Völgyes, I. and Toma, P. 1976. *Politics in Hungary*. San Francisco, W. H. Freeman
Yoon, S. 1975. Provencal Wine Cooperatives *in* J. Boissevain and J. Friedl (eds.), *Beyond the Community: Social Process in Europe*.
Zám, T. 1973. *Bács-Kiskunból jövök* ('Magyarország Felfedezése' series). Budapest, Szépirodalmi Könyvkiadó
1974a. Szociográfia a borhamisitásról. *Forrás*, Vol. vi, No. 4, pp. 31–9
1974b. Szeszmesterek (Szociográfia a tiltott pálinkafőzésről). *Forrás* Vol. vi, No. 5/6, pp. 51–64
Zsigmond, G. 1978. Az 1960–70-es évek fordulójának családtipusa *in* T. Bodrogi (ed.), *Varsány*, pp. 151–72. Budapest, Akadémiai Kiadó

Index

administration
   'administrative methods' against the
     peasantry, 37
   in pre-socialist period, 5, 8, 106–8
   in socialist period, 109–12
   manipulated from outside, 10, 127,
     129–31, 134–6
agriculture, *see* farming
artisans, 67–70

bisztró, 11, 22, 67, 100 (plate)
búcsú, 118–19

capital
   as a factor of farm production, 66,
     149
   'capitalist' farmers, 31–2, 97; *see
     also* farming, maximisers
capitalism
   current perceptions of, 163
   development of in pre-socialist
     Tázlár, 16–18, 19–20
Chayanov, A.V., 19–20, 94–5, 169,
    171, 174(n), 181(n)
children
   contribution to farming, 58–9, 146
church
   in pre-socialist period, 12, 116, 119
   in socialist period, 115–22
   personal religious convictions, 114,
     158
climate, 7–8
collectivisation (*see also under* land,
    peasant economy, szakszövet-
    zeket, tanya)
   general rationality of, 37, 39–40, 48,
     170–1
   in Tázlár, 30–2, 39–40, 131–2, 136,
     166
Communist Party, 50, 111, 112–15
community
   absence of in pre-socialist period, 5,
     15, 17–20, (173(n)), 174(n)
   limited emergence of in socialist
     period, 23–4, 157, 164–6

Consumers' Cooperative, 12, 71, 123,
    178(n)
cooperation
   informal, 17, 23, 90, 144
corruption, 150, 160–1
council chairman, 109–10, 111, 112,
    132, 134, 159, 193 (plate)
cultural development, 115, 123–5,
    163–4
Cumanians, 4

democratic centralism, 108–9
'distressed' elements, 151–4
dual residence, 27–8

economic reform, 45–7, 175(n), 185(n)
education, 159–60
   political, 114
   religious, 118
elections, 111, 129–30, 135–6
Erdei, F., 15, 17–18, 19, 31, 174(n),
    175(n)

family (*see also under* households,
    labour, women)
   as a productive unit, 27–8, 36, 77,
     144–6
   continued isolation of, 146–7
farming
   determined by environment, 7–8,
     58–60
   development of cooperatives, 34–8;
     see also under production co-
     operative, production cooperative
     group, szakszövetkezet
   fruit and wine production, 8, 18, 26,
     44, 47, 60–2, 84–5, 99–103
   milk production, 26–7, 29, 62–4,
     81–2
   pig-fattening, 26, 29, 47, 64–6, 81–
     2, 85
   small-farm sector: full-time farms,
     76, 85–8, 91, 98; integration at
     local level, 78–80, 82, 91–4,
     95–8; integration at national level,